Salads for All Seasons

Salads
for
All Seasons

Barbara Gibbons

Macmillan Publishing Co., Inc.
NEW YORK
Collier Macmillan Publishers
LONDON

Macmillan Publishing Co., Inc.
866 Third Avenue, New York, N.Y. 10022
Collier Macmillan Canada, Inc.

Library of Congress Cataloging in Publication Data
Gibbons, Barbara.
  Salads for all seasons.
  Includes index.
  1. Salads. I. Title.
TX740.G46   641.8′3   82-255
ISBN 0-02-543130-7   AACR2

10 9 8 7 6 5 4 3 2 1

Printed in the United States of America

Contents

Acknowledgments

I'd like to express my appreciation to Ilka Shore Cooper and everyone else at Macmillan for their topnotch work in getting this book together, and to my home economist, Dorothea Fast, and typist, Moira McKaig, for their tireless aid in getting it right . . . and getting it done! Cookbooks are like salads: both need the right ingredients.

1

Introduction

Welcome to "green cuisine"! In case you hadn't noticed, "salad days" are here . . . for good. Vegetables are indisputably in. Fresh is fashionable. Among the beautiful people, the greengrocer has replaced the butcher and baker as the required first place to shop for food. Now, eating light is eating right. Fiber has displaced protein as the good-stuff fad food you can't get too much of.

Vegetables? You probably remember negotiating with Mom over string beans for chocolate cookies. Where did all this trendy appreciation of garden goodies come from?

I submit that it's all tied in with our national preoccupation with the avoidance of pudginess. If we are what we eat, string beans take on new appeal. We may rankle over the impossible and sometimes downright dangerous standards of slimness that prevail in our society, but let's face it, anything easily accomplished is never valued very much. And most of us grew up in a world where nothing was as easily accomplished as getting fat. In fact, few things were harder to avoid. If you ask me, the whole skinnymania serves a valuable purpose: It keeps us from eating our way into terminal obesity. As we stride deeper into the eighties, some sort of anthropological correction of the "funfood era" was bound to occur.

Fattening Fast Foods

Most of us emerged into adulthood during the heyday of fast foods, the era when franchisers, food processors, supermarkets and advertisers grew financially fat by feeding us good-tasting empty calories that cost more to promote and package than they did to produce. We grew up on heat-and-eat, thaw-and-serve, drive-in, take-out, nutritionally neutered nibbles that were high in fat, sugar, starch and synthetics. They allayed our appetites without feeding our hunger. Modern life grew increasingly complex; conflicting demands, double jobs, long commutes, fractured family life kept us chained to the desk, workbench and driver's seat, with little time to prepare "proper" meals. And our own seats showed an alarming tendency to spread in a most unflattering manner!

Meanwhile, television and magazine ads held up images of anorexically slender models to taunt us with impossible-to-meet standards of desirability. As thin grew increasingly in, promoters found new ways to mine the American wallet. Fad diet books, commercial weight-loss clubs, protein fasts, expensive spas and "miracle" medications were marketed as instant answers to melt away the accumulating bulges.

The Changing American Menu

But things are changing. After decades of crash diets, Americans seem to be waking up and understanding that we really are what we eat. Fashion magazine diet articles today are more likely to be rooted in sound nutritional advice. We are finally beginning to accept the self-evident, knew-it-all-along answer: Lifelong vitality and good looks depend on eating vital, good-looking foods!

Uncle Sam Wants You . . . to Be Slim

Though we're entering an era of federal withdrawal from interference with our lives, it was preceded by intense preoccupation with the American diet. Recent government policy has had an important influence on food habits. In the late seventies Uncle Sam stepped in to repeat what mother always told you: Eat your vegetables! The message of the Senate Subcommittee on Nutrition was that whole grain was better than white bread and apples were better than pie. The new message was that long life and leanness lay in less meat and more potatoes—less fat, butter, eggs and cream. We were urged to use the salt shaker and sugar bowl sparingly, and to fill up on Mother Nature's harvest of grains, fruits and vegetables. Above all, the experts told us, calories *do* count. And we should consume no more of them than necessary to keep us at the weight we should be.

The Greening of the American Menu

How do all these vitality prescriptions fit in with an eat-and-run lifestyle weaned on vending machines and Big Macs? America focused new attention on the original "fast foods": raw fruits and vegetables.

It's a natural!

Those of us who grew up despising the mushy olive-drab offerings of our mothers and the can-opener concoctions of school cafeteria steam tables have always welcomed the salad side dish as the alternative to unappetizing overcooked "greens."

Do-It-Yourself Salad Bars

Meanwhile, restaurant operators were discovering the way to save work for themselves and their staff while keeping their patrons occupied: the salad bar! Let the patrons pitch in and concoct their own first course while awaiting the main event. If some customers were opportunistic and greedy in the way they heaped their plates, no matter. Overfed on greenery, patrons would accept smaller portions of the expensive steaks and roast beef. Owners soon discovered that many patrons were willing to forgo the "main course" and pay a premium price to feed themselves from a trough of greenery. Making a meal of salad became increasingly common.

Making a meal of salad, in fact, has become the new American way! Food critics often focus on the negative aspects of America's vast food distribution system, and ignore its virtues. Yes, we have pink tomatoes, but we also have mangoes in Maine and strawberries in February. Americans have easy access to a dazzling harvest of fresh fruits and vegetables from all over the world all year long. In less than an hour most of us can wheel in and out of a supermarket and fill our baskets with the fruits of four seasons and all corners of the world. What's in store for you at the supermarket may not match the best you can grow next summer, but the point is that you don't have to wait until next summer—you can have it right now! Making a meal of salad is the quickest, easiest, least fattening, most nutritious "fast food" available.

Salads for All Seasons

With today's fresh emphasis on eating for fitness, salad is no longer anchored to side-dish status before or after a meal. More often today, salad is the meal! What's more, salad meals know no season. "Green Cuisine" needn't be captive to the calendar or clock. Your salad can be served hot in winter or modified to brighten your breakfast. After all, many of today's trendy, vegetable-rich hot dishes are really salads in disguise: chunky soups with undercooked vegetables, stir-fry mixtures in which the vegetables are merely heated through and served still crisp, pita bread sandwiches packed with sprouts and other veggies, blender beverages that are purees of garden fruits or vegetables. These newly popular choices are certainly in keeping with the spirit of salad cuisine.

In My Book, Salad Can Be *Any* Meal!

What is salad, anyway?

The word has a history of ever-widening usage. It actually derives from the word "salt." Originally it meant nothing more than fresh, salted greens. Freshness in taste and texture continue to be associated with the idea of salad, even though salad needn't be raw, or even cold. And, of course, it needn't be salted. The current dictionary definition is sufficiently loose to allow the word "salad" to be applied to many mixtures, even by the most literal minded.

> sal'ad, n. (OFr. salade; Pr. salada; L. salata, pp. of salare, to salt, from sal, salt.)
> 1. a dish, usually cold, of sea food, chicken, eggs, raw or cooked fruits or vegetables, especially lettuce, etc., in various combinations, prepared with a dressing of oil, vinegar, and spices or mayonnaise, etc.
> 2. any green plant or herb used for such a dish or eaten raw; especially, (Dial.), lettuce.
> 3. a finely chopped or ground food, as egg, ham, or chicken, mixed with mayonnaise and served on a bed of lettuce or in a sandwich. *

This book goes beyond even that wide-ranging definition in concerning itself with the spirit behind today's green revolution . . . the desire to eat wisely and well from Mother Nature's bounty. With that in mind, *Salads for All Seasons* doesn't confine itself to the predictable categories you might expect in a cookbook devoted to salads. My aim

* *Webster's New Twentieth Century Dictionary of the English Language,* Unabridged, 2nd Ed., 1980.

is to awaken your imagination to the endless possibilities of "Green Cuisine"—to invite a fresh approach to every meal all year long. With this book as a guide, the cook-in-a-hurry can cook in minutes (or not at all), yet doesn't have to rely on the usual processed junk foods and convenience mixes, or on franchised fast foods that fatten without filling.

About the Recipes

Each recipe in this book lists the calories for each serving. The calorie counts are intentionally kept low by minimizing the use of fats, oils and other high-calorie ingredients. In developing recipes for this book, my aim was to meet the needs and desires of busy Americans who are looking for healthier, less calorie-costly alternatives in hurry-up meals. So, you'll find that this book is long on shortcuts, and short on troublesome techniques and exotic or hard-to-find ingredients. Even though its aim is to help find imaginative, appealing ways to use fresh foods, you'll find that some of the recipes do make use of such handy "convenience foods" as frozen vegetables, bottled dressings, seasonings and some mixes. It's not the convenience aspect of processed foods that causes us trouble; it's the excess fats, fillers and calories that are substituted for substance in them. When such a product is relatively low in calories and can be handily incorporated into a recipe that's nutritious and nonfattening, I have made use of it, with alternatives for those who want them.

Calorie counts in this book are based on U.S. Department of Agriculture data and the nutrition labels of the most widely available brands. Portion sizes have been calculated to match standard serving sizes. Keep in mind that if a recipe serves four and you eat it all yourself, the calorie count quadruples!

2

Salad Basics

How's your salad savvy? Do you know the answers to these questions:

- Can lettuce be sliced instead of torn? (Yes, sometimes)
- Is it always necessary to peel carrots? (No)
- Should you trim the tops from radishes before you store them?(Yes)
- Can mushrooms, peas and beets be eaten raw? (Absolutely!)
- Which has more calories, red peppers or green? (Red)
- What's the least fattening salad oil? (They're all the same)

If you're bewildered by "butterhead" and confounded by "cos," let's start our crash course in salad ingredients right here!

Let's Start with Lettuce

Not because lettuce is absolutely essential in a salad (it isn't), but because lettuce is the one green that most tossed salads have in common! And speaking of common, we might as well start with that most common of all lettuces: plain old ordinary iceberg.

Iceberg Lettuce

Food snobs and self-styled gourmets consider iceberg the polyester of lettuce. Why? Simply because it *is* so widely available—in other words, common! Iceberg is a victim of its own virtues: affordability, availability, durability and practicality. Restaurants and supermarkets love iceberg lettuce for its long-wearing and easy-care qualities. Iceberg stays as fresh and crisp as a permanent press shirt!

But don't let disdain for the ordinary blind you to iceberg's genuine culinary advantages: It *is* uncommonly crisp. It has a crunchy texture unequaled by any other lettuce. Its pleasant, mild flavor is the perfect foil for other, more assertive greens. Its delicate light green color contrasts well with darker or brighter ingredients. In fact, iceberg is the lettuce of choice in many types of dishes where crunchy texture is paramount. It's *the* lettuce to shred as a topping for tacos, a garnish for enchiladas, the base for a Tex-Mex salad; to stuff into pita pockets or hero sandwiches; to cube into stir-fried hot Chinese salads. Iceberg is the bedding lettuce that can cradle other salad mixtures without losing its crunch. It's the limp-proof workaday lettuce that stays crisp in your lunchbox sandwich.

Let's face it: Practical advantages *do* count for something! If you've got more important things to do than food-shop, iceberg is the lettuce you can buy this week and still use next week. For every-other-week supermarketers, iceberg lettuce can mean the difference between lettuce and no lettuce.

HOW TO BUY IT: Unlike other produce choices, the best heads of iceberg lettuce are light for their size, indicating looseness and crispness. Heavy heads of iceberg will be tight and dense. (However, dense iceberg *is* good for cutting into cubes for Chinese stir-fry dishes.) Iceberg lettuce should be stored in the refrigerator in its wrapper; if unwrapped, put it in a plastic bag. It's the longest-lasting lettuce, since it's still usable after a week or ten days, and sometimes even longer. Mushy outer leaves can be stripped away to reveal fresh, usable inner leaves.

HOMEMADE SALAD MIXTURES: Iceberg is the one lettuce you can use in make-ahead, keep-on-hand salad mixtures. Simply tear it into bite-size pieces and combine it with chopped onions, diced pepper or other *dry* salad vegetables. Refrigerate the *unwashed* mixture in a plastic bag or covered bowl. Crisp the salad mixture in icy water for a few minutes at dinner time, and drain it well. Then add leaky vegetables like tomatoes and cucumbers *just before serving*.

STORAGE TIP: Don't slice iceberg with a knife if you plan to store it, because the leaves will develop rust spots. However, it's perfectly all right to shred or slice iceberg *with a stainless steel knife* if you plan to use it right away.

Calories: 59 per pound.

Boston and Butterhead Lettuce

If iceberg is polyester, then Boston lettuce is silk: delicate, soft and status-y, a crushy crinkle of leaves that gently unfold like pretty gift-wrapping in shades of jade and celadon. Definitely first class! (Like silk, Boston lettuce is also expensive, fragile, easily wilted and hard to clean!)

Also known as butterhead lettuce, Boston lettuce has a sweet, mild flavor and a soft texture that's delicious alone, or combined with other high quality salad ingredients.

Because Boston lettuce is extremely perishable, you should plan to use it as soon as possible, within a day or two of purchase. Store the heads—unwashed—in a plastic bag in the refrigerator, and do not attempt to prepare it until just before dinner time. *Never* slice Boston lettuce with a knife because the leaves will blacken along the edges. Simply tear the leaves from their base. Wash the torn pieces in several changes of cold running water (Boston lettuce tends to be full of sooty soil). Drain well, and postpone adding dressing until immediately before serving because this lettuce wilts quickly.

Calories: 64 per pound.

Bibb and Limestone Lettuce

Bibb lettuce—also known as limestone—is a smaller relative of Boston lettuce, with leaves that are somewhat darker and crisper. In terms of taste, texture, price and perishability, Bibb shares most of its cousin's advantages and disadvantages. A tiny whole head of Bibb lettuce makes an elegant single serving salad with no other ingredients except a zesty dressing. Wash the whole head under running tap water, separating the leaves carefully to flush out the soil.

Calories: 64 per pound.

Leaf Lettuce

Leaf lettuce comes in many varieties, all characterized by the tendency to grow in loose-leaf bunches rather than forming heads. Some of these varieties are pretty indeed, particularly *red lettuce*: dark green leaves with frilly ruby-red edges, a knockout in any salad bowl! Leaf lettuce varieties are much loved by home gardeners; they're easy to grow in most areas. Leaf lettuce grows quickly, can be picked continuously, takes little space, and is attractive as a border or tucked in among flowers.

Most varieties of leaf lettuce are mild and sweet, with a texture that's firmer and crisper than Boston or Bibb. In terms of perishability, leaf lettuce is midway between iceberg and Boston. Wrap leaf lettuce loosely in plastic or put it in a large uncrowded plastic bag in your refrigerator. Undressed leaf lettuce salads can be made several hours ahead of time, if necessary (but leaf lettuce does not have the keep-ability of iceberg). Leaf lettuce should be torn rather than cut, al-though a last-minute slicing job with a stainless steel knife won't do it any real harm if you're pressed for time.

Calories: 82 per pound.

Romaine and Cos Lettuce

Romaine lettuce, also known as cos, is the most ubiquitous of the loose-leaf lettuces. It's the lettuce that's de rigueur in Caesar salad! Its flavor is stronger and its leaves are crisper than most of the preceding lettuces, particularly the darker outer leaves. Romaine should be torn rather than cut; then the outer leaves should be torn away from their tougher center ribs. Discard the ribs if they tend to toughness. The tiny inner leaves can be left whole. Whole heads of romaine should be wrapped or bagged loosely in plastic in the refrigerator; romaine will last a few days. Undressed salads can be made a few hours ahead of time, if necessary; add dressing at the last minute.

Calories: 82 per pound.

A Bit of the Bitter

All of the preceding lettuces are mild in flavor. The following lettuces provide a touch of bitterness for flavor accent.

Curly endive, also known as *chicory*, is a frilly dark green lettuce with a white stem. It's added to salad for its attractive appearance and bitter flavor. (A little goes a long way!) Less bitter in flavor is *escarole* (also known as *broad leaf endive* because it looks a bit like curly endive, but is less curly). Another bitter green is *radicchio*, or *red Italian chic-ory*. It's similar in taste and appearance to curly endive, except that its leaves are fringed in dark red.

Belgian endive is a pale green, mildly flavored sprout of the chicory plant (the lighter the color, the less bitter the flavor). Elegant and expensive, this lettuce forms small tightly folded heads consisting of graceful plume-shaped leaves. Use Belgian endive promptly.

Calories: 91 per pound for both curly and Belgian endive.

Other Salad Greens

Arugula is a peppery-flavored green of Italian descent that's becom-ing more available in supermarkets. *Watercress* is another peppery-sharp green that can add accent to salad mixtures. *Dandelions* are a tasty, slightly bitter ingredient that may be found "free" on your own lawn! Gather only the tiny leaves that emerge in the spring; mature dandelion leaves are too bitter. *Spinach* leaves have grown so popular as salad greens that many people eat them more often raw than cooked. Tear the leaves away from the stems and discard the stems. *Mustard Greens* are another of the vegetables traditionally cooked that are now becoming popular as raw ingredients in the salad bowl. Mustard greens are somewhat bitter; use only the tender tips.

Cabbage—particularly *red cabbage*—is often shredded into salad green mixtures to add color as well as crispness. However, cabbage has such an assertive flavor that it tends to overpower delicate lettuces. Another cabbage-flavored green is *Chinese celery cabbage*; in appearance it resembles romaine lettuce. The texture (as well as the taste) is crisply cabbage-like.

Salad Red, Yellows, Purples, Oranges

Tomatoes

Tomatoes are an exquisite delicacy when sun-ripened on the vine. Out of season, however, they're likely to be a cosmetic abomination! The tasteless pink tennis balls that blight the supermarket produce case most of the year result from the discovery that unripe green tomatoes can be artificially reddened by ethylene gas. Colored to look ripe and refrigerated to prevent them from maturing (and becoming soft, perishable and difficult to handle from the retailer's point of view), these hard, dry, tart, tasteless travesties add little to a salad other than an irritating reminder of what the tomato could have been had it not been cut down before its prime. If produce marketers were discouraged from peddling tasteless, artificially colored tomatoes—by a widespread boycott—the pink tennis balls would eventually disappear and be replaced by fewer, better-tasting but costlier tomatoes. Speaking for myself, I'd rather have one real tomato a week than a whole carton of waxy pink imposters.

Tomatoes should *never* be refrigerated until they are fully ripe. The color of ripe tomatoes is a rich red with no remaining touches of yellowness, and the flesh yields to gentle pressure. Firm tomatoes may be easier to slice, but their flavor is not yet fully developed. Once a tomato is refrigerated, ripening is suspended and it will never reach its full flavor.

SHOPPING FOR TOMATOES: When you shop, try to select a variety of tomatoes in several stages of near-ripeness so that you have a steady supply of ready-to-use tomatoes until your next shopping trip. You can manipulate the home-ripening of tomatoes by storing some covered and some uncovered. Those stored covered in a paper bag (or a ripening bowl) will ripen more quickly than those left in an open bowl, exposed to the air. You can further speed up the ripening of tomatoes by enclosing them with an apple; the apple emits a ripening compound that will speed maturation.

Off season, cherry tomatoes are likely to be the only tomatoes available that will ripen acceptably. When you come home from shopping, unwrap the pint package of cherry tomatoes and separate the ready-to-use from the not-yet-ripe. Refrigerate only the ripe tomatoes.

When acceptable tomatoes are unavailable, keep in mind that cubes of eating oranges added to a salad can stand in for the sweet-tart taste of tomatoes.

Calories: 91 per pound.

Onions and Their Kissing Cousins

Depending on your point of view or plans for the evening, the presence (or absence) of onions can make a salad inedible. "Onions in the salad?" is a question that invites definite opinions! For that reason, the safest way to serve onions with salad is on the side, allowing others to partake or not, according to their preference.

Some tips: *Yellow onions* are more strongly flavored than the big, mild, sweet onions known as *Spanish* or *Bermuda* onions. *Red* or *purple* onions add a dash of color to a salad as well as flavor. *Scallions*, also known as *green onions* or *spring onions*, are young onion plants with immature bulbs and dark tubular green leaves. Simply cut off the roots and slice the rest: bulb and leaves both. They make an attractive alternative to chopped onion. *Chives* are a grass-like cousin of the onion, often sold growing in small pots. Snip off the leaves as needed and use them minced, like scallions. Onions can be stored in a cool dark place, or refrigerated to prevent them from sprouting. Scallions should be refrigerated.

Calories: onions, 172 per pound; scallions (green onions), 163 per pound (bulb and top); chives, 127 per pound.

Cucumbers

Cucumbers are best when they're immature and have soft seeds; fully ripened cucumbers have hard seeds. Avoid overly large cucumbers, those with a tinge of yellowness, soft or puffy cucumbers and those with shriveled ends. A glossy appearance and slippery, greasy feel indicates that the cucumbers have been coated with wax. Unwaxed cucumbers should not be peeled before slicing; much of the valuable fiber is in the skin.

Calories: 68 per pound not pared; 64 per pound pared.

Sweet Bell Peppers

Bell peppers are extra high in fiber. *Red bell peppers* are nothing other than *green bell peppers*, fully ripened. Red peppers cost more than green ones because the farmer has them in his custody longer. Sometimes you can get red peppers for the price of green ones merely by being patient. Keep the peppers a few days in a paper bag or ripening bowl at room temperature, and the green peppers may continue to mature and change color, from green to red. Green peppers will ripen to red only if they have been picked relatively close to maturity. Light green peppers are very young and will never ripen to red. Red peppers are sweeter and more flavorful than green, and therefore have a few more calories. Other sweet peppers that can be added to salads include the long sweet *Italian-frying peppers* (available in both green and red) and the sweet *yellow pepper*.

Calories: green, 100 per pound; red, 141 per pound.

More Salad Vegetables

Sweet fennel has a flattened bulb, celery-like ribs and feathery, fern-like leaves. The bulb is tender, sweet and crunchy with a faintly licorice-like anise flavor. Slice it like celery and serve it with a dip, or add it to salads or use it instead of celery in fruit salads, or stir-fry it in Oriental combinations. This bulb is popular in Italian cuisine where it's known as *finocchio*. Fennel is traditionally served during the Christmas-New Year season.

Calories: bulb, 158 per pound; leaves, 118 per pound.

Green beans, also known as *snap beans* or *string beans*, should break with a "snap" indicating freshness (and they should not have any "strings"). Slice off the tips and cut the beans on the diagonal; use the sliced beans raw in salad where their sweetness adds flavor as well as crunch. *Yellow wax beans* can also be sliced and served raw in salads, adding a pretty yellow color. Long raw beans—yellow and green—make a colorful addition to a dip tray.

Calories: green raw, 145 per pound; yellow, raw, 122 per pound.

Beets are usually cooked and served hot, or marinated in a sweet and sour sauce and chilled. Now, thanks to the food processor, shredded raw beet "confetti" has become a popular addition to appetizer plates (often accompanied by shredded raw carrot, turnip or other raw root vegetables). The tops *(beet greens)* should be removed from fresh beets before they are stored in the refrigerator. Otherwise the tops continue to draw moisture from the beets.

Calories: 195 per pound.

Broccoli is another "cooked" vegetable that's increasingly being served raw. Only the young florets or bud clusters should be used for salads or raw appetizer trays. Simply break them off and rinse them in cold water. Some varieties of broccoli have purple florets.

Calories: 145 per pound.

Cabbage is strongly flavored, popular in coleslaw, and a good source of vitamin C. The dark green outer leaves are more nutritious than the light white inner leaves, although the latter are more tender and delicately flavored. *Red cabbage* is similar in flavor and nutrition; its rosy-purple color makes it a popular addition to tossed salads. *Green savoy cabbage* has crinkly, wrinkled leaves.

Calories: green, 109 per pound; red, 141 per pound.

Carrots should be refrigerated with their tops removed (to prevent the foliage from drawing moisture and nutrients from the carrot). The best carrots for salads are small, young and tender. Older, tougher carrots should be cooked. It's not necessary to pare raw carrots for salad if you scrub them well and slice them wafer thin, or if you shred them in a food processor. Carrot "curls" are made by slicing pared carrots lengthwise with a peeler into thin wafer-strips. Then drop the strips in icewater.

Calories: 191 per pound.

Cauliflower has a strong flavor and fragrance when cooked. However, none of this assertiveness is apparent when cauliflower florets are served raw. Raw cauliflower has a pleasant sweet flavor and a snappy crispness. Simply break off the florets, or slice them into "chips." Raw florets or chips make a nice vegetable nibble on dip trays.

Calories: 122 per pound.

Celery has a pleasant, distinctive flavor and crunch that makes it popular on appetizer trays. Thinly sliced celery is popular in fruit salads, but often overlooked as an addition to tossed salads. Celery that is served raw should always be crisp. Limp celery can be restored to crispness by standing the cut ribs of celery in a glass of tepid water three or four hours, until the moisture has been absorbed. A "vase" of cut celery can be kept in the refrigerator ready to serve (or to nibble).

Calories: 77 per pound.

Jerusalem artichokes are the tuberous root of a type of sunflower. It is not an artichoke and doesn't come from Jerusalem. Another name for it is *sunchoke*. With brown skin and white flesh, these sweet, crisply fleshed tubers look a bit like knobby potatoes. The brown skin should be pared away. Then slice or dice the crisp white flesh and add it raw to salads. Jerusalem artichoke should be kept in the refrigerator, unpared; wrap it tightly in plastic to prevent shriveling.

Calories: 129 per pound (average).

Mushrooms are now very popular eaten raw, in salads (particularly spinach salads) and on appetizer trays. Mushrooms should not be washed until ready to serve, and then they should be washed well to remove all bits of the "dirt" (actually, the culture medium) that clings to their stems. Mushrooms do not need to be peeled. The best mushrooms for salad are young, clean, smooth and unwilted, with caps closed or just beginning to open. They can be thinly sliced, or left whole if small. *Enok* or *enoki mushrooms* are tiny long-stemmed mushrooms with a peppery flavor, popular in Oriental cuisine . . . a delicious addition to any salad.

Calories: 127–159 per pound.

Peas. Young sweet tender peas are delicious raw. Once peapods are harvested, they must be kept refrigerated to prevent their sweetness from turning to starchy toughness. Leave the peas in their pods, stored in the refrigerator, until serving time. Shell the peas and discard the pods at the last minute.

Calories: 381 per pound.

Radishes add peppery crunch and color to any salad. In addition to the familiar red radishes, there are long *white "icicle" radishes.* Some long white *oriental radishes* are bigger than carrots. If fresh and crisp, the green radish tops can also be used in salad, adding spicy radish flavor. The leaves should be removed before radishes are stored in the refrigerator.

Calories: 77 per pound.

Sprouts are popular in salads. The most commonly available are the fine green shoots of *alfalfa,* and the familiar "Oriental bean sprouts" grown from *mung beans.* Mung sprouts can be eaten raw in salads as well as stir-fried. Rye, wheat, soybeans and a number of other types of sprouts are available in health food stores. Growing your own sprouts takes only a few days and some simple household equipment —you don't even need sunlight or soil! Seeds or beans for sprouting are packaged with directions and sold in health food stores. Whether purchased or home-grown, raw, ready-to-use sprouts should be stored in the refrigerator. Rinse them well in cold water before using.

Calories: mung bean sprouts, 159 per pound; alfalfa sprouts, approximately the same.

Summer squashes include the soft-skinned *yellow squash* and the dark green *zucchini.* Both can be eaten raw: Dice or slice them like cucumbers and add to salads. Both yellow squash and zucchini are milder in flavor and less crisp than cucumbers.

Calories: 86 per pound.

Spices, Herbs and Seasonings

If "something for nothing" appeals to you—calorically speaking—consider the value of spices and herbs. Imaginative seasoning is the spice of slim cooking, a culinary sleight of hand for anyone who prefers meals with more creativity than calories!

Herbs and spices aren't calorie-free—no food really is—but because they're used in such small quantities, they make up the one category of ingredients where the calories literally "don't count."

Consider this: Most dried herbs and spices range between 3 and 10 calories per teaspoon (or per tablespoon for fresh herbs), yet their flavor is so potent that you would rarely use more than 5 or 10 calories worth in a recipe that serves six or eight. So the seasonings usually add barely a calorie per person. Yet the flavor they provide far outweighs the flavor contribution of other "heavier" ingredients in your salad bowl. A tablespoon of tasteless oil, for example, is 120 calories!

Spiceshelf Calories

Seasonings that are 5 calories per teaspoon include basil, bay leaf, garlic powder, marjoram, parsley flakes, rosemary, sage, savory, tarragon and thyme.

Seasonings that are 6 to 10 calories per teaspoon include allspice, caraway, cardamom, cinnamon, clove, coriander, cumin, dill, fennel, ginger, mace, dry mustard, onion powder, oregano, paprika, pepper, sesame seeds and turmeric. Celery seed and nutmeg are 11 calories a teaspoon. Poppy seeds are the highest on the list at 13 calories a teaspoon.

Using Spices, Herbs and Seasonings

Like wine, seasonings are meant to be enjoyed and experimented with, so the rules about what goes with what should be taken with a grain of salt, so to speak! One guideline for appropriateness is to pair seasonings with other foods native to the regions where the particular seasoning grows well and is used abundantly. Allspice, for example, is a leading export of Jamaica, so you could hardly go wrong if you were to sprinkle tropical fruits like pineapple and mango with a dusting of allspice. Chicken and seafood are also popular in Jamaican cuisine. A seafood or cold chicken salad garnished with fruit or seasoned with lime and spiced with allspice would be a logical combination. By combining them, you have given ordinary ingredients a Caribbean flair!

More food for thought:

Allspice (whole berries or ground powder). Similar to a blend of cinnamon, nutmeg and clove. Used in Jamaica, Mexico, Caribbean, Central America. Try it with seafood, poultry, fruit salads, use it in pickled foods.

Anise (whole seeds). Sweet and licorice-like, similar to fennel. Used in Middle East, China, Italy, Spain, Southern Europe. Try it in pork and veal dishes, with eggplant, chickpeas, zucchini and citrus fruits. Use it as a substitute for *star anise* in Oriental combinations.

Basil (leaves). Sweet and pungent with a faintly licorice-like flavor. Used in Italy, France, Southern Europe. Try it with tomatoes, blended into cottage or pot cheese, in *pesto* dressings, with Creole or seafood salads, combined with oregano and garlic in Italian combinations.

Bay (leaves). Strong-but-pleasant flavor and fragrance. Used in France, Spain, Portugal, Italy, Greece, Turkey. Use it with poultry, fish, meat, in marinated dishes and dressings, soups and sauces.

Caraway (seeds). Mild, similar to dill seeds. Used in Holland, Poland, Middle Europe. Use in cheese dips and spreads, cheese dressings, coleslaw and potato salads, with ham and pork, in cottage cheese.

Cardamom (seeds and ground). Sharp, pungent, cinnamon-like. Used in South America, India. Add it to marinades, pickles, curry mixtures, spicy Oriental combinations.

Celery (seeds, salt and powder). Celery-like flavor. Used in France, other Western European countries, India, Middle East, Far East. Add it to potato and macaroni salads, tuna and other seafood salads; use it in coleslaw, pickles, salad dressings.

Chervil (leaves). Mild parsley-like flavor, very aromatic. Used in Middle Europe. Try it with fish, in macaroni and potato salad, Caesar salad, coleslaw, pickles; add to mayonnaise.

Chili powder (a blend of hot pepper, cumin and oregano, plus other seasonings; ranges from hot to mild depending on ingredients and proportions). For Mexican, Tex-Mex, South American, Caribbean dishes. Add to tomato mixtures, spicy meat or poultry salads; use it on shellfish, with avocado or peppers, in cheese spread and dips.

Cilantro (fresh leaves of the coriander plant, also known as Chinese or Mexican parsley). Distinctively pungent flavor, parsley-like leaves. Use it in Mexican, Tex-Mex and Oriental combinations.

Cinnamon (tree bark sold in "sticks," ground powder). Sweet fragrant spice that's widely used. Add it to fruit mixtures, Mexican and Greek salads, spicy tomato marinades for meat, poultry, or seafood. Use it in curry and chili combinations, in pickles.

Coriander (seeds and ground). Spicy and citrus-like. Used in Middle East, Orient, South America. Try in chili and curry combinations, spicy Oriental salads and stir-fry mixtures; add to pickles and coleslaw.

Cumin (seeds and ground). Cumin is the predominant flavor in most commercial chili and curry powders; popular in Middle Eastern and South American cuisines. Add it to tomatoes and tomato-based sauces and marinades, spicy yogurt sauces, dressings and bastes, chickpea dips, marinated eggplant. Sprinkle cumin on spicy meat mixtures for pita or pocket sandwiches.

Curry powder (a blend of hot pepper, cumin and sweet spices plus ground turmeric, which provides the intense yellow color). Flavor and hotness varies according to ingredients and proportions. Add curry to Indian, Middle Eastern and Polynesian combinations; use it to spice up mild cheese dips; mix with yogurt and lime juice as an Indian-style marinade or barbecue baste for meat or poultry.

Dill seed. Distinctive caraway-like flavor and fragrance, slightly bitter—widely used in Middle European cuisines. Sprinkle dill seed on potato and macaroni salads, use in pickles, coleslaw, on fish, pork and ham, in savory cottage cheese mixtures.

Dill weed. The feathery leaves of the dill plant; pleasant, pungent flavor, distinctive fragrance—widely used—add to potato and macaroni salads, seafood and fish sauces, with cucumbers. Pickled vegetables; stir into yogurt or sour cream sauces; sprinkle on cold soups, add to cottage cheese, mayonnaise or marinated vegetables. Use dill weed leaves in cold, uncooked dishes; use dill seeds in hot dishes (heat will bring out their flavor) or when the texture of seeds is desired.

Fennel (seeds). Sweet and licorice-like, similar to anise. Used in Middle East, Italy, other parts of Europe. Sprinkle on pork, poultry or seafood salads; use it with tomatoes, sweet peppers and other raw vegetables and fruit salads. Add fennel to stir-fry Oriental combinations and spaghetti sauce.

Fenugreek (seeds). Spicy slightly bitter maple-like flavor. Common in Asia, Morocco, North Africa, Middle East. Use in pickles, marinated vegetables, cold meats and poultry and seafood, add to curry mixtures.

Garlic (fresh, powdered, dried minced garlic, garlic juice). Widely used, especially in Southern Europe. Distinctively pungent flavor and fragrance, add to any savory salad or dressing combination. Use with meats, poultry, seafood, vegetables, dips, sauces and marinades.

Ginger (ground powder, fresh or dried minced ginger root). Widely used. Sprinkle on fruits, particularly peaches and pears, add to Oriental stir-fry combinations or soy-based marinades and sauces. Combine with tomato and lime juice for Caribbean baste for poultry or seafood; add to pickles.

Mace (ground, outer coating of the nutmeg). Similar to nutmeg, but stronger flavor and fragrance. Widely used in many regions. Add a pinch to dressings and sauces, to the poaching liquid for seafood, the cooking liquid for vegetables, particularly spinach.

Marjoram (leaf). Similar to oregano. Used in Europe, Middle East. Try with lamb, veal, other meats or poultry; with tomatoes, eggplant, mixed green salads, dips and sauces; with green beans and peas.

Mint (leaf). Fragrant and flavorful. Widely used especially in Britain, Greece. Good with lamb, red meats, chicken, peas, carrots, cheese, fresh fruit, creamy cold soups, tossed green salads, iced drinks.

Mustard (ground powder, whole seeds, prepared mustard). Widely used in many countries. Hot and spicy flavor. Add a pinch to liven up mild and creamy sauces, bland dressing; use in cheese dips; add to mayonnaise, seafood sauces. Use the seeds in pickle mixtures.

Nutmeg (ground). Distinctive fragrance and flavor. Widely used, particularly in French, Northern Italian and Caribbean cuisines, add to creamy sauces, salad dressing, stuffings, mild cheese dips. Use with cabbage, cauliflower and spinach, chicken, seafood, mildly flavored meats like veal. Add to fruits, fruit salads, fruit sauces, sweet cottage cheese combinations, milk drinks and creamed soups.

Oregano (leaf, ground and crumbled). Most familiar as the predominant herb in pizza or spaghetti sauce; also widely used in Mexican, Greek, Middle Eastern and other Mediterranean cuisines. Use with tomatoes, pepper, zucchini, eggplant; all meats, poultry and seafood; with mild cheeses, sauces, salad dressing and dips.

Paprika (ground red sweet pepper). Mild flavor, bright red color. Widely used, particularly in Hungary, Western Europe and Spain. Sprinkle on coleslaw, potato salad, macaroni salads and cottage cheese, to season mild spreads and dips, to add color to poached seafood or white sauces. Use with yogurt or sour cream dressings and sauces for cucumbers, peppers, poultry, seafood, meat mixtures.

Pepper, Black (whole peppercorns, coarsely ground, finely ground). Hot and biting flavor. Freshly ground pepper has a distinctive flavor. Widely used as a table seasoning on all types of food.

Pepper, White (ground). The fully ripened peppercorns, with a flavor similar to black pepper, widely used in white, light and creamy foods when the appearance of black pepper specks is not wanted.

Pepper, Red Cayenne (ground red pepper). Very hot, tongue-burning taste; widely used in many hot cuisines. Add it, along with other appropriate herbs and seasonings, to Mexican, Indian, Polynesian,

Caribbean, South American, Tex-Mex, Chinese (Szechuan), African and Creole combinations. Add just a pinch to liven mild and creamy foods, sauces, salad dressings.

Poppy seeds. Tiny navy-blue seeds with a distinctively pleasant taste and texture, widely used in many European cuisines. Add them to macaroni and potato salads, crunchy vegetable dips, cheese spreads; sprinkle on cottage cheese; serve on hot noodles; add to yogurt or sour cream toppings.

Rosemary (dried whole or crumbled leaf). Found in French, Italian, Spanish and other Mediterranean cuisines. Pleasant, slightly mint-like flavor. Use with poultry, pork, tomatoes, most vegetables, cheeses, salad dressings.

Sage (dried whole or crumbled leaf). Widely used in European cuisines; strong, but pleasant sweet herbal fragrance and flavor, good with poultry, pork, mushrooms, fillings and stuffings, tomatoes, mixed green salads, dressings, bastes and sauces, beans, soups and stews.

Savory (dried whole or crumbled leaf). Used in France, Spain, Italy, Western and Southern Europe. Somewhat like thyme in flavor and fragrance.

Sesame (seeds). Sometimes toasted, delicious nutty fragrance and flavor. Widely used in European, Middle Eastern and Oriental cuisines. Sprinkle on salads for flavorful crunch. Use in stir-fry dishes.

Tarragon (leaves). Distinctive herbal flavor a bit like anise, popular in French cooking and most Continental cuisines. Good with chicken, seafoods (particularly shellfish), meats, tomato and egg dishes, mild cheeses, mushrooms, wine-basted foods, soups, creamy dairy dishes.

Thyme (whole dried or crumbled leaf). Distinctive pleasant herbal flavor and fragrance widely used. Good with most meats, poultry, seafood with tomatoes and tomato-based sauces, in salad dressings; also in marinades and bastes.

Turmeric (ground yellow powder, the main coloring ingredient in curry powder and prepared mild mustards). Slightly ginger-like in flavor; used in Indian, Caribbean, Middle Eastern cuisines. Adds mild flavor and distinct yellow saffron-like color to sauces and dressings; use it in rice, marinades, soups. Combine it with spices to create your own mild curry powder.

Salad Oils

Most salad dressings, both commercial and homemade, contain large amounts of fat in the form of oil. In fact, fat accounts for most or even all the calories in conventional dressing. (In homemade oil and vinegar mixtures, the oil contributes 120 calories a tablespoon while the vinegar accounts for only 2 calories a tablespoon.)

The "right" oil for your salads and dressings depends on where you put your priorities: flavor (or the lack of it), cholesterol considerations and calories. How you might rank these considerations depends on your point of view and the state of your arteries and waistline.

Calories

As the chart on page 23 indicates, there's no significant difference in the calorie counts of various salad oils. Keep in mind that oil *is* fat, and there's no such thing as a low-fat or nonfattening salad oil that's "light" in calories. The only practical way to cut down on the calories in salad dressings is to *cut down* on oil, not switch from one brand or type to another.

What about mineral oil? In older diet books (and in some European diet cookbooks) you may encounter the outdated suggestion of substituting noncaloric, pharmaceutical-grade mineral oil (the type sold in drugstores for constipation problems). Because mineral oil isn't used by the body, it adds no calories, so this may seem like a workable diet idea. However, it is nutritionally unsound because mineral oil also interferes with the absorption of necessary vitamins. Thus, substitution of enough mineral oil to make a difference in your diet would also carry with it the risk of significantly interfering with your vitamin levels.

Nutrition researchers are currently investigating another "no-calorie" fat you may have heard about. Known as "sucrose polyester," this is a synthetic fat that the body cannot absorb. Medical researchers are interested because it also seems to lower cholesterol levels. However, much more research will be needed to determine all the possible effects on the human body. This synthetic fat is not available now and may never be. So for the foreseeable future, there is no way to save calories on salad oils except by using them sparingly!

Saturated Fat, Unsaturated Fat and Your Cholesterol

Oil doesn't contain cholesterol, so what's the big debate? The argument is not over the cholesterol content of oil, but rather how various types of fat might affect the amount of cholesterol circulating in your bloodstream. The cholesterol in your blood comes from two sources: the food you eat (animal foods like meats, eggs, cheese, milk, etc.) and from your body itself, which makes its *own* cholesterol!

What is important about the types of fats and oils you use is that different types of fat seem to affect the way your body handles its cholesterol. Saturated fats seem to increase cholesterol levels while polyunsaturated fats seem to lower them. Which is which? *Saturated fats* are hard at room temperature; they include animal fats like lard and butter, and vegetable fats that have been treated with hydrogen to make them hard, such as shortenings and stick margarines. Most salad oils on the other hand, are *polyunsaturated*—liquid at room temperature! However, some salad oils are higher in polyunsaturates than others. If your doctor has prescribed a cholesterol-lowering regimen, you will probably want to select your salad oils from those with the lowest percentage of saturated fat.

Should people in good health switch to polyunsaturated oils in an attempt to stave off a heart attack? That's a question to take up with your doctor, who can help you assess your own risk factors and reach an informed decision.

Flavor

If you don't care about calories or cholesterol—or even if you do—flavor (or the lack of it) is a prime consideration in *any* recipe! The flavors of different types of oil range from tasteless to quite strong. The marketers of flavorless oils have sought to turn the lack of taste into an advantage ("won't interfere with flavor," "so light," "no oily taste"). Americans have become so used to highly processed oils devoid of flavor that nothing is lost in terms of flavor by decreasing the fat content of popular commercial dressings.

If you like to taste and smell the olives in olive oil, Spanish, Portuguese and Greek imported virgin olive oils are generally more flavorful, aromatic and full-bodied than either the Italian imports or those from France. French olive oils are the lightest in flavor. What does this mean to calorie counters or cholesterol watchers? You can increase the *perception* of olive oil by using a stronger-tasting brand, but less of it. Make up for the missing volume by diluting your olive oil with a tasteless polyunsaturated oil (to lower your cholesterol count) or with nonoily ingredients (to cut calories). Another way to increase the olive oil flavor—without olive oil calories—is to add olives to your salad! Or add some of the packing liquid from canned or bottled olives to your dressing mixtures. If you want to make a small amount of peanut oil seem like more, add a teaspoon or so of peanut butter to any blender dressing, and you can use a lot less peanut oil!

Storing Salad Oils

Unopened containers of salad oils will keep without refrigeration for years, but all oils (and other foods high in oils, like nuts) eventually become rancid. Development of off-flavors is speeded up by exposure to air, light and heat. For that reason, once you open a bottle of oil it should be resealed tightly and stored in a cool, dark place. Canned salad oils should be transferred to tightly capped bottles.

If you use salad oil sparingly because of calorie considerations, do buy it in small amounts that will be used within several weeks of opening. If you open a larger container than you can use promptly, refrigerate it. While most cookbooks advise against storing salad oil in the refrigerator (it becomes cloudy and thick), refrigeration *is* suggested for opened containers of oil that you expect to have on hand for several months. Cloudiness is harmless and will disappear once the oil warms up to room temperature. Because *any* high fat ingredient may become rancid at room temperature, calorie watchers should refrigerate all infrequently used high-oil ingredients—nuts, sesame seeds, flavored soy bits and peanut butter, for example.

Oil	Calories per Tablespoon	% Cholesterol	% Fat	% Saturated	Flavor
Corn	120	0	100	10	None
Cotton Seed	120	0	100	25	None
Coconut	120	0	100	80	Slight
Olive	119	0	100	11	Mild-to-strong
Peanut	119	0	100	18	Mild, nutty
Safflower	120	0	100	8	None
Sesame	120	0	100	14	Mild, nutty
Soybean	120	0	100	15	Mild
Sunflower	120	0	100	11	None

Sour Power: Vinegars, Lemon, Lime and Other Fruit Juices

The tartness in salad dressings is generally provided by the addition of acid, usually in the form of vinegar—a diluted acid.

The word "vinegar" comes from the French word *vinaigre*, meaning "sour wine." In addition to wine, vinegar is also made from beer, grains, apples and other fermentable fruits. The tart taste is due to the acid content. In fact, most commercial vinegars are a mild 5 percent solution of acetic acid, which explains why ordinary white vinegar is so useful as a household cleaning acid. (Vinegar can remove light tarnish from brass or dissolve the hard water deposits on your shower door.)

Vinegar is also a preservative; it slows the growth of harmful bacteria in pickled foods. While vinegar is added to salads for its sharp flavor accent, the practice is also rooted in the belief that mild acid aids the digestion of coarse, fibrous or stringy vegetables. Apple cider vinegar is particularly favored as a folk remedy.

When to Use Which

While white, cider and wine vinegars can be used interchangeably in a pinch, there are flavor and color differences that favor the use of one over the other in different recipes.

White vinegar is colorless and has the sharpest, purest flavor. When would you use it? It's perfectly clear! White vinegar is best when you want to add pure, one-dimensional sourness with no other color or flavor notes. Because white vinegar is pure sour power, its flavor is decidedly sharper than other vinegars, so you probably want to use less of it.

Apple cider vinegar is the traditional salad favorite. It has a milder, fruity flavor and tawny tone. *Red wine vinegar* has a deep wine flavor and color. It has escalated in popularity during the last two decades. Less widely available but also growing in popularity are *white wine vinegar* and Oriental *rice wine vinegar*. Both are clear and colorless, so they won't tint a dressing or salad with a tawny or wine tone. Rice wine vinegar is much milder than other vinegars, a fact that should interest calorie counters. Because it's less vinegary you can dress your salad with more of it and use less high-calorie oil.

Flavored Vinegars

Flavored vinegars are made by adding herbs, seasonings or other highly flavored ingredients to any favorite vinegar. Commercially bottled varieties usually fetch fancy prices, but seasoned vinegars are easy to make at home with fresh or dried ingredients. Vinegars seasoned with fresh ingredients should be stored in the refrigerator.

Some suggestions:

Garlic vinegar. Mash one or two cloves of peeled garlic and put them into a small, narrow-necked bottle or cruet. Then fill it with white, wine or cider vinegar. Store in the refrigerator. The longer you store it, the more pronounced the flavor! Replenish the bottle with a little vinegar to dilute the flavor if it becomes too strong. Another way to add garlic to plain vinegar is to add a teaspoon or two of instant dried minced garlic to any favorite vinegar and wait a day or two for the flavors to blend.

Herb vinegar. Wash and dry freshly gathered young herb leaves (mint, oregano, basil, tarragon, thyme or any favorite). Bruise the leaves slightly to speed up the release of flavor. Half-fill a small bottle or jar loosely with the leaves, then fill it to the top with any favorite vinegar. Store it in the refrigerator. Or, add a tablespoon or two of dried herbs to a pint of any favorite vinegar. Dilute with additional vinegar if the flavor becomes too strong. Use the vinegar strained, if you prefer.

Hot pepper vinegar. Wash a small hot pepper, then chop it or cut it into strips. Put it in a bottle or cruet and fill with white or cider vinegar. Store in the refrigerator.

Flower vinegar. Wash and dry freshly gathered rose or nasturtium petals, loosely half-fill a small bottle with the petals, then fill it with white vinegar. Refrigerate two or three weeks, then strain off the vinegar. It will have a distinctly floral flavor and fragrance.

Berry vinegar. Half-fill a bottle with crushed raspberries, strawberries or other berries, then cover with white vinegar. Refrigerate one or two weeks, then strain. Store in the refrigerator.

Horseradish or ginger vinegar. Wash and dry a few pieces of the root and place in a small bottle. Cover with white or white wine vinegar. Store in the refrigerator.

Spicy vinegar. Season cider, white or white wine vinegar by adding a few cinnamon sticks, a whole nutmeg, allspice, berries, cloves or a few tablespoons mixed pickling spices. Try mixed crab or "shrimpboil" spices added to vinegar for a nice seasoning for seafood salads.

Mild wine vinegar. For a wine vinegar that is milder than the commercial products, combine equal parts leftover red wine and commercial red wine vinegar (or vary the proportions to suit your taste). To make the vinegar nonalcoholic (and reduce calories as well) simply heat the wine to boiling and simmer one minute. De-alcoholized, homemade, mild wine vinegar can help you save calories because you can use more vinegar and less oil in your salads! This is a good use for leftover, bottom of the bottle wine.

Mild cider vinegar. For a less sharp product, dilute equal parts cider vinegar and canned apple juice (vary the proportions to suit your taste).

Lemon Juice and Other Fruity Favorites

Another way to add tartness to salads is with lemon or other citrus juices. Lemon juice in place of vinegar is particularly appropriate in Greek salads, Middle Eastern mixtures and cold seafood plates. Lime juice is less sharp than lemon, and they can be used interchangeably in any dressing. Lime juice is particularly appropriate in fruit salads. Or try it in any combination with a Caribbean flavor!

Another idea: Try using grapefruit juice instead of lemon or lime, or use as a milder substitute for vinegar in any favorite salad dressing. For a touch of sweetness and less puckerpower, orange juice can replace all or part of the lemon juice in any dressing mixture.

Buttermilk, Yogurt and Sour Creamy Smoothness

Many salads and dressings call for the creamy texture and tangy tartness of such cultured dairy foods as yogurt, buttermilk and sour cream. While there are differences in taste and texture, for the sake of convenience or calorie-savings, you can use these products interchangeably.

Buttermilk does *not* contain butter! It's made from skim milk and is the least fattening of these cultured products, having only 88 calories in a cupful. However, buttermilk has lost out to yogurt in popularity and is less widely available than it was a few generations ago. If a recipe calls for a small amount of buttermilk and you have none on hand or don't want to purchase a whole quart, simply substitute *yogurt*. To give yogurt the liquid consistency of buttermilk, shake the container vigorously or beat the yogurt smooth in your blender, food processor or electric mixer bowl.

If you want the taste and texture of sour cream without the calories, yogurt can stand in here as well. To keep the thick texture, gently fold ingredients into the yogurt using a wire whip or the tines of a fork. If you are using yogurt as a sour cream substitute to save calories, be sure to read the label carefully. Choose plain low-fat yogurt (120–125 calories a cupful) not whole milk yogurt (150 calories) or fruit-flavored sweetened yogurt (150 to 260 calories or more!).

Blender-whipped *cottage cheese* is another substitute for sour cream. When whipped smooth in the blender or food processor, cottage cheese develops a thick creaminess that is closer to the texture of sour cream than yogurt is. Choose a tangy cottage cheese for a flavor that's more like sour cream, or spike your homemade sour cream with a little lemon juice for added tartness.

True *sour cream* has 416 calories a cupful. A slimmer alternative with true sour cream taste and texture is *sour half-and-half* (320 calories a cupful), available in some areas. Nondairy sour dressings are synthetic products that may cost you even more calories than real sour cream. If cutting calories is your chief concern, don't buy any product without checking the label for calorie data. Some of these products are made with large amounts of vegetable oil (and sometimes with highly saturated coconut oil) and contain 475 or more calories a cupful!

Natural Thickeners and Stabilizers

One feature of commercial salad dressings and mixes that makes them so popular is their homogenized texture, due to the presence of thickeners, emulsifiers and stabilizers. Remember, water and oil don't mix!

Liquid pectin is a simple, low-calorie, natural emulsifier you can add to homemade oil and vinegar mixtures. It is available on the canning supply shelf of your supermarket. Pectin is a natural product derived from orange peel; it's used in jam and jelly making to augment the natural pectin in fruits so that they will set. Liquid pectin is thick and syrupy in texture, cloudy in appearance; its flavor is slightly tart and citrusy. If you add some liquid pectin to oil and vinegar mixtures, your salad dressing will be thicker and won't separate immediately after you shake it up. Liquid pectin is only 2 calories a tablespoon and promises other health benefits as well. It is high in natural fiber; experiments suggest that it can help lower cholesterol. The addition of pectin may even prevent the complete absorption of other fats or fatty ingredients in the same salad, thereby saving more calories than it adds!

How much to add? My favorite proportion for low calorie oil and vinegar dressings is one part oil, one part vinegar, one part water and one part liquid pectin, plus herbs and seasonings to taste. If you're not calorie-wary, use two parts oil and omit the water. Or vary the proportions and additional seasonings to suit your taste.

If you're cholesterol-wary, you won't want to use *eggs* as a thickener in salad dressings. However, eggs are a natural emulsifier that help to keep fat and fluid mixtures in suspension. Mayonnaise is the chief example. No-cholesterol *egg substitutes* work the same way.

Another way to increase the density and homogeneity of your salad dressing mixtures is to add a small amount of *plain gelatin*. The gelatin granules must first be softened and melted before they are added; then the dressing must chill until the gelatin sets. Sprinkle one teaspoon (one third of a single packet) on ¼ cup cold water. Wait one minute until gelatin granules swell; then heat the mixture gently until gelatin melts and becomes clear. Stir melted gelatin into two cups of salad dressing and chill several hours.

Commercial Salad Dressing and Mixes . . . Regular, Light and Low Calorie

Commercial salad dressings tend to be high in calories, fat and salt; they usually contain artificial colors, flavors and preservatives, even sugar! Most are expensive in view of the relative cheapness of their ingredients. Nevertheless, they are unbeatably convenient. And fattening! (See chart on page 23.) But you have alternatives.

With Americans' compulsive concern for calories, the less fattening salad dressing alternatives have moved off the dietetic shelf and into the mainstream of the supermarket. Not so many years ago, calorie watchers were confined to just a few basics in bottled diet dressings: Italian, French and maybe blue cheese. Today nearly every popular type of commercial dressing is also available in a calorie-reduced version.

However, many "low-cal" dressings are not as low calorie as you might think! While government nutrition guides continue to publish scanty calorie counts for special dietary dressings, the nutrition labels of brands actually available reveal that popular "calorie-reduced" and "light" bottled dressings can range up to 50 calories a tablespoon. Luckily for the diet conscious, federal law requires that nutrition information—including calorie counts—be disclosed on the label of any product that makes nutritional claims. So there's no need to be deceived about how different types and brands of dressings compare. Simply put on your glasses and check the label! If nutritional information—*including* the calorie count—is not printed on the label, it's a safe assumption that the product is not low in calories!

With so many types and brands of calorie-reduced dressings to choose from, some are sure to please you more than others. If a particular brand disappoints you, don't give up on the whole low-cal category! Another brand's version may be more to your liking. Why not take the time to taste several types and brands at once, so you can make a valid judgment. Join with several other diet-minded friends and make it an afternoon or lunchtime project, sharing the cost of several bottles or jars of dressing. Pour or spoon the samples into small paper cups and provide celery sticks or other vegetable dippers. Score your choices. Each person will come away from such an experiment with a list of personal favorites.

3

Salad Dressings, Toppings and Sauces

Over 2,000 years ago the Babylonians tossed their vegetables with oil and vinegar, that most basic of salad dressings. Unfortunately for the calorie-wary, salad oil is the most fattening ingredient in your kitchen: almost 2,000 calories a cupful. A single tablespoon of oil is 120 calories and generally outweighs the caloric content of an entire salad bowl! Advertising implications notwithstanding, there is no such thing as a salad oil that's "light" in calories. Whether the oil comes from sunflower, safflower or sesame seeds, from soybeans, corn or peanuts, all oil is equally "heavy" in calories.

That's the bad news. The good news is that most oils used in salad dressings are polyunsaturated vegetable fats, the "good guys" in the cholesterol controversy. Butter, cream, meat, cheeses and dairy products contain the hard, saturated animal fats we have been cautioned to limit.

What should be pointed out, however, is that government nutrition experts now counsel Americans to restrict their consumption of *all* types of fat and to vary the sources of their fat intake so that polyunsaturated vegetable fats account for a greater ratio. In other words, we should be thinking of ways to use vegetable oil as a *substitute* for animal fat, not merely adding more fat to our diet. The recommendations do not suggest, as some advertisers imply, that an orgy of salad oil and soft margarine is in order.

31

The same set of recommendations also urges Americans to eat more fresh fruits and vegetables, so the well-dressed salad seems to be just what the doctor ordered: a good way to combine the needed fiber in vegetables with a modest amount of polyunsaturated fat. Since fat and oil are natural components of so many foods, the amount of oil added to salad can be modest, indeed—and probably should be, if your weight indicates the need to be careful about calories.

Many of the dressings, toppings and sauces collected in this section are sparing in fat and careful about calories and demonstrate the ways favorite-but-fattening dressings can be slimmed down.

Basic Vinaigrette (French or Oil and Vinegar) Salad Dressing

⅓ cup any vinegar (cider, wine, white, herb-seasoned, etc.)
⅔ cup any salad oil (olive, corn, safflower, sunflower, etc.)
½ to 1 tsp. dry mustard *or* 1 to 2 tsp. any favorite prepared
    mustard, such as yellow, brown, Dijon-style (optional)
1 clove minced garlic *or* pinch of dried garlic *or* squeezed garlic
    juice *or* use garlic salt instead of plain salt (optional)
Salt and coarsely ground pepper to taste
Pinch of sugar or granulated fructose *or* a few drops of honey or
    liquid sugar substitute

Combine ingredients in a covered jar; shake well just before serving.
Makes 1 cup, 80 calories per Tbs.

Lemon Vinaigrette—Substitute lemon juice for the vinegar.

Orange Vinaigrette—Combine 3 Tbs. vinegar and 2 Tbs. orange juice in place of the vinegar. Omit sugar or other sweetener.

Lower-Fat Vinaigrette
With water—Reduce oil to ⅓ cup or less; add ⅓ cup ice water; 40 calories per Tbs.
With liquid pectin—Reduce oil to ⅓ cup; add ⅓ cup liquid pectin; 45 calories per Tbs.
With fruit juice—Reduce oil to ⅓ cup; omit sugar. Add ⅓ cup apple juice or any other fruit juice; 45 calories per Tbs.

Blender or Food Processor Real Mayonnaise

1 egg
2 Tbs. lemon juice
1 tsp. dry mustard *or* 2 tsp. prepared
1 tsp. salt
Pinch of white or red cayenne pepper
1 cup any vegetable oil (olive, corn, soy, safflower, sunflower, etc.)

Combine all ingredients except oil in blender or food processor, using the steel blade. Process until blended. With the motor at high speed, slowly add the oil in a thin steady stream through the opening in the cover. Transfer to a covered container and store in the refrigerator. Use within one week.
Makes 1 cup, 125 calories per Tbs.

Calorie-Reduced Yogurt Mayonnaise—Gently fold 1 cup plain low-fat yogurt into 1 cup chilled real mayonnaise. Or make smaller amounts as needed by blending equal parts yogurt and mayonnaise with a fork. Each Tbs. 55 calories.

Cottage "Mayonnaise"

1 cup creamed California-style cottage cheese
2 Tbs. lemon juice
2 hard-cooked eggs, peeled
1 tsp. prepared mustard
1 tsp. celery salt
½ tsp. sugar (optional)

Combine in blender or food processor; whip until smooth.
Makes approximately 1½ cups, 15 calories per Tbs.

Yogurt, Mayonnaise Sauce—Substitute yogurt for cottage cheese (dressing will be thin); 15 calories per Tbs.

Italian Ricotta Mayonnaise—Substitute part-skim ricotta cheese for cottage cheese; 15 calories per Tbs.

Green (Avocado) Mayonnaise

1 very ripe medium avocado, peeled
1 large egg
¼ cup lemon juice
2 tsp. prepared mustard
1 tsp. celery salt
Dash of Tabasco sauce *or* pinch of red cayenne pepper

Cut avocado flesh into cubes and combine with remaining ingredients in electric mixer bowl or food processor, using the plastic or steel blade. Beat in electric mixer or process just until dressing is thick as whipped cream. Cover and store in the refrigerator. Use within a day or two.

Makes 1½ cups (approximately), about 20 calories per Tbs.

Zesty Mayonnaise

¾ cup mayonnaise (regular or low-fat)
¼ cup red wine vinegar
1½ Tbs. sugar *or* equivalent sugar substitute
1 Tbs. paprika
1 Tbs. prepared mustard
Salt or garlic salt to taste

Combine ingredients; beat smooth. Chill. Serve on greens or fruit chunks.

Makes approximately 1 cup, 80 calories per Tbs. with regular ingredients; 30 calories per Tbs. with lower-calorie alternatives.

Mock Mayonnaise

1 envelope unflavored gelatin
½ cup cold water
1 Tbs. dry mustard
1 Tbs. salt
¼ tsp. paprika
1⅓ cups boiling water
2 Tbs. butter or margarine
2 eggs, beaten
½ cup lemon juice or vinegar

To soften, sprinkle gelatin on cold water in top of double boiler, off heat. Mix together dry mustard, salt and paprika. Add to softened gelatin with boiling water and butter. Add small amount of hot mixture to beaten eggs, stirring rapidly. Return eggs to double boiler and cook, stirring constantly, until mixture begins to thicken. Remove from heat; gradually stir in lemon juice or vinegar. Chill until slightly thickened. Beat with rotary beater until well blended. Pour into jar; cover and store in refrigerator. To serve, beat again with rotary beater.

Makes 2¾ cups, 10 calories per Tbs.

Creamy Cooked Salad Dressing

2 eggs
¾ cup skim milk
2 Tbs. olive or salad oil
1 Tbs. all-purpose flour
4 to 5 tsp. sugar or fruit sugar (optional)
1 tsp. dry *or* 2 tsp. prepared mustard
Dash of Tabasco sauce *or* pinch of red cayenne pepper
3 to 4 Tbs. lemon juice or vinegar
Salt or celery salt to taste

Off heat, beat eggs and milk in the top of a double boiler. Beat in the oil, flour, (sugar), mustard and Tabasco sauce.

Place the double boiler top over hot (not boiling) water. Cook, stirring constantly, until mixture is thick. Stir in lemon juice or vinegar and salt to taste. Don't allow mixture to boil. Remove from heat and cool. Chill thoroughly.

(If desired, thin dressing with cold milk or water. For a more mayonnaise-like flavor, omit sugar and use lemon juice instead of vinegar.)

Makes 1½ cups, 20 calories per Tbs. without sugar; 25 calories per Tbs. with sugar.

Oil-Free Dressing—Omit oil—if desired, substitute 2 Tbs. olive liquid (from a jar of olives) for the oil—15 calories less per Tbs.

Sour Cream Dressing—Prepare previous dressing as directed. Gently fold in 1 cup sour cream (or sour half-and-half) when cold. Makes 2½ cups, 30 calories per Tbs. with sour cream; 20 calories per Tbs. with sour half-and-half.

Yogurt Dressing—Substitute plain low-fat yogurt for the sour cream; 15 calories per Tbs.

Oil-Free Cooked Salad Dressing

2 Tbs. sugar
1 Tbs. cornstarch
2 tsp. salt
1 cup water
2 egg yolks, lightly beaten
4 Tbs. lemon juice
3 Tbs. cider vinegar
1 Tbs. prepared mustard

In top of double boiler off heat, thoroughly combine dry ingredients; gradually add water, blending until smooth. Stir in remaining ingredients.

Place over boiling water; stirring constantly, cook 7 to 8 minutes until thick and smooth.

Cover and reduce to very low heat; cook 5 minutes, stirring occasionally. Chill before using. Store in refrigerator.

Makes approximately 1⅓ cups, 15 calories per Tbs.

Mayonnaise Piquante

½ cup mayonnaise (regular or low-fat)
¼ cup low-fat lemon yogurt
1 Tbs. lemon juice
½ tsp. fennel seed
½ tsp. Worcestershire sauce

Combine ingredients. Chill. Good with mixed greens or fruit chunks.

Makes approximately ¾ cup, 70 calories per Tbs. with regular mayonnaise; 30 calories per Tbs. with low-fat mayonnaise.

Red Wine Dressing I

¼ cup olive or any salad oil
¼ cup red wine vinegar
¼ cup dry red wine
¼ cup water
1 clove garlic, minced
2 tsp. fresh thyme or tarragon leaves *or* ½ tsp. dried
Salt and pepper to taste

Combine in a covered jar and shake well.
Makes 1 cup, 35 calories per Tbs.

Roquefort—Add 5 Tbs. crumbled Roquefort cheese (25 additional calories per Tbs.).

Caesar Dressing—Add 1 raw (or coddled) egg and 2 Tbs. grated Parmesan cheese (¼ cup defrosted no-cholesterol egg substitute may be used in place of the egg).

Anchovy Dressing—Add 1 Tbs. anchovy paste and 2 tsp. parsley flakes.

Vinaigrette—Add 2 tsp. chopped chives, 1 Tbs. chopped fresh parsley, 1 Tbs. chopped dill pickle, 1 tsp. capers and 2 chopped hard-cooked eggs (same count).

Red Wine Dressing II

½ cup dry red wine
4 Tbs. vinegar
½ cup water
4 Tbs. olive oil
2 tsp. cornstarch or arrowroot
1 tsp. salt or garlic or onion salt
Pinch of cayenne pepper

Combine all ingredients. Heat and stir over low heat until mixture simmers and thickens, about 5 minutes. Refrigerate in covered container.
Makes approximately 1½ cups, 25 calories per Tbs.

White Wine—Use dry white wine in place of red wine.

Dressing Diable—Add 2 tsp. dry mustard.

Curry Dressing—Add 1 tsp. curry powder.

Tarragon Dressing—Add 1 tsp. dried tarragon.

Chili-Hot Dressing—Add 1 tsp. chili powder and 2 tsp. prepared mustard.

Low-Fat Italian Wine Dressing

½ cup red wine vinegar
½ cup olive oil
½ cup liquid pectin (1 packet)
½ cup water
1 clove garlic, mashed
1 Tbs. chopped fresh basil or oregano *or* 1 tsp. dried
1 tsp. salt or garlic salt

Shake up in a covered jar; store in refrigerator. Shake again before using. Serve with tossed salad.

Makes a little more than 2 cups, approximately 30 calories per Tbs.

Blue Cheese Dressing

¼ cup cold milk (regular or skim)
1½ cups uncreamed cottage cheese (regular or low-fat)
⅓ cup (1½ oz.) crumbled blue cheese
3 Tbs. lemon juice
¾ tsp. onion salt
¼ tsp. garlic salt

Combine all ingredients in electric blender or food processor, using the metal blade. Process with short on-off bursts until fairly smooth. Cover and chill.

Makes approximately 2 cups, 15 calories per Tbs.

Speedy Gonzalez Guacamole Dressing

½ small very ripe avocado
½ cup bottled Italian salad dressing (regular or low-fat)
Pinch cumin seed (optional)

Mash peeled avocado and blend in salad dressing and seasoning, if desired. (Or whip ingredients smooth in blender or food processor, using the steel blade.) Store leftovers in refrigerator. Use over shredded iceberg lettuce or tossed salad. Makes 1 cup dressing, 50 calories per Tbs. with regular dressing; 25 calories per Tbs. with low-fat dressing.

Low-Sodium Salad Dressing

1 can (7¼ oz.) ready-to-serve, low-sodium tomato soup
¼ cup salad oil
2 Tbs. wine vinegar
1 Tbs. lemon juice
1 Tbs. finely chopped onion
1 Tbs. sugar
1 large clove garlic, minced
Generous dash pepper

Combine all ingredients in a jar. Chill. Shake well before using.
Makes about 1¼ cups, 30 calories per Tbs.

Many easy, creamy salad dressings are based on commercial mayonnaise, either regular or the low-fat, calorie-reduced variety.

Creamy Mustard Dressing

1 cup mayonnaise (regular or low-fat)
¼ cup prepared mustard
¼ cup orange juice
Salt or garlic salt and pepper to taste

Combine all ingredients. Cover; chill 1 hour. Serve over grapefruit sections, avocado slices, ham slices and Boston lettuce.
Makes 1⅓ cups, 80 calories per Tbs. with regular mayonnaise; 35 calories per Tbs. with low-fat mayonnaise.

Lemon Caesar Salad Dressing

½ cup mayonnaise (regular or low-fat)
½ cup fresh lemon juice
1 tsp. Worcestershire sauce
1 clove minced garlic *or* pinch of instant garlic (optional)
2 Tbs. grated Parmesan cheese
¼ cup minced fresh parsley

Stir or blend ingredients together; toss with romaine lettuce or raw spinach leaves.
Makes approximately 1 cup dressing, 55 calories per Tbs. with regular mayonnaise; 25 calories per Tbs. with low-fat mayonnaise.

Creamy Italian Salad Dressing

⅓ cup mayonnaise (regular or low-fat)
⅓ cup cider or white vinegar
⅓ cup water
1 clove garlic, mashed (optional)
Salt or garlic salt and pepper to taste
2 tsp. crushed fresh oregano *or* ½ tsp. dried

Combine ingredients and whip them with a fork until blended. Store in a covered container in the refrigerator.

Makes 1 cup, 35 calories per Tbs. with regular mayonnaise; 15 calories per Tbs. with low-fat mayonnaise.

Creamy Italian Cheese—Reduce mayonnaise to ¼ cupful. Stir in 3 Tbs. grated Parmesan cheese. Additional calories: 5 per Tbs.

Creamy Cucumber Dressing

1 cup mayonnaise (regular or low-fat)
1 cup pared, seeded cucumber, chopped
2 Tbs. minced parsley
1 clove garlic, minced
1 Tbs. minced chives or scallions
½ tsp. salt
Pinch of coarse-ground pepper
1 cup plain low-fat yogurt

Stir together mayonnaise, cucumber, parsley, garlic, chives, salt and pepper. Fold in yogurt. Chill.

Makes approximately 2¾ cups, 40 calories per Tbs. with regular mayonnaise; 20 calories per Tbs. with low-fat mayonnaise.

Low-Fat Creamy Onion Salad Dressing

½ large sweet (Spanish) onion, coarsely chopped
¼ cup olive or salad oil
½ cup cider or white vinegar
¼ cup part-skim ricotta cheese
½ cup cold water
¼ cup fresh parsley
1 Tbs. fresh oregano or basil *or* 1 tsp. dried
Salt and pepper to taste

Combine onion with the other ingredients in blender or food processor using the steel blade. Cover and process until creamy. Store in a covered jar in the refrigerator; shake before using.

Makes 1¾ cups, 20 calories per Tbs.

Thousand Island Dressing

1 cup mayonnaise (regular or low-fat)
⅓ cup skim milk
2 Tbs. chili sauce
2 Tbs. sweet relish
1 hard-cooked egg, chopped

Combine ingredients. Chill.

Makes approximately 1½ cups, 45 calories per Tbs. with regular mayonnaise; 25 calories per Tbs. with low-fat mayonnaise.

Low-Fat Thousand Island Dressing

½ cup low-fat mayonnaise
⅓ cup low-fat plain yogurt
¼ cup cold water
¼ cup catsup
2 Tbs. pickle relish
2 Tbs. minced fresh parsley
2 Tbs. minced chives or onions

Stir together until blended. Refrigerate.

Makes approximately 1⅔ cups, 20 calories per Tbs.

Creamy Curry Dressing

1 cup mayonnaise (regular or low-fat)
2 tsp. curry powder (or more to taste)
1 cup applesauce (regular or unsweetened)
8 oz. plain low-fat yogurt

Combine mayonnaise with curry and applesauce. Fold in yogurt. Chill. Serve over fruit.

Makes approximately 3 cups dressing, 40 calories per Tbs. with regular mayonnaise and applesauce; 20 calories per Tbs. with low-fat mayonnaise and unsweetened applesauce.

Creamy Horseradish Dressing

1 cup mayonnaise (regular or low-fat)
½ cup plain low-fat yogurt
2 Tbs. finely chopped onion
1 to 2 Tbs. prepared white horseradish to taste
½ tsp. salt
⅛ tsp. pepper
2 Tbs. fresh parsley

Combine all ingredients. Cover; chill 1 hour. Serve over slices of beef, tomato, and onions.

Makes 1⅔ cups, 60 calories per Tbs. with regular mayonnaise; 25 calories per Tbs. with low-fat mayonnaise.

Creamy Mexican-Style Salad Dressing

½ cup mayonnaise (regular or low-fat)
½ cup tomato juice (regular or spicy for making a Bloody Mary)
1 Tbs. lime or lemon juice
2 tsp. cumin seeds *or* 1 tsp. ground cumin
Pinch of dried oregano
Chili powder or Tabasco sauce to taste

Stir together until blended. Cover and chill in refrigerator. Serve with shredded iceberg lettuce or iceberg plus sliced peppers, onions and tomatoes.

Makes 1 cup, 50 calories per Tbs. with regular mayonnaise; 25 calories per Tbs. with low-fat mayonnaise.

Creamy Italian Cheese Dressing

4 Tbs. part-skim ricotta cheese
3 Tbs. grated Parmesan cheese
3 Tbs. mayonnaise (regular or low-calorie)
3 Tbs. wine or cider vinegar
2 Tbs. lemon juice *or* additional vinegar
⅓ cup cold water
1 clove garlic, peeled
2 tsp. fresh oregano leaves *or* ½ tsp. dried

Combine ingredients in blender or food processor using the steel blade. Process until smooth. Store covered in the refrigerator.

Makes about 1 cup, 30 calories per Tbs. with regular mayonnaise; 20 calories per Tbs. with low-fat mayonnaise.

Pronto Creamy Italian Salad Dressing

    1 cup part-skim ricotta cheese
    1 envelope seasoned salad dressing mix

Combine in your blender. Blend on low speed, scraping down sides of container frequently with a rubber scraper. Pour into a covered jar and refrigerate.

Makes 1¼ cups, 20 calories per Tbs.

Mediterranean Dressing

    ½ cup plain low-fat yogurt
    ½ cup mayonnaise (regular or low-fat)
    2 Tbs. lemon or lime juice
    1 tsp. ground turmeric
    Salt or garlic salt and pepper to taste

Combine; beat smooth. Chill.

Makes approximately 1 cup, 55 calories per Tbs. with regular mayonnaise; 25 calories per Tbs. with low-fat mayonnaise.

Spicy French Salad Dressing

    ½ cup mayonnaise or French salad dressing (regular or low-fat)
    2 Tbs. chili sauce
    1 tsp. Worcestershire sauce
    1 tsp. prepared mustard
    Few drops Tabasco sauce

Thoroughly mix ingredients. Refrigerate. Stir again before using.

Makes approximately ⅔ cup, 75 calories per Tbs. with regular mayonnaise; 35 calories per Tbs. with low-fat mayonnaise; 50 calories per Tbs. with regular French dressing; 15 calories per Tbs. with low-fat French dressing.

Dressings based on low-fat yogurt.

Presto Yogurt Russian Dressing

½ cup plain low-fat yogurt
½ cup catsup
1 tsp. lemon juice or vinegar
Salt and pepper

Mix all ingredients, seasoning to taste.
Makes 1 cup dressing, 15 calories per Tbs.

Restaurant-Style Yogurt Russian Dressing

½ cup bottled chili sauce or catsup
½ cup plain low-fat yogurt
3 Tbs. vinegar
1 tsp. salt or garlic salt
1 tsp. ground turmeric *or* 1–2 drops yellow food coloring
    (optional)

Combine and stir well.
Makes approximately 1 cup, 15 calories per Tbs.

Yogurt Russian Dressing

1 cup plain low-fat yogurt
1 hard-cooked egg, peeled
5 Tbs. catsup
2 Tbs. chopped sweet bell peppers
Salt and pepper

In a blender, combine yogurt, egg, and catsup until smooth. Stir in
bell pepper, and season to taste.
Makes approximately 1½ cups dressing, about 15 calories per Tbs.

Yogurt Blue Cheese Dressing

1 cup plain low-fat yogurt
4 oz. blue or Roquefort cheese
3 Tbs. vinegar
1 clove garlic (optional)
1 tsp. salt or garlic salt
¼ tsp. coarsely ground pepper

Whip in blender on high speed until smooth.
 Makes 1½ cups, 25 calories per Tbs.

Creamy Greek Feta Cheese Dressing—Substitute feta for blue
cheese, lemon juice for vinegar. Add a few fresh mint and oregano
leaves or a pinch of dried, if desired (20 calories per Tbs.).

Yogurt Roquefort Dressing

½ cup mayonnaise (regular or low-fat)
1 cup plain low-fat yogurt
2 Tbs. milk
⅓ cup crumbled Roquefort or blue cheese
Salt and pepper
Thyme

Stir mayonnaise, yogurt and milk together until smooth. Mix in
cheese and seasonings to taste.
 Makes approximately 2 cups, 35 calories per Tbs. with regular
mayonnaise; 20 calories per Tbs. with low-fat mayonnaise.

Yogurt Green Goddess Dressing I

1 cup plain low-fat yogurt
1 hard-cooked egg, peeled
1 tsp. Worcestershire sauce
1 Tbs. lemon juice
1 tsp. celery salt
1 tsp. prepared hot mustard
¾ cup fresh parsley without stems, loosely packed
¼ cup chopped chive or scallion

Combine in covered blender and blend until smooth.
 Makes about 1½ cups dressing, approximately 10 calories per Tbs.

Yogurt Green Goddess Dressing II

¼ cup mayonnaise (regular or low-fat)
¼ cup plain low-fat yogurt
2 Tbs. dry white wine
Dash of Worcestershire sauce
1 cup parsley, minced
2 Tbs. minced chives

Beat ingredients together. Chill.

Makes approximately 1 cup, 30 calories per Tbs. with regular mayonnaise; 15 calories per Tbs. with low-fat mayonnaise.

Yogurt Caesar Dressing I

½ cup plain low-fat yogurt
1 egg yolk, raw
2 Tbs. lemon or lime juice
2 Tbs. grated Parmesan cheese
1 tsp. Worcestershire sauce
½ tsp. garlic salt
Freshly cracked pepper
Minced fresh parsley (optional)

Blend ingredients together with a fork. Spoon over romaine lettuce or raw spinach, and garnish with purple onion rings and toasted bread croutons, if desired.

Makes approximately ¾ cup dressing, 15 calories per Tbs.

Yogurt Caesar Dressing II

1 cup plain low-fat yogurt
1 hard-cooked egg, peeled
2 Tbs. lemon juice
1 clove garlic, peeled
1 tsp. Worcestershire sauce
2 Tbs. Parmesan cheese
Salt and pepper to taste

Combine all ingredients in covered blender; beat until smooth. Refrigerate.

Makes about 1¼ cups dressing, approximately 15 calories per Tbs.

Low-Fat Creamy Greek-Style Salad Dressing

⅓ cup low-fat mayonnaise
⅓ cup plain low-fat yogurt
¼ cup cold water
¼ cup lemon juice
Salt or onion salt and pepper to taste
2 Tbs. minced fresh parsley
½ tsp. dried mint or marjoram *or* 2 tsp. minced fresh
½ tsp. dried oregano *or* 2 tsp. minced fresh

Stir together until blended. Refrigerate.
Makes approximately 1 cup, 20 calories per Tbs.

Pronto Green Goddess Dressing

1 envelope Green Goddess dressing mix
1 cup plain low-fat yogurt

Stir contents of envelope into yogurt. Mix thoroughly.
Makes 1¼ cups, 10 calories per Tbs.

Farmer Cheese and Onion Dressing

4 oz. fresh farmer cheese
1 Tbs. minced onion
1 cup plain low-fat yogurt
½ tsp. Worcestershire sauce
¼ tsp. dry mustard

Combine all ingredients in blender or food processor, using steel blade. Cover and process until smooth. Chill.
Makes approximately 1½ cups, 15 calories per Tbs.

Spicy Tomato Dressing

1 cup tomato-vegetable juice
¼ cup chili sauce
2 Tbs. salad oil
1 Tbs. lemon or lime juice
2 tsp. prepared horseradish

Combine ingredients; chill. Serve with meat or vegetable salads.
Makes approximately 1⅓ cups, 15 calories per Tbs.

Tangy Tomato Dressing

12 oz. can tomato juice
½ cup red wine vinegar
¼ cup salad oil
2 tsp. Worcestershire sauce
1 tsp. sugar (optional)
1 Tbs. minced onion *or* 1 tsp. onion flakes
1 clove garlic, minced
2 tsp. prepared mustard
Salt and pepper to taste
Splash of hot pepper sauce (optional)

In blender: Cover; blend all ingredients until smooth. Chill.
By hand: Place tomato juice, vinegar, oil and Worcestershire sauce
in a jar with a tight-fitting lid. Cover and shake. Add remaining
ingredients; shake or stir until smooth. Chill.
Makes approximately 2¼ cups, 15 calories per Tbs.

Italian Variation—Omit Worcestershire and mustard. Add 2 tsp.
mixed Italian seasonings, or 1 tsp. dried oregano and 1 tsp. dried
basil.

Chinese Dressing

1 can (6 oz.) tomato-vegetable juice
1 Tbs. white or rice vinegar
2 tsp. soy sauce
1 tsp. prepared mustard
2 Tbs. salad oil (optional)

In covered container, shake all ingredients until well blended. Chill.
Makes ¾ cup, 5 calories per Tbs.; 25 calories per Tbs. when made
with oil.

Japanese Dressing

  1 Tbs. cornstarch
  ¾ cup fat-skimmed chicken broth
  ¼ cup dry sherry
  3 Tbs. soy sauce
  1 tsp. sugar
  1 tsp. sesame seeds

Mix the cornstarch into the chicken broth. Combine all ingredients
in a saucepan. Cook and stir over low heat about 5 minutes until
thickened and clear.
Makes approximately 1 cup dressing, 15 calories per Tbs.

Spicy Florida Grapefruit Dressing

  2 tsp. cornstarch
  1 tsp. sugar
  ¾ tsp. salt
  ⅛ tsp. pepper
  ½ tsp. paprika
  ½ tsp. dry mustard
  1 cup grapefruit juice
  2 Tbs. salad oil
  ¼ cup catsup

Combine dry ingredients in saucepan; stir in grapefruit juice. Place
over medium heat and bring to a boil, stirring constantly. Boil 1
minute.
Remove from heat. Stir in remaining ingredients. Chill. Stir again
before serving.
Makes 1¼ cups, 20 calories per Tbs.

Peachy-Keen Fruit Dressing

1 large or 2 small very ripe peeled peaches *or* ¾ cup peach puree
  (baby food)
¼ cup mayonnaise (regular or low-fat)
3 to 4 Tbs. plain or vanilla low-fat yogurt

Beat, blend or process ingredients together until smooth. Refrigerate
in a covered container; use promptly.

Makes 1 cup (approximately), about 30 calories per Tbs. with regular mayonnaise; 15 calories per Tbs. with low-fat mayonnaise.

Raspberry (or Strawberry) Dressing—Substitute ¾ cup pureed
fresh or defrosted unsweetened berries for the peaches. Calories: 30
per Tbs. with raspberries and regular mayonnaise; 15 per Tbs. with
low-fat mayonnaise.

Banana Dressing for Fruit Salads

2 very ripe bananas, peeled
2 Tbs. lime or lemon juice
½ cup plain low-fat yogurt or buttermilk or skim milk
½ tsp. salt
3 tsp. sugar or fructose *or* equivalent sugar substitute (optional)

In blender or electric mixing bowl, beat bananas until smooth. Add
remaining ingredients and beat until blended.

Makes 1 cup, 20 calories per Tbs.; sugar or fructose adds 5 calories
per Tbs.

Fruity Salad Dressing

½ cup mayonnaise (regular or low-fat)
½ cup any fruit-flavored low-fat yogurt
2 Tbs. ice water

Fold ingredients together, adding only enough water to achieve desired consistency.

Makes about 1 cup, 55 calories per Tbs. with regular mayonnaise;
25 calories per Tbs. with low-fat mayonnaise.

Whipped Cream Dressing for Fruit Salads

½ cup plain low-fat yogurt
½ cup mayonnaise (regular or low-fat)
½ cup pressurized whipped cream (regular or light)

Fold yogurt and mayonnaise together. Spray whipped cream into a ½-cup measure. Fold into mayonnaise mixture.

Makes 1½ cups, 40 calories per Tbs. with regular mayonnaise; 20 calories per Tbs. with low-fat mayonnaise.

Honey and Yogurt Dressing

¼ cup plain low-fat yogurt
4 Tbs. honey
1 Tbs. lemon juice
½ tsp. celery seed
¼ tsp. paprika

Combine all ingredients. Mix thoroughly. Chill.

A delicious sweet dressing particularly appropriate for salads with fresh fruit.

Makes approximately ½ cup, 40 calories per Tbs.

Yogurt Hollandaise Sauce for Hot Cooked Vegetables

3 egg yolks *or* 6 Tbs. no-cholesterol egg substitute
1 cup plain low-fat yogurt
1 Tbs. lemon juice
Butter-flavored salt or butter flavoring

Beat the egg yolks. Beat in yogurt and lemon juice. Heat, stirring constantly, in the top of a double boiler, over hot water, until thick and smooth. Add seasonings to taste.

Makes about 1¼ cups, 15 calories per Tbs. with egg yolks; 10 calories per Tbs. with egg substitute.

Mustard Sauce

¼ cup plain low-fat yogurt
2 tsp. dried instant onion
2 tsp. hot (Dijon-style) mustard or more to taste
Salt to taste (optional)

Stir ingredients together; chill until serving time. Serve with cold fish, chicken or beef.

Makes ¼ cup, 12 calories per Tbs.

Creamy Horseradish Sauce for Cold Meats

½ cup part-skim ricotta cheese
2 Tbs. mayonnaise (regular or low-fat)
2 to 3 Tbs. cold water
2 Tbs. prepared white horseradish or more to taste
3 or 4 tsp. capers (optional)
Salt and white pepper to taste (optional)

Blend ingredients until smooth in blender or food processor, using the steel blade. Use with cold ham, beef, corned beef, tongue, chicken or fish. Good with raw vegetables, too.

Makes a scant cup, 25 calories per Tbs. with regular mayonnaise; 20 calories per Tbs. with low-fat mayonnaise.

Fresh Cucumber Sauce for Cold Seafood

1 cup coarsely chopped unpeeled unwaxed cucumber
2 tsp. lemon juice
½ cup plain low-fat yogurt
4 Tbs. mayonnaise (regular or low-fat)
1 tsp. prepared mustard
1 Tbs. minced onion *or* 1 tsp. onion flakes
Salt and pepper to taste

Chop cucumber coarsely, without peeling, then leave in a colander about 30 minutes to drain. Squeeze out moisture, then combine with remaining ingredients. Chill in the refrigerator a few hours for flavors to blend.

Makes about 1½ cups, 20 calories per Tbs. with regular mayonnaise; 10 calories per Tbs. with low-fat mayonnaise.

Spicy Seafood Sauce

⅔ cup chili sauce
3 Tbs. dill pickle relish
1 Tbs. prepared horseradish

Mix together all ingredients and chill. Serve with raw small clams or oysters on the half shell or small cooked shrimp (1 tsp. for each).
Makes approximately 1 cup; 4 calories per tsp.

Fresh Dill Sauce for Cold Fish

2 Tbs. minced fresh dill weed
2 Tbs. minced fresh parsley
2 Tbs. minced pickle or drained relish
¼ cup mayonnaise (regular or low-fat)

Stir ingredients together and serve.
Makes ½ cup, approximately 55 calories per Tbs. with regular mayonnaise; 20 calories per Tbs. with low-fat mayonnaise.

Russian Dill Sauce—Combine 6 Tbs. Russian dressing (regular or low-fat) with 3 Tbs. minced fresh dill and 2 Tbs. minced fresh parsley. Makes ½ cup, approximately 55 calories per Tbs. with regular dressing; 25 calories per Tbs. with low-fat dressing.

Garden Tartar Sauce

5 Tbs. mayonnaise (regular or low-fat)
Lemon juice
1 Tbs. minced fresh parsley
1 Tbs. minced fresh chives or scallions
1 tsp. prepared yellow mustard
1 Tbs. minced pickle or drained relish
1 tsp. capers (optional)
Salt and pepper to taste

Stir together; refrigerate until serving time.
Makes ½ cup, under 35 calories per Tbs. with regular mayonnaise; 15 calories per Tbs. with low-fat mayonnaise.

Low-Fat Tartar Sauce for Cold Fish

5 Tbs. plain low-fat yogurt
5 Tbs. mayonnaise (regular or low-fat)
1 Tbs. lemon juice
2 Tbs. minced fresh parsley
2 tsp. minced fresh dill weed (optional)
2 Tbs. minced chives or scallions
1 tsp. prepared mustard
2 Tbs. minced pickle relish
Salt and pepper to taste

Stir together. Store in the refrigerator.

Makes 1 cup, 35 calories per Tbs. with regular mayonnaise; 18 calories per Tbs. with low-fat mayonnaise. (Regular tartar sauce has 74 calories per Tbs.)

Thyme Sauce

½ cup mayonnaise (regular or low-fat)
½ cup low-fat plain yogurt
2 Tbs. minced chives or scallions or onions
4 Tbs. minced fresh thyme *or* 1 Tbs. fresh parsley and 1 tsp. dried thyme
Salt and pepper to taste

Stir ingredients together and serve. Delicious with fish, seafood or chilled chicken.

Makes 1 cup, approximately 50 calories per Tbs. with regular mayonnaise; 20 calories per Tbs. with low-fat mayonnaise.

Greek Seafood Sauce

½ medium cucumber, peeled and minced
4 Tbs. plain low-fat yogurt
1 Tbs. lemon or lime juice
2 Tbs. minced fresh mint or marjoram
Salt and pepper to taste

Peel cucumber, and mince finely or shred coarsely. Wrap in a clean white towel and squeeze out moisture. Combine with remaining ingredients; chill until serving time.

Makes approximately ⅔ cup, approximately 7 calories per Tbs.

Greek Minted Cucumber and Parsley Sauce—Substitute finely minced fresh parsley for mint.

4

Make-Ahead and Marinated Salads

A ready-to-serve salad that waits in the refrigerator until serving time is a boon to any busy cook. Unlike freshly tossed salads composed of lettuce or other fresh greens, marinated salads require no last-minute attention; they're all ready "dressed to go." Another advantage: leftover marinated salads can be saved and served again, while tossed salad will wilt in its dressing if you attempt to reclaim the leftovers for another meal.

Marinated salads are also versatile. They can be made from either raw or crisply cooked vegetables. In fact, they can even be based on leftover hot vegetables, thereby providing the thrifty cook with a way to recycle tonight's cooked vegetables into tomorrow's marinated side dish. Any favorite bottled dressing poured on vegetables remaining after dinner can give you a head start on tomorrow's menu!

Serving vegetables cold in a spicy dressing can be a quick salvation for the "salad course" when there's no fresh greenery in your crisper. Canned or frozen vegetables can be the starting point. If you have no time to shop, check your pantry or freezer for inspiration.

A final point about marinated salads: they travel well! Tossed greens might be difficult to manage at a picnic, at your weekend retreat or in your lunchbox, but a Thermos bottle full of marinated vegetables can add crunch to your lunch. With cold cooked meat, poultry or seafood added, a marinated salad can *be* your lunch.

Artichoke Salad

Marinade
  2 Tbs. olive oil
  2 Tbs. white wine vinegar
  1 Tbs. minced fresh oregano *or* 1 tsp. dried
  1 Tbs. minced fresh basil *or* 1 tsp. dried
  Garlic salt and pepper

Salad
  1 package (10 oz.) frozen artichoke hearts, defrosted
  1 green bell pepper, seeded and diced
  10 ripe olives, pitted and sliced
  10 green stuffed olives, sliced
  12 cherry tomatoes

Mix marinade ingredients. Cook artichoke hearts according to package directions; drain. Add artichokes to marinade, turning to coat completely. Marinate several hours in the refrigerator, turning occasionally.

At serving time, toss artichoke hearts and marinade with remaining salad ingredients. Serve on a bed of lettuce, if desired.

Makes 4 servings, 130 calories each.

Savory Marinated Slaw

  2 carrots, sliced
  1 package (10 oz.) coleslaw mix *or* 1 small head cabbage, shredded
  1 cucumber, chopped

Dressing
  ½ cup cider vinegar
  ¼ cup sugar
  ¼ cup salad oil
  1 tsp. celery salt
  2 tsp. dried savory
  1 clove garlic, minced
  A few drops of Tabasco sauce

Combine salad ingredients. Shake dressing ingredients in a jar with a tight-fitting lid; toss with salad. Refrigerate several hours to allow flavors to blend.

Makes 8 servings, 105 calories each.

Dilled Florets

2 cups broccoli florets
2 cups cauliflower florets
1 carrot, pared and sliced
1 unpared cucumber, sliced
¼ cup snipped dill weed
½ cup creamy cucumber salad dressing (regular or low-fat)

Toss all ingredients together. Refrigerate several hours before serving so that flavors will blend.

Makes 4 servings, 185 calories each, with regular salad dressing; 120 calories each with low-fat dressing.

Corn and Broccoli Salad

1 package (10 oz.) frozen broccoli cuts, defrosted
1 package (10 oz.) frozen corn kernels, defrosted
2 Tbs. diced pimiento
4 Tbs. Italian salad dressing (regular or low-fat)

Cook broccoli and corn according to package directions, until barely tender. Drain thoroughly. Toss with remaining ingredients. Chill.

Makes 6 servings, 105 calories each with regular salad dressing; 75 calories each with low-fat dressing.

Cabbage-Carrot Slaw

2 cups shredded cabbage
2 cups shredded carrots
½ cup minced green bell pepper
1 cup plain low-fat yogurt
1 Tbs. orange juice
1 Tbs. minced onion
1 tsp. celery seed
2 tsp. caraway seed
Salt or garlic salt

Thoroughly mix all ingredients, seasoning to taste. Chill.
Makes 4 servings, 80 calories each.

Deviled Carrot Salad

3 cups grated carrots
¼ cup orange juice
1 Tbs. brown sugar
1 tsp. prepared mustard
Salt to taste
Dash of cayenne pepper (optional)

Toss all ingredients together lightly. Serve chilled or cook in a large skillet until just heated through and serve hot.
Makes 6 servings, 35 calories each.

Israeli Pickled Cauliflower

½ cup cider vinegar
⅔ cup water
1 tsp. salt
1 tsp. sugar
Small bay leaf
¼ tsp. mustard seed
Pinch of white pepper
10 oz. raw cauliflower florets, about 1½ cups
1 carrot, pared and sliced

Boil together vinegar, water, salt, sugar, bay leaf, mustard seed and pepper, for 2 minutes. Remove from heat. Pour over vegetables in a refrigerator container. Chill for several hours at least. Serve as a relish, with salads, or as a garnish for cold meat, poultry or fish.
Makes approximately 2 cups, 4 servings, 35 calories each.

Yogurt-Cucumber Salad

½ cup plain low-fat yogurt
2 Tbs. lemon juice
½ tsp. salt
1 tsp. sugar
2 cucumbers, sliced

Blend yogurt, juice, salt and sugar. Toss with cucumbers; chill several hours.
Makes 4 servings, 40 calories each.

Quickie French-Dressed Carrots

1 package (10 oz.) frozen sliced carrots or canned tiny Belgian
    carrots
4 Tbs. French dressing (regular or low-fat)
3 Tbs. water or orange juice
Pinch of ground cinnamon or nutmeg (optional)

Combine ingredients. Allow carrots to defrost and marinate in the dressing several hours before serving.

Makes 3 servings, 115 calories each with regular dressing; 65 calories each with low-fat dressing; orange juice adds 10 calories per serving.

Marinated Cucumbers and Onion

2 cucumbers, peeled and sliced
1 small sweet onion, sliced into thin rings
Equal parts cider and cider vinegar
Salt and coarse pepper to taste

Combine cucumbers and onion in a glass or ceramic bowl, adding just enough of the liquids to cover. Add salt and pepper. Cover; refrigerate several hours. Drain and serve.

Makes 4 servings, approximately 25 calories each.

Oriental Marinated Cucumber

2 tsp. grated fresh ginger *or* 1 tsp. ground ginger
3 Tbs. rice or white vinegar
3 Tbs. soy sauce
1 medium unpared cucumber, raw
1 or 2 scallions *or* 1 small red onion, sliced
Pinch of red cayenne pepper (optional)

Soak grated ginger in vinegar 1 hour, or mix ground ginger with vinegar. Then combine with soy sauce and mix well. Slice unpared cucumber into spears, then slice spears into bite-size chunks. Thinly slice the scallions. Combine all ingredients in a glass bowl and chill in the refrigerator before serving.

Makes 4 servings, approximately 20 calories each.

Oriental Marinated Squash—Substitute raw yellow summer squash or green zucchini for the cucumber.

Bread and Butter Pickles

4 cups sliced cucumbers
1 cup sliced onion
½ cup diced red bell pepper
3 Tbs. uniodized salt
1 cup unsweetened cider or apple juice
½ cup sugar
½ tsp. ground turmeric
1 tsp. celery seeds
1 tsp. dry mustard

Stir cucumbers, onion and bell pepper with salt, until well coated. Refrigerate 2 to 3 hours. Remove from refrigerator and rinse off salt. Combine remaining ingredients and heat to boiling. When mixture boils, stir in vegetables, then reheat to boiling. Allow to cool, then pour into a nonmetallic container. Cover and store in the refrigerator. Wait 2 or 3 days before serving.

About 25 calories per ¼ cup.

Sugar-Free Bread and Butter Refrigerator Pickles—Omit sugar. After the vegetables are reheated to boiling, remove from the heat and stir in noncaloric sugar substitute to equal ¾ cup sugar (36 quarter-grain saccharin tablets or 18 packets of granulated sweetener). Approximately 10 calories per quarter-cup.

Bread and Butter Pickles with Fructose—Substitute 4 Tbs. granulated fructose for the sugar.

New Pickles

4 cups small whole pickling cucumbers
1 Tbs. mixed pickling spices
1 clove garlic, mashed
4 Tbs. uniodized salt
¼ cup white or cider vinegar
4 cups water

Wash unpeeled cucumbers and put them in a nonmetal container. Combine remaining ingredients and boil 5 minutes. Pour over cucumbers. Cover and refrigerate; wait 2 to 3 days before serving. Store in refrigerator.

About 7 calories per pickle.

Eggplant Caponata

1 small or ½ large eggplant, pared
2 ribs celery
2 medium onions, peeled
2 cloves garlic, minced
1 can (16 oz.) peeled tomatoes
½ cup pitted black olives
¼ cup olive liquid (from can of olives)
2 Tbs. olive or salad oil
2 Tbs. cider or wine vinegar
1 tsp. mixed dried Italian herbs *or* a few oregano, basil and thyme
  leaves
Salt and pepper to taste

Cut eggplant into ½-inch cubes. Slice celery in half lengthwise, then mince. Halve onions, then slice. Combine all remaining ingredients in a pan; add eggplant, celery and onions; heat to boiling. Cover and simmer 10 to 15 minutes, until vegetables are just tender. Remove from heat and cool. Chill until serving time.

Makes 8 side-dish servings, 75 calories each.

Mediterranean Eggplant Salad or Spread

1 small eggplant (about 1 lb.)
1 green bell pepper, seeded
1 onion, peeled
1 tomato
3 Tbs. snipped parsley
1 clove garlic, minced
2 Tbs. Italian dressing (regular or low-fat)
2 or 3 black pitted olives, sliced

Bake eggplant in a moderate 375° oven until softened, about 45 minutes. Peel the eggplant when cool enough to handle. Combine with bell pepper, onion, tomato, parsley and garlic; chop together until finely minced. Mix in salad dressing. Garnish with olive slices.

Makes approximately 2 cups, about 10 calories per Tbs.

Grapefruit-Avocado Slaw

1 cup grapefruit, diced
1 avocado, diced
½ cup coleslaw dressing
1 red bell pepper, seeded and diced
2 cups shredded cabbage

Mix together the grapefruit and avocado; combine with dressing, and refrigerate. Just before serving, toss with bell pepper and cabbage.
Makes 8 servings, 95 calories each.

French Green Bean Salad

2 cups green beans, diagonally sliced, raw or crisply cooked
1 small onion, sliced into rings
1 tomato, seeded and chopped
¼ cup diced green bell pepper
¼ cup sliced celery
1 Tbs. minced fresh dill
¼ cup French salad dressing (regular or low-fat)
Salt and coarse-ground pepper

Combine ingredients, add seasonings to taste. Refrigerate several hours to allow flavors to blend.
Makes 6 servings, 65 calories each with regular dressing; 45 calories with low-fat dressing.

Raw Green Beans with Italian Cheese Dressing

2 cups fresh whole green beans
½ cup cottage cheese
2 Tbs. grated Parmesan cheese
1 Tbs. vinegar
2 Tbs. minced chives
1 hard-cooked egg
Salt and pepper to taste

Wash and remove tips of green beans; refrigerate.
Place remaining ingredients in blender or food processor, using the metal blade, and process until almost smooth.
To serve, arrange green beans on serving dish; pour dressing over

them. Or put dressing in a serving cup, and surround with green beans for dipping.

Makes approximately ¾ cup dressing, 20 calories per Tbs. Green beans are 10 calories per ¼ cup.

Quickie Marinated Green Beans Oreganato

    1 can (16 oz.) green beans, undrained
    2 Tbs. minced fresh onion *or* 2 tsp. dried (optional)
    ¼ cup diced sweet red bell pepper, fresh or canned
    Salt or garlic salt and pepper to taste
    ¼ tsp. dried oregano
    1 Tbs. olive or salad oil
    2 Tbs. cider vinegar

Combine ingredients and chill several hours.
    Makes 4 servings, 55 calories each.

Green and Yellow Two Bean Salad—Substitute 1 can (8 oz.) green beans and 1 can (8 oz.) yellow wax beans for the 1 can (16 oz.) green beans.

Two Bean Salad

    1 can (16 oz.) cut green beans, drained
    1 can (8 oz.) yellow wax beans, drained
    ½ cup sliced scallions
    ¼ cup minced fresh parsley
    3 Tbs. cider vinegar
    1 Tbs. minced oregano
    Salt and pepper

Mix all ingredients, seasoning to taste. Chill several hours to blend flavors.
    Makes 6 servings, 35 calories each.

Marinated Green Beans to Go

1 package (10 oz.) frozen green beans
¼ cup Italian salad dressing (regular or low-fat)
¼ cup cold water

Transfer the frozen green beans to an insulated container while the beans are still frozen. Add Italian salad dressing and cold water. Vegetables will defrost but stay chilled in the marinade. (Other vegetables or combinations may be substituted.)

Makes 3 servings, 135 calories each with regular dressing; 65 calories each with low-fat dressing.

Lettuce Slaw

1 medium head very crisp, firm iceberg lettuce
1 small onion
1 unpared cucumber
4 or 5 radishes
1 red or green sweet bell pepper (optional)
½ cup mayonnaise (regular or low-fat)
1 Tbs. lemon juice or vinegar
Salt or seasoned salt to taste

Shred the lettuce by hand or in a food processor. (To use food processor, cut the head of lettuce in half and remove the core. Slice each half into wedges to fit into the feeding tube of food processor. Shred the wedges; be sure to empty the container before it becomes too crowded.) Shred the remaining vegetables. Rinse lettuce and other vegetables in cold water and drain. Combine the rinsed vegetables with mayonnaise, lemon juice or vinegar, and salt just before serving.

Makes 6 servings, approximately 160 calories each with regular mayonnaise; 80 calories each with low-fat mayonnaise.

Italian Summer Mushroom Salad

½ lb. fresh mushrooms, sliced
1 yellow summer squash, peeled, sliced
1 tomato, chopped
¼ cup diced green bell pepper

Dressing
2 Tbs. olive oil
2 Tbs. white vinegar
1 Tbs. fresh oregano *or* 1 tsp. dried
Salt and pepper to taste

Combine salad ingredients. Shake dressing ingredients in a jar with a tight-fitting lid. Toss together.
Makes 4 servings, 95 calories each.

Spinach Salad with Oriental Five-Spice Dressing

6 cups torn raw spinach
½ cup diagonally sliced scallions
1 eating orange, seeded, peeled and diced
½ cup thinly sliced water chestnuts, sun chokes or jicama *or*
   12 thinly sliced radishes

Dressing
6 Tbs. French dressing (regular or low-fat)
2 Tbs. soy sauce
1 tsp. five-spice powder or pumpkin pie spice plus a pinch of anise
   seed
6 tsp. toasted sunflower seeds

Toss salad ingredients together. Stir dressing, soy sauce and five-spice powder together and drizzle over prepared salad. Sprinkle with sunflower seeds.
Makes 6 servings, 130 calories each with regular dressing; 95 calories each with low-fat dressing.

Five-Spice Turkey Salad Bowl—Add 1½ cups (7½ oz.) diced cooked white meat turkey (or chicken) to the preceding recipe.
Makes 3 meal-size salads, 395 calories each with regular dressing; 320 calories each with low-fat dressing.

Herbed Tomato Salad

3 vine-ripened tomatoes, cubed
2 Tbs. minced onion
Salt or garlic salt and coarse pepper to taste
1 Tbs. minced fresh thyme or sage *or* ½ tsp. dried
1 Tbs. olive oil
2 Tbs. olive liquid (from jar of olives)
3 Tbs. cider vinegar
1 tsp. prepared mustard *or* ¼ tsp. dry

Combine tomatoes and onion in a bowl or jar. Combine remaining ingredients in blender or food processor and blend a few seconds. Or combine herbs with dressing in a covered jar; shake until blended. Pour over vegetables. Cover and marinate several hours.

Makes 4 servings, 75 calories each.

Sicilian Salad

3 vine-ripened tomatoes, seeded and diced
2 green bell peppers, seeded and diced
1 cup sliced sweet onion
¼ cup flat Italian parsley, minced
1 small clove garlic, minced
½ cup pitted ripe olives, sliced
½ cup Italian salad dressing (regular or low-fat)

Combine ingredients; chill.

Makes 6 servings, 160 calories per serving with regular salad dressing; 95 calories per serving with low-fat dressing.

Marinated Tomatoes Italian-Style

3 large vine-ripened tomatoes
2 Tbs. parsley or Italian flat parsley
1 Tbs. olive oil
3 Tbs. red wine vinegar
1 small onion, peeled and chopped
1 Tbs. minced fresh basil or oregano *or* ½ tsp. dried
1 small clove garlic (optional)
Salt and pepper to taste

Peel and dice tomatoes; set aside. Combine remaining ingredients in blender or food processor using steel blade; process until finely minced. Pour dressing over tomatoes and mix well. Cover and refrigerate several hours before serving.

By hand: Mince onion, garlic and basil. Combine with oil and vinegar. Add diced tomatoes and mix well. Cover and refrigerate.

Makes 6 servings, 50 calories each.

Mexican Tomato Salad

3 large vine-ripened tomatoes
1 small onion, minced
1 rib celery, minced
1 small green bell pepper, seeded, chopped
1 to 2 Tbs. minced fresh or canned hot chili peppers (optional)

Dressing
1 clove garlic, minced
1 Tbs. oil
3 Tbs. red wine vinegar
1 tsp. cumin seeds *or* ½ tsp. ground cumin
1 Tbs. minced fresh oregano *or* ½ tsp. dried
Salt and pepper to taste

Peel and dice tomatoes. Combine with onion, celery, bell peppers and chili peppers. Combine dressing ingredients and pour over tomato mixture. Chill several hours.

Makes 8 servings, 45 calories each.

Minted Marinated Tomatoes

3 cups diced vine-ripened tomatoes
½ cup chopped parsley
¼ cup chopped fresh mint *or* 1 Tbs. dried mint leaves plus 2 Tbs.
    additional parsley
¼ cup thinly sliced scallions or chopped onion
3 Tbs. olive oil
3 Tbs. lemon juice
Salt and pepper to taste

Combine ingredients. Cover and chill several hours.

Makes 4 servings, 80 calories each.

Pickled Zucchini

4 medium zucchini, unpeeled
2 Tbs. uniodized salt
Ice cubes
¼ cup cider or white vinegar
1½ cups unsweetened apple juice or cider
1 onion, thinly sliced
1 clove garlic mashed *or* pinch of instant
1 Tbs. dill seeds
Few sprigs fresh dill leaves (optional)

Slice zucchini; sprinkle with salt and add to bowl containing a tray of ice cubes. Mix well. Leave at room temperature until ice melts. Drain off ice water.

Combine drained zucchini with remaining ingredients in a jar, crock or other nonmetal container. Cover and refrigerate 2 days before serving. Store in refrigerator.

Approximately 15 calories per ¼ cup.

Zucchini Pickles

4 medium zucchini, sliced (3–4 cups)
1 cup broccoli florets
2 onions, sliced
1 green bell pepper, sliced
½ cup sugar or equivalent sugar substitute
1 cup vinegar
1 tsp. celery salt
¼ tsp. ground cloves

Mix vegetables in storage container. Bring sugar, vinegar, celery salt and cloves to a boil in a small saucepan. Pour over vegetables. Store in refrigerator for two days before serving.

Makes 10 ½-cup servings, 65 calories each with sugar; 30 calories each with sugar substitute.

Lazy Deli Salad

2 cups chopped raw celery
2 cups finely chopped raw carrot
½ cup chopped sweet onion
Minced parsley (optional)
1 cup bottled low-fat Italian salad dressing

Combine, cover and refrigerate 24 hours before serving. Stir occasionally.

Note: If desired, in place of the Italian salad dressing, substitute 3 Tbs. olive oil, 5 Tbs. cider vinegar, ½ cup water, and salt, pepper and oregano or Italian herbs to taste.

Makes 8 servings, under 40 calories per serving with bottled low-fat dressing; 70 calories per serving with salad dressing alternatives.

5

Salads to Heat and Eat

On first thought, hot salad may seem to have all the appeal of cold potatoes. But come to think of it, we *do* enjoy cold potatoes, in the form of potato salad! And we also enjoy hot German-style potato salad. In my book, any combination of vegetables can be a salad, hot or cold!

What makes hot vegetables a salad rather than simply being cooked vegetables? It's a matter of degree. Vegetables that have been cooked to death surely do not qualify, but those that have been heated rather than cooked—that retain their living color and crunch, their fresh flavor—can still be considered salad, even though served hot.

Oriental stir-fried vegetable combinations constitute a prime example of a salad that we heat and eat. The vegetables are only heated through, without destroying any of the taste or texture they would have if served in a tossed salad. Nutritionally speaking, vegetables that are merely heated rather than thoroughly cooked retain most of the vitamin value they have when raw.

Considering the popularity of fresh salad over conventionally cooked vegetables (and the prevailing preference for crunch over mush), you may never wish to cook vegetables again.

Easy Frozen Vegetables with Hollandaise Sauce

¾ lb. fresh, or 1 package (10 oz.) frozen, broccoli or green beans,
    etc.
½ cup water
2 Tbs. lemon juice
¼ cup mayonnaise (regular or low-fat)
Salt or seasoned salt and pepper

Cook vegetables in unsalted water until tender but still crisp. Transfer
to a bowl and cover to keep warm. Turn heat high and simmer cooking water until reduced to a few tablespoons. Combine hot cooking
water with lemon juice, mayonnaise and seasonings to taste; blend
smooth with a fork. Pour over hot vegetables.

Makes 3 servings, 170 calories each, with broccoli and regular
mayonnaise; 80 calories less per serving with low-fat mayonnaise.

Cold Asparagus in Yogurt Sauce

1½ lbs. fresh asparagus

Sauce
8 oz. plain low-fat yogurt
1 Tbs. minced fresh parsley
1 tsp. prepared mustard
1 tsp. chives or onion
½ tsp. dried tarragon or dill leaves
Salt and pepper and paprika to taste
Dash cayenne pepper or Tabasco sauce

Lay asparagus in a skillet; add 1 inch water. Cover and simmer 2 to 4
minutes, just until tender. Cool. Cut into 2-inch pieces. Refrigerate.

Combine remaining ingredients and refrigerate 1 hour or more. Just
before serving, toss asparagus with sauce.

Makes 6 servings, 55 calories each.

Blue Cheesy Asparagus Salad

2 packages (10 oz. each) frozen asparagus spears, defrosted
2 hard-cooked eggs, cut in wedges
⅓ cup blue cheese dressing (regular or low-fat)
1 cup cherry tomatoes

Cook asparagus according to package directions. Drain and chill. Arrange on salad plates, bordered by egg wedges. Pour dressing over top. Garnish with tomatoes.

Makes 6 servings, 125 calories each with regular salad dressing; 70 calories each with low-fat dressing.

Cold Broccoli Italian

(To keep broccoli a bright green color, don't add salad dressing until just before serving)

1 package (10 oz.) frozen whole broccoli spears
½ cup water
Pinch of oregano or mixed herbs (optional)
1 Tbs. minced onion
3 Tbs. Italian salad dressing (regular or low-fat)

For even cooking, defrost broccoli first. Heat water in a nonstick saucepan. Add broccoli (and oregano or herbs if desired). Cover and cook 3 minutes, uncover and continue to cook until nearly all the liquid has evaporated. Do not drain. Add onion and chill thoroughly. Add salad dressing just before serving.

Makes 3 servings, 110 calories per serving with regular salad dressing; 60 calories per serving with low-fat dressing.

Green Beans Pronto—Substitute a package (10 oz.) of defrosted whole green beans for the broccoli. Do not cover. Cook uncovered until tender but still crisp; about 3 to 4 minutes. Makes 3 servings, 105 calories each with regular salad dressing; 55 calories each with low-fat dressing.

Baked Chicken and Broccoli Salad

1 package (10 oz.) frozen broccoli spears, defrosted
4 frying chicken cutlets (skinless, boneless breasts), poached
¾ cup creamy cucumber salad dressing
4 Tbs. shredded, sharp cheddar cheese.

Preheat oven to 400°. Arrange broccoli in a single layer in a nonstick baking dish. Place chicken over the broccoli. Pour on the salad dressing. Top with shredded cheese.

Bake in 400° oven for 15 minutes. Serve directly from the baking dish.

Makes 4 servings, 370 calories per serving.

Lower-Calorie Variation—Use low-fat creamy cucumber salad dressing and substitute low-fat cheese for the cheddar; 240 calories per serving.

Springtime Variation—Substitute very thin, tender asparagus tips for the broccoli; 370 calories per serving.

Brussels Sprouts and Tomato Salad

1 package (10 oz.) frozen brussels sprouts
2 Tbs. salad oil
3 Tbs. cider vinegar
Salt and pepper to taste
12 small cherry tomatoes
Lettuce

Cook brussels sprouts according to package directions. Drain, cool and slice each in half lengthwise. Mix oil, vinegar, salt and pepper. Toss with brussels sprouts and cherry tomatoes. Arrange on beds of lettuce.

Makes 4 servings, 110 calories each.

Hot Brussels Sprouts Salad

1 carton (1 pt.) fresh brussels sprouts
1 cup water
3 Tbs. mayonnaise (regular or low-fat)
2 to 3 tsp. lemon juice
Salt and pepper

Put a steaming basket, rack or trivet in a saucepan that has a cover. Arrange the brussels sprouts in the basket or on the rack. Add water. Cover tightly and cook over moderate heat until sprouts are tender but firm, about 8 to 10 minutes.

To prepare sauce, combine mayonnaise with the hot liquid the vegetables were cooked in, and beat smooth. Add lemon juice, salt and pepper to taste.

Makes 4 servings, 105 calories each with regular mayonnaise; 60 calories each with low-fat mayonnaise.

Hot Dilled Brussels Sprouts

1 carton (1 pt.) fresh brussels sprouts *or* 10 oz. package frozen, defrosted
½ tsp. dill seeds
1 cup chicken broth with fat skimmed off
Salt and pepper to taste
1 Tbs. minced fresh dill weed

Spray a nonstick skillet with cooking spray. Spread the brussels sprouts in a single layer. Sprinkle with dill seed. Add the broth. Heat to boiling. Cover and cook 2 minutes. Uncover and continue to cook, turning brussels sprouts occasionally, until most of the liquid has evaporated. Season to taste. Sprinkle with dill weed before serving.

Makes 3 servings, 45 calories each.

Carrots Harvard-Style (Sweet and Sour)

2 cups sliced carrots
2 Tbs. cider vinegar
¼ cup pineapple juice
2 Tbs. sugar
Pinch of ginger
Salt
2 tsp. cornstarch
¼ cup water

Cook carrots in a mixture of the vinegar, juice, sugar, ginger and salt, just until tender or about 5 minutes. In a small cup combine cornstarch with water until well mixed. Pour into carrots and stir until thickened and cleared. Serve warm or chilled.

Makes 4 servings, 60 calories each.

Carrots in Pineapple Sauce

3 cups sliced carrots, fresh or frozen
1 cup unsweetened pineapple juice
½ cup fat-skimmed chicken broth or water
Pinch of ground cinnamon
Salt and pepper to taste

Combine ingredients in nonstick saucepan. Cover tightly and simmer 10 to 15 minutes. Uncover and continue to simmer until most of the liquid has evaporated.

Makes 4 servings, under 80 calories each.

Hot "Confetti" Carrots

2 medium unpared carrots
1 rib celery (optional)
2 or 3 slices onion (optional)
½ cup fat-skimmed chicken broth, undiluted
Salt and pepper

Shred carrots, celery and onion (if used) with the coarse grating disk of a food processor, the shredding attachment of a mixer, or by hand. Combine vegetables and broth in a nonstick saucepan or small skillet.

Cover tightly and simmer 5 minutes. Uncover and continue to simmer until nearly all the liquid has evaporated. Season to taste.

Makes 2 servings, 45 calories each. (Recipe may be doubled for 4 servings.)

Cauliflower Salad

1 head cauliflower (2 lbs.) broken into florets
1 cup sliced scallions
3 ripe tomatoes, seeded and diced
1 cup tomato juice
1 to 2 Tbs. lemon juice
1 garlic clove, chopped
Salt and pepper to taste

In salted water, simmer cauliflower 5 or 6 minutes, just until tender but still crisp. Drain and cool.

Mix drained cauliflower with remaining ingredients. Chill until ready to serve.

Makes 6 servings, 80 calories each.

Italian Oven-Fried Cauliflowerets

2 cups fresh cauliflower florets
¼ cup Italian salad dressing (regular or low-fat)
3 Tbs. grated Italian cheese
3 Tbs. Italian-seasoned breadcrumbs

Moisten individual florets with Italian salad dressing. Combine cheese and breadcrumbs, then roll florets in the mixture. Arrange in a single layer, not touching, on a shallow nonstick baking tray, well sprayed with cooking spray or lightly wiped with oil. Bake uncovered in a preheated very hot 475° oven, until tender but still crisp, about 5 to 7 minutes.

Makes 4 servings, 130 calories each with regular salad dressing; 80 calories each with low-fat dressing.

Japanese Style—Roll the florets in soy sauce, then in a combination of Parmesan cheese and unseasoned breadcrumbs; 65 calories per serving.

Oven-Fried Eggplant Steaks—Cut fresh unpared eggplant into ¾-inch slices. Moisten with lemon or tomato juice. Press each steak in a mixture of equal parts grated cheese and Italian-seasoned breadcrumbs. Arrange on a nonstick baking tray which has been sprayed with cooking spray or lightly wiped with oil. Bake uncovered in a preheated 475° oven 5 to 6 minutes each side. Calories: 65 per serving.

Skillet Celery and Green Beans

2 cups celery, cut in ¼-inch diagonal slices
1 clove garlic, minced
1 Tbs. salad oil
1 cup chicken broth or bouillon
1 package (10 oz.) frozen cut green beans, defrosted
¼ lb. fresh mushrooms, sliced
3 Tbs. sliced almonds
Grated peel of ½ fresh lemon
1 Tbs. fresh squeezed lemon juice

Spray a nonstick skillet with cooking spray. Combine celery, garlic, oil and ¼ cup of the broth. Cook and stir, uncovered, just until celery is tender (about 5 to 6 minutes). Add green beans, mushrooms and remaining broth; stir-fry 2 to 3 minutes more. Stir in almonds, lemon peel and juice. Garnish with lemon slices, if desired.

Makes 4 servings, 110 calories each.

Crunchy Green Beans, Mushrooms and Almonds

2 Tbs. butter or margarine or diet margarine
1 small clove garlic, minced
1 cup celery, sliced diagonally
1 cup raw sliced green beans
½ cup raw sliced mushrooms
1 envelope chicken bouillon granules
½ lemon, in very thin slices
2 Tbs. sliced almonds

Melt butter or margarine in a large nonstick skillet. Add garlic, cook 2 minutes. Add vegetables along with bouillon granules; stir-fry 2 to 3 minutes. Stir in lemon slices and almonds; heat through. Serve immediately.

Makes 4 servings, 95 calories each with butter or margarine; 70 calories each with diet margarine.

Garden Peas in Butter Sauce

2 cups shelled fresh young peas (about 1½ lbs. in shells)
1 Tbs. butter or diet margarine
Salt and pepper

Put the peas in a nonstick pot or skillet large enough so that they are in one very shallow layer. Add the butter and about ½ cup water. Season to taste. Cook over high heat, stirring often, until most of the water evaporates and peas are heated through. (If peas are mature, add more water and cook until tender.) Serve peas coated with the reduced cooking liquid.

Makes 4 servings, approximately 85 calories per serving with butter, 75 calories per serving with diet margarine.

Garden Ratatouille

1 Tbs. olive oil
1 large onion, peeled, sliced
1 medium zucchini, sliced
1 yellow summer squash, sliced
1 or 2 cloves garlic, minced (to taste)
1 medium eggplant, pared and sliced into 1-inch cubes
1 red bell pepper, seeded and sliced
1 green bell pepper, seeded and sliced
6 medium vine-ripened tomatoes, diced
3 Tbs. minced parsley
1 cup water or fat-skimmed chicken broth
Salt and pepper

Heat the oil in a large nonstick skillet or electric frypan (or spray with cooking spray until slick). Spread the onion, zucchini, yellow squash slices and garlic in a shallow layer. Cook over low heat just until vegetables begin to brown. Turn to brown evenly. Stir in remaining vegetables. Stir in water or chicken broth. Add salt and pepper to taste. (If desired, add 1 Tbs. minced fresh thyme, savory, marjoram, basil or oregano, or ½ tsp. dried herbs.) Cover tightly and simmer 30 minutes for crunchy texture, or 40 to 50 minutes for a softer texture. (Add more water or broth, if needed.) Uncover and continue to simmer until most of the liquid has evaporated. Serve hot or chilled. Makes 12 side-dish servings, 55 calories each.

Skewered Ratatouille Vegetables

1 small eggplant, pared
2 medium zucchini, unpeeled
2 bell peppers, seeded
4 small onions, peeled
16 cherry tomatoes
½ cup Italian salad dressing (regular or low-calorie)
4 Tbs. grated sharp Romano cheese
4 Tbs. plain or Italian-seasoned breadcrumbs

Slice eggplant and zucchini into 1-inch bite-size chunks. Slice bell peppers into 1-inch squares. Quarter small onions; separate into leaves. Leave cherry tomatoes whole. Alternate vegetables on skewers.

Roll in Italian salad dressing to moisten. Mix grated cheese and breadcrumbs; roll vegetables in mixture to coat lightly.

Broil or barbecue 3 inches from heat source, turning every few minutes, just until lightly browned. Or arrange skewers on a nonstick cookie sheet that has been sprayed until slick with cooking spray or wiped lightly with oil. Place uncovered in a preheated 500° oven. Bake 6 to 8 minutes, just until golden and crisp.

Makes 8 servings, approximately 155 calories each with regular salad dressing; 105 calories each with low-calorie dressing.

Quick-Cooked Corn in Butter Sauce

1 cup water
6 medium ears of corn
3 Tbs. butter or diet margarine
Salt and pepper to taste

Put a small wire grid in the bottom of a large pot to keep the corn above the water. Pour in water. Add the corn. Cover pan tightly. Steam the corn just until the kernels are tender but still firm, about 5 to 15 minutes (depending on the size of the kernels, the thickness of the ears, and the freshness and maturity of the corn). Remove cover, rack and corn. Add butter to remaining liquid. Raise heat to high. Cook until most of the liquid has evaporated. Season with salt and coarsely ground pepper. Pour over corn and serve at once. Each ear, about 120 calories, 95 calories with diet margarine.

Stuffed Tomatoes with Mushrooms

3 firm, well-shaped tomatoes
1 Tbs. diet margarine
1 Tbs. Italian salad dressing (regular or low-fat)
1½ cups sliced fresh mushrooms
1 egg
2 Tbs. minced chives
Salt and pepper to taste

Preheat oven to 350°. Cut tomatoes in half; scoop out pulp, discard seeds. Set pulp and tomato shells aside.

Heat margarine and salad dressing in a small nonstick skillet. Add mushrooms; saute until liquid evaporates and mushrooms begin to brown. In the skillet, mix mushrooms with tomato pulp, egg, chives, salt and pepper. Fill tomato shells with this mixture. Place in a nonstick baking dish.

Bake in 350° oven 20 minutes.

Makes 6 servings, 55 calories each with regular salad dressing; 45 calories each with low-fat dressing.

Baked Vegetables Niçoise

1 zucchini, sliced
1 yellow summer squash, sliced
1 small onion, minced
1 small eggplant, peeled and cubed
1 tomato, peeled and cubed
1 green bell pepper, seeded and diced
5 pitted black olives, sliced
1 clove garlic, minced
3 Tbs. Italian salad dressing (regular or low-fat)
3 eggs
½ cup milk (regular or low-fat)
1 Tbs. flour

Preheat oven to 350°. Mix vegetables, olives and garlic with salad dressing in a 3-qt. nonstick baking dish. Beat together eggs, milk and flour, and pour over vegetables.

Bake in 350° oven for 1 hour.

Makes 6 servings, 145 calories each with regular ingredients; 115 calories each with low-fat ingredients.

Hot Zucchini "Confetti"

(Very quick cooking!)

> 1 unpared medium zucchini, shredded
> ½ small onion, peeled (optional)
> 1 tsp. oil (optional)
> Salt or seasoned salt
> Coarsely ground pepper
> 1 tsp. grated cheese

Shred zucchini (and onion) with the coarse grating disk of a food processor or the shredding attachment of mixer (or by hand). Heat oil in a nonstick saucepan or small skillet (or spray with cooking spray). Spread the vegetables in a shallow layer. Cover tightly and cook 1 minute. Uncover and continue cooking an additional minute or 2, stirring often, until most of the liquid in the pan has evaporated. Watch carefully to prevent sticking. Stir in seasonings to taste. Sprinkle with grated cheese.

Makes 2 servings, 25 calories each (oil adds 20 calories per serving).

Shredded Yellow Squash—Substitute summer squash for zucchini. For a colorful "confetti," combine shredded zucchini, summer squash and minced sweet red pepper.

Hot or Cold Zucchini à la Grecque

> 1 medium zucchini, cubed
> 1 Tbs. minced onion *or* 1 tsp. dried
> Squeeze of garlic juice *or* pinch of instant garlic
> 1 Tbs. minced fresh parsley
> Pinch of dried mint and oregano *or* a few fresh leaves, minced
> 2 Tbs. mayonnaise (regular or low-fat)
> 1 Tbs. grated Parmesan or Romano cheese
> Salt and pepper to taste

Quarter zucchini lengthwise, then cut into bite-size cubes. Combine with remaining ingredients and mix lightly. Chill until serving time.

For a hot, crunchy vegetable: Preheat oven to 400°. Prepare zucchini as above. Spoon mixture into a shallow nonstick baking dish. Place uncovered in a 400° oven about 8 to 10 minutes, or until zucchini is heated through but still crisp.

Makes 3 servings, 85 calories each with regular mayonnaise; 45 calories each with low-fat mayonnaise.

Crock Pot for Crunchy Low-Cal Vegetables

By now, everyone who ever wanted one already has one. In fact, you may have one even if you didn't want one! In the mid-seventies, slow-cooking crock pots became the quintessential shower and Mother's Day gift, the universal gadget to give to somebody who had everything else.

Where is yours today? In constant use? Or stashed behind the fondue set and crepe maker? If you are tired of all-day, one-dish dinners, you might like to explore some other uses for these pots that need no watching.

One of my favorite ways to use a crock pot is for crunchy Oriental vegetables that taste and look stir-fried. That's right, "stir-fried"! But without stirring. And without frying. No oil!

Sounds hard to believe, but you can slow-cook vegetables for an hour or two and get the same fresh taste, texture and color you get with quick-cooking in a frying pan or a wok. Why would you want to spend an hour or two to get the same results that take minutes in a skillet? Because this method requires absolutely no attention, leaving you free to attend to other matters, your guests, for example. If dinner is delayed 15 or 20 minutes, your crunchy crock-pot-cooked vegetables won't overcook or get cold.

Crunchy Oriental Crocked Vegetables

> 2 unpared zucchini, cubed
> 2 red or green bell peppers, seeded and diced
> Pinch of ground ginger (optional)
> 1 Tbs. soy sauce, broth (beef or chicken) or water

In electric crock pot: Combine ingredients. Cover and cook on low setting 1 to 2 hours.

In oven: Combine ingredients in an ovenproof crockery pot (bean-pot, cookie jar, etc.) or a heavy casserole. Cover tightly and place on a rack in cold oven. Set the thermostat on lowest setting ("warm" or 150° to 200°). Cook at low temperature 1 to 2 hours.

Makes 6 servings, 25 calories each.

Crocked Acorn Squash

Acorn squash
¼ to ½ cup apple juice or cider per whole squash
Cinnamon or pumpkin pie spice

Cut each acorn squash into quarters and scrape away seeds. Place squash in a crock pot with the skin down. Pour ¼ to ½ cup apple juice over the squashes and sprinkle very lightly with ground cinnamon. Cover and cook on low setting 2 to 4 hours.
Each ¼ squash, 55 calories.

Greek-Style Crocked Green Beans

2 packages (10 oz. each) whole or sliced (not French cut) frozen
   green beans
2 cups (16 oz.) plain tomato sauce
2 tsp. dried onion flakes (optional)
Pinch of dried mint or marjoram or oregano
Pinch ground nutmeg and cinnamon

Combine ingredients in crock pot. Cover and cook on low setting 2 to 4 hours if beans are defrosted, 1 hour longer if frozen. If softer green beans are desired, extend cooking time 1 hour.
Makes 6 servings, 45 calories each.

Broccoli Parmesan

2 packages (10 oz. each) frozen chopped broccoli
½ cup fat-skimmed chicken broth or water
3 Tbs. mayonnaise (regular or low-fat)
1 Tbs. grated Parmesan cheese

Combine broccoli and broth in crock pot. Cover and cook on low heat 1 to 2 hours (2 to 3 hours, if broccoli is frozen). Stir in remaining ingredients until blended, and leave vegetable mixture in crock pot until ready to serve.
Makes 6 servings, 85 calories per serving with regular mayonnaise; 55 calories per serving with low-fat mayonnaise.

6

Potato, Pasta and Rice Salads

Not so long ago, most waistline-watchers thought of starch as a bad word—okay for shirts, maybe, but not so hot for the body underneath. All those best-selling carbohydrate-counting diet books convinced Americans that the road to slimness was paved with "protein," and that calories somehow "didn't count." So, despite the fact that potatoes, pasta and rice are virtually fat-free (and therefore lower in calories than such fat-marbled protein foods as steaks and chops), starchy foods were banished from the plates of the weight-wary and the vacant space was filled in with *more* "protein." Luncheonettes still pair a fried hamburger with cottage cheese and label it a "diet plate"!

Today we know better—or should! All meat and no potatoes makes Jack a fat boy, and a prime candidate for a heart attack. And Mrs. Spratt, who fills up on fat, is likelier than her leaner sisters to develop breast cancer. What's more, we have discovered that the pound-provoking image of starchy foods is unwarranted. To the degree that they displace fatty, cholesterol-laden high-calorie foods, carbohydrate foods can actually *promote* slimness, just the reverse of what the fad diets told us! Today, the very foods we had been told to avoid have emerged as allies in our battle of the bulge!

One way to increase the effectiveness of these allies is to serve them in salads. Served hot, potatoes, pasta and rice have an affinity for attracting calories in the form of butter, sour cream or calorie-laden sauces. But as salads, their companions are more likely to be lean low-calorie vegetables.

In this section I have included a variety of salads based on potatoes, pasta and rice, plus a number of combination dishes and casseroles.

Creamy Cucumber Potato Salad

4 Tbs. creamy cucumber salad dressing (regular or low-fat)
4 cups cooked, peeled and thinly sliced potatoes
½ cup diced celery
4 Tbs. minced red or green bell pepper (optional)
3 or 4 scallions, thinly sliced
1 small or ½ large unpared cucumber, chopped
1 hard-cooked egg, chopped (optional)
1 Tbs. minced fresh parsley or fresh dill
2 to 3 Tbs. plain low-fat yogurt (optional)
Paprika

Stir salad dressing into potatoes while still warm. Chill several hours. Stir in remaining ingredients at serving time.

Makes 8 servings, 90 calories per serving with regular salad dressing; 70 calories per serving with low-fat dressing (optional ingredients add 15 calories per serving).

Yogurt Potato Salad

3 potatoes, pared, boiled, drained and sliced
½ onion, sliced thin

Dressing
2 cups plain low-fat yogurt
2 Tbs. lemon juice
1 tsp. prepared mustard
Salt and pepper to taste
Sugar or sugar substitute to taste (optional)
Pinch of paprika (optional)

Combine potatoes and onion.

Mix the dressing ingredients thoroughly; toss with potato mixture. Chill.

Before serving, sprinkle with additional paprika, if desired.

Makes 6 servings, 105 calories each.

Green Pickle Potato Salad

6 cups cooked, peeled and thinly sliced potatoes
1 small raw carrot, shredded
1 cup chopped celery
1 small onion, minced
2 Tbs. minced fresh parsley
1 small or ½ medium green or new pickle, minced
2 hard-cooked eggs, thinly sliced (optional)
Paprika (optional)

Dressing
4 Tbs. pickle juice
⅔ cup mayonnaise (regular or low-fat)
⅔ cup plain low-fat yogurt
Pinch of prepared horseradish *or* dash of Tabasco
Pinch of dry mustard *or* ½ tsp. prepared
Salt or celery salt and pepper to taste
1 Tbs. dill seeds (or more to taste)

Combine vegetables, parsley and minced pickle in a bowl. Blend pickle juice, mayonnaise, yogurt, horseradish and mustard together; add to vegetables. Toss lightly to mix. Add salt, pepper and dill seeds to taste. Chill. Garnish with egg slices and paprika, if desired.

Makes 12 servings, 150 calories each with regular mayonnaise; 100 calories each with low-fat mayonnaise; eggs add 15 calories per serving.

Potato Salad Caesar

1 raw egg *or* ¼ cup no-cholesterol egg substitute
¼ cup Italian salad dressing (regular or low-fat)
4 Tbs. grated Parmesan cheese
1 Tbs. Worcestershire sauce
2 tsp. prepared mustard
1 tsp. garlic salt
4 potatoes, peeled, cooked and cubed
4 pitted black olives, sliced

Blend egg and salad dressing. Combine with remaining ingredients; chill.

Makes 8 servings, 120 calories per serving with egg and regular salad dressing; 90 calories per serving with egg substitute and low-fat dressing.

Primavera Potato Salad

2 potatoes, cooked, peeled and thinly sliced
¾ cup bottled Italian-style salad dressing (regular or low-fat)
Small purple onion, peeled and sliced into rings
1 large or 2 small vine-ripened tomatoes, in wedges
1 small sweet bell pepper, seeded and sliced into rings
1 cup thinly sliced raw mushrooms
Salt or seasoned salt and pepper
Boston lettuce or any tender variety

Marinate sliced potatoes in salad dressing until serving time. Stir remaining vegetables into marinated potatoes, mix lightly and season to taste. Arrange on beds of lettuce on salad plates.

Makes 4 servings, 340 calories per serving with regular salad dressing; 190 calories per serving with low-fat dressing.

Food Processor Potato Salad

4 cups cooked, peeled and diced potatoes
1 cup unpared raw carrots
½ cup onion
½ cup green pickle
½ cup very thinly sliced celery
¼ cup very thinly sliced stuffed green olives
Salt and pepper
Few sprigs fresh parsley (optional)

Dressing
½ cup low-fat cottage cheese
⅓ cup plain low-fat yogurt
¼ cup mayonnaise (regular or low-fat)
1 Tbs. lemon juice or vinegar
2 tsp. prepared mustard
Dash of Tabasco sauce *or* pinch of red cayenne pepper
2 tsp. dill seed *or* a few sprigs fresh dill weed

Put diced potatoes in a large mixing bowl. Shred the carrots, onion and pickle, using the shredding disk of a food processor. Add to the potatoes. Replace disk with slicing disk and thinly slice the celery and olives. Add to the potatoes.

Replace the disk with the steel blade. Combine dressing ingredients in the food processor bowl and process until dressing is completely smooth. Add to salad and mix lightly. Season with salt and pepper to taste. Refrigerate until serving time. Garnish with parsley.

Makes 8 servings, 135 calories per serving with regular mayonnaise; 105 calories per serving with low-fat mayonnaise.

Casino Potato Salad

4 cups cooked, diced potatoes
1 cup sliced celery
4 Tbs. chopped pimiento

Dressing
¾ cup low-fat cottage cheese
1 Tbs. wine vinegar
3 Tbs. French dressing (regular or low-fat)
Salt and pepper
Paprika

Combine the potatoes, celery and pimiento.

In blender or food processor (using the steel blade), combine the dressing ingredients with seasonings to taste. Process until smooth. Toss with the vegetable mixture. Chill.

Makes 10 servings, 75 calories per serving with regular dressing; 65 calories per serving with low-fat dressing.

Egg-and-Potato Salad

6 medium potatoes, cooked, peeled and cubed
3 Tbs. lemon juice
5 Tbs. mayonnaise (regular or low-fat)
1 green bell pepper, seeded and diced
1 onion, peeled and chopped
Salt or seasoned salt and pepper
6 hard-cooked eggs, peeled and quartered

Combine potatoes, lemon juice and mayonnaise. Cover and chill.

At serving time, toss with bell pepper and onion. Season to taste. Garnish with egg quarters.

Makes 6 lunch-size servings, 280 calories per serving with regular mayonnaise; 230 calories per serving with low-fat mayonnaise (or 12 side-dish servings at half the calories).

Brenda's Low-Calorie Potato Salad

2½ lbs. potatoes, peeled and cubed
3 Tbs. low-calorie French dressing
1 hard-cooked egg, peeled
¾ cup finely shredded carrots
¾ cup finely sliced celery
¼ cup finely sliced scallions
2 Tbs. chopped dill pickle

Dressing
8 oz. plain low-fat yogurt
1 tsp. prepared mustard
1 tsp. prepared horseradish
1 tsp. Worcestershire sauce
Salt and pepper to taste

Cook potatoes in boiling (salted) water to cover, until tender, about 15 minutes. Drain and cool. Toss with French dressing until lightly coated.

Separate yolk from white of hard-cooked egg. Reserve yolk. Chop white and add to potatoes, along with carrots, celery, scallions and pickle.

Combine dressing ingredients; toss with salad. Cover and chill several hours. Before serving, toss again lightly, garnish with sieved egg yolk.

Makes 8 servings, 130 calories each.

Potato Salad with Sour Cream and Egg

3 cups cooked, peeled and diced potatoes
½ cup minced celery
2 Tbs. minced chives or onion
3 Tbs. minced red or green sweet pepper
1 Tbs. minced fresh dill or parsley
3 Tbs. sour cream or sour half-and-half or plain low-fat yogurt
3 Tbs. bottled Italian salad dressing (regular or low-fat)
½ tsp. prepared mustard (optional)
Salt and pepper
1 hard-cooked egg, shredded
Paprika (optional)

Combine vegetables and dill in a mixing bowl. Blend sour cream, salad dressing and mustard together in a small bowl, and add to salad.

Toss lightly. Add salt and pepper to taste. At serving time, sprinkle with shredded egg and paprika.

Makes 6 servings, 120 calories per serving with sour cream and regular salad dressing; 90 calories per serving with yogurt and low-fat salad dressing.

Steak-and-Potato Salad Lunch

2 oz. leftover lean broiled steak, trimmed of fat
1 small leftover cold cooked potato, peeled and cubed
3 or 4 fresh mushrooms, sliced

Dressing
2 tsp. red wine vinegar
1 tsp. table wine (red or white)
1 tsp. catsup
2 Tbs. plain low-fat yogurt
2 tsp. minced onion *or* ½ tsp. onion flakes
Salt and pepper

Slice steak into julienne strips; mix with potato cubes and mushroom slices.

Combine dressing ingredients; toss lightly with salad ingredients. Season to taste. Serve on lettuce leaves, if desired.

Makes 1 serving, 235 calories.

Potato, Ham and Artichoke Salad

1 pkg. (9 oz.) frozen artichoke hearts
3 potatoes, pared, boiled and thinly sliced
1 lb. lean cooked ham, cubed
4 Tbs. thinly sliced sweet pickles

Dressing
¾ cup plain, low-fat yogurt
4 Tbs. French dressing (regular or low-fat)
2 Tbs. minced fresh dill or parsley (optional)

Cook artichoke hearts according to the package directions, drain and cut in halves. Combine with potatoes, ham and pickles.

Mix dressing ingredients; toss with salad ingredients. Chill.

Makes 12 servings, 135 calories per serving with regular dressing; 120 calories per serving with low-fat dressing.

Blender-Slender Vichyssoise

    3 cups pared and cubed raw potatoes
    1¼ cups (10 oz.) undiluted, fat-skimmed chicken broth (canned
        or homemade)
    1½ cups chopped onions
    ⅔ cup part-skim ricotta cheese
    2 Tbs. minced fresh parsley or chives
    1 cup (approximately) cold skim milk
    Salt and pepper
    Parsley or minced chives (optional)

Combine potatoes, chicken broth and onions in a heavy pot. Cover
tightly and simmer 25 to 30 minutes, until potatoes are tender.

Combine ricotta, parsley and ¼ cup cold milk in blender. Cover
and blend until smooth. Add potato mixture, a little at a time; blend
until pureed. (If your blender capacity is not large enough to accom-
modate all ingredients in one processing, process half of the mixture
at a time.) Stir in remaining cold milk to achieve desired consistency.
Season to taste. Chill thoroughly before serving. Garnish with a few
additional sprigs of parsley or minced chives, if desired.

Makes 8 servings, 95 calories each.

Hot Yogurt Scalloped Potatoes

    4 potatoes, unpared
    Boiling salted water
    ½ cup plain low-fat yogurt (at room temperature)
    Small clove garlic, squeezed for juice *or* pinch of instant garlic
    1 Tbs. finely minced fresh parsley
    Salt and pepper

Place the potatoes in a pot with about an inch of boiling water. Cover
tightly and simmer 30 minutes, or until potatoes test tender with a
fork. Drain and discard water. Return the potatoes to the pan over
low heat. Shake the pan until the surfaces of the potatoes are dry.
Remove the potatoes and peel them, using a fork to hold them and a
small knife and your fingers to pull off the peel. Slice the potatoes and
return them to the pot.

Combine yogurt, garlic juice and parsley. Add to the potatoes over
very low heat, just until sauce is warmed (do not boil). Season to
taste.

Makes 8 servings, 60 calories each.

Chiliburger Baked Potatoes

4 baking potatoes
½ lb. lean beef round, ground
1 small onion, minced
½ sweet green bell pepper, seeded and minced
2 vine-ripened tomatoes, peeled and cubed
2 Tbs. water or tomato juice
Salt or garlic salt and pepper to taste
2 to 4 tsp. chili powder (to taste)
¼ tsp. dried oregano *or* ½ tsp. minced fresh oregano (optional)
½ tsp. cumin seeds *or* ¼ tsp. ground cumin (optional)

Preheat oven to 400°.

Puncture potatoes 4 or 5 times with a fork. Place them on the rack in the oven. (Do not wrap them.) Bake 50 to 60 minutes at 400°, until potatoes feel tender when gently squeezed.

While potatoes are baking, combine the remaining ingredients in a shallow nonstick baking pan. Cover the pan with foil and bake 20 to 25 minutes. Remove foil and continue baking, stirring often, until the mixture is thick, about 15 minutes. Remove from the oven to prevent overcooking. Cover to keep warm.

When potatoes are tender, squeeze them with a gloved mitt. Split potatoes open and fill them with the beef mixture. Serve immediately.

Makes 4 meal-size servings, 205 calories each.

Potato-Lover's Cottage Cheese Lunch

1 medium baking potato
½ cup low-fat cottage cheese
3 Tbs. finely minced red or green sweet bell pepper
Salt or onion salt and pepper to taste
2 tsp. grated Parmesan or Romano cheese
Pinch of dried thyme or oregano

Preheat oven to 400°.

Scrub potato; bake unwrapped and uncovered in a 400° oven for 1 hour or until potato feels soft when gently pressed.

Meanwhile, combine remaining ingredients and leave at room temperature so that the filling will not be chilled. When potato is baked, squeeze it gently to soften, then slit open and fill with the cottage cheese mixture.

Makes 1 serving, 210 calories.

Potatoes Genovese

4 cups cooked, pared and sliced hot potatoes
1 cup part-skim ricotta cheese
¼ cup fresh basil leaves or fresh parsley
Small clove garlic
Pinch of ground nutmeg (optional)
Pinch of grated lemon peel (optional)
Salt or butter-flavored salt and pepper to taste
¼ to ⅓ cup hot chicken broth or hot water from cooking potatoes
Grated Parmesan cheese (optional)

While potatoes are cooking, combine remaining ingredients except broth or water (and grated cheese) in blender or food processor using the steel blade. Cover and blend until completely smooth. Just before serving, add the boiling broth or cooking water to the ricotta cheese mixture; blend until mixture is the consistency of a thick sauce. Pour over potatoes. Sprinkle with grated Parmesan cheese, if desired.

Makes 6 servings, approximately 130 calories per serving. (Parmesan cheese is approximately 8 calories per tsp.)

Parsley Potatoes

6 potatoes, pared and sliced thin
½ cup minced onion
1 clove garlic, minced
1 chicken bouillon cube
Water
½ cup parsley, chopped

Place potatoes, onion, garlic and bouillon cube in saucepan with enough water to cover. Cook 10 minutes, or until potatoes are tender; drain. Toss with parsley.

Makes 12 servings, 55 calories each.

Potato-Tomato Pot

1 Tbs. olive oil
2 raw potatoes, pared
1 tomato
1 onion
Salt and pepper to taste

Preheat oven to 400°.

Pour the olive oil into a small nonstick baking dish. Cut the potatoes and tomato into 1-inch chunks. Slice the onions. Toss the vegetables, salt and pepper with the oil in the baking dish.

Cover and bake 30 minutes at 400°. Uncover; bake 30 minutes longer.

Makes 4 servings, 100 calories each.

Hot Tuna Skillet Niçoise

1 sweet onion, peeled, halved and thinly sliced
1 tsp. olive or salad oil
1 Tbs. olive liquid (from jar of olives)
¾ cup (6 oz.) tomato or tomato-vegetable juice
1 cup fat-skimmed chicken broth (canned or homemade) or water
1 can (6½ or 7 oz.) water-packed solid white meat tuna, undrained
1 potato, peeled and thinly sliced
Squeeze of garlic juice *or* pinch of instant garlic
Dash of Worcestershire sauce
4 or 5 pitted black olives, thinly sliced, or stuffed green olives
1 package (10 oz.) frozen whole green beans, defrosted
Few fresh basil leaves, minced, *or* ¼ tsp. dried basil
Few sprigs fresh parsley, minced

Combine onion, oil and olive liquid in a nonstick frying pan or electric skillet which has been sprayed with cooking spray or wiped lightly with oil. Cook uncovered over moderate heat until onion begins to brown.

Stir in tomato juice and broth (or water). Add liquid from canned tuna. Add potato, garlic juice and Worcestershire sauce. Cover tightly and simmer 15 to 20 minutes, until potatoes are just tender.

Remove cover and stir in sliced olives and defrosted green beans. Simmer, stirring occasionally, just until green beans are tender (about 3 or 4 minutes) and liquid has reduced by half. Flake tuna into the skillet and add basil and parsley; mix gently without breaking up the tuna. Heat just until warmed through.

Makes 2 meal-size servings, 300 calories per serving with broth; 285 calories per serving with water.

Primavera Potato Casserole

4 cooked potatoes, peeled and diced
1 green or red bell pepper, seeded and minced
2 onions, peeled and chopped
2 ribs celery, minced
1 cup plain low-fat yogurt
Salt or butter-flavored salt
Dash of Tabasco sauce

Topping
3 Tbs. seasoned bread crumbs
2 Tbs. grated American or Parmesan cheese

Preheat oven to 350°.

Combine casserole ingredients in a nonstick baking dish which has been sprayed with cooking spray or wiped lightly with oil. Combine topping ingredients; sprinkle over the top of the casserole. Bake uncovered, in a 350° oven for 15 to 18 minutes, until warmed through and topping is bubbly and lightly browned.

Makes 6 servings, 135 calories each.

Ratatouille Topping for Baked Potatoes

1 small eggplant, pared and diced
½ medium unpeeled zucchini, diced
1 onion, peeled and minced
1 Tbs. chopped fresh basil or oregano *or* 1 tsp. dried
1 clove garlic, peeled and minced (optional)
Salt or garlic salt and pepper to taste
1 can (6 oz.) tomato paste
1 can (10 oz.) chicken broth, fat-skimmed
Grated Romano cheese (optional)

Stir all ingredients except cheese together in a pot. Cover tightly and simmer 45 to 60 minutes. Uncover and continue to simmer until sauce is thick. Serve over hot drained high-protein pasta, or spoon over baked potatoes or fluffy rice. Sprinkle grated Romano cheese on top before serving (if desired).

Makes 4 servings, 80 calories each (sauce only). (Grated Romano cheese adds 25 calories per Tbs.)

Sweet Potato Salad

2 sweet potatoes
Salt (optional)
2 apples
2 large ribs celery
2 Tbs. orange juice
2 Tbs. mayonnaise (regular or low-fat)
2 Tbs. plain low-fat yogurt
Cinnamon

Pare potatoes and cut in 1-inch chunks; cook in simmering (salted) water to cover, until just tender, about 15 minutes. Drain and cool.

Core and cut unpared apples in 1-inch chunks. Slice celery.

Combine juice, mayonnaise and yogurt. Toss with other ingredients. Sprinkle with cinnamon. Chill.

Makes 6 servings, 120 calories per serving with regular mayonnaise; 100 calories per serving with low-fat mayonnaise.

Herbed Macaroni Salad

4 cups water
4 bouillon cubes (beef, chicken or vegetarian)
4 oz. uncooked elbow macaroni
⅓ cup plain low-fat yogurt
2 Tbs. minced onion
⅓ cup chopped celery
⅓ cup grated raw carrots
2 Tbs. minced fresh parsley
¼ cup mayonnaise (regular or low-fat)
2 tsp. tarragon vinegar
½ tsp. prepared mustard

Bring water and bouillon cubes to a boil in a large pot. Add macaroni; simmer 15 minutes until tender. Drain, but do not rinse. Add yogurt and onion to hot macaroni. Stir thoroughly; let stand 15 minutes, stirring occasionally. Mix in celery, carrots and parsley.

Combine mayonnaise, vinegar and mustard. Stir into macaroni mixture. Chill.

Makes 4 servings, 215 calories per serving with regular mayonnaise; 165 calories per serving with low-fat mayonnaise.

Macaroni Salad

2 cups uncooked elbow macaroni
2 ribs celery, chopped
1 onion, chopped
1 Tbs. mayonnaise (regular or low-fat)
2 Tbs. plain low-fat yogurt
3 Tbs. chopped fresh red sweet bell pepper or canned pimiento
2 Tbs. fresh chopped parsley
Salt and pepper
Paprika

Cook the macaroni in 2 qts. of salted boiling water for 15 minutes, or until tender. Rinse under cold running water.

Combine macaroni, celery and onion. Stir in mayonnaise, yogurt, bell pepper (or pimiento) and parsley. Salt and pepper to taste. Sprinkle with paprika. Chill well before serving.

Makes 6 side-dish servings, 115 calories per serving with regular mayonnaise; 105 calories per serving with low-fat mayonnaise.

Lunchtime Macaroni Salads—For lean protein, top each serving of macaroni salad with one of the following (additional calories given):

1 hard-cooked egg, in wedges (80 calories)
½ cup diced cooked white meat chicken (115 calories)
3½ oz. drained and flaked water-packed tuna (125 calories)
½ cup cooked shrimp (75 calories) or crabmeat (70 calories)

Macaroni Slaw

3 cups cold, tender-cooked elbow macaroni
1 large carrot, unpared
1 large rib celery, trimmed
½ red onion
4 or 5 radishes
½ green bell pepper
4 or 5 stuffed green olives
¼ cup bottled creamy cucumber salad dressing (regular or low-fat)
1 Tbs. mayonnaise (regular or low-fat) or plain low-fat yogurt
Salt and pepper to taste
Paprika, minced fresh dill weed or dill seed (optional)

Rinse and drain cooked macaroni. Shred vegetables and olives in a food processor or vegetable shredder. (By hand, grate the carrot, celery, onion and bell pepper; slice the radishes and olives.)

Stir all ingredients together; season to taste. Chill. If desired, sprinkle with paprika, dill weed or dill seed before serving.

Makes 10 servings, 85 calories per serving with regular ingredients; 60 calories per serving with low-fat salad dressing and yogurt.

Chicken and Macaroni Salad with Olives

    3 cups cooked, rinsed and drained elbow macaroni
    2 cups diced cooked chicken or turkey
    2 hard-cooked eggs, chopped
    ¼ cup chopped dill pickles
    3 Tbs. sliced green olives

Dressing
    ⅓ cup olive liquid (from jar of olives)
    ⅓ cup mayonnaise or salad dressing (regular or low-fat)
    ⅓ cup plain low-fat yogurt
    1 Tbs. fresh dill weed *or* 1 tsp. dried
    Salt or onion salt to taste
    Pinch of pepper

Combine macaroni, chicken (or turkey), eggs, pickles and olives. Mix well and set aside.

In a covered jar, combine remaining ingredients. Shake well. Pour over macaroni mixture and toss lightly. Cover and refrigerate until serving time.

Makes 4 meal-size servings, 405 calories per serving with regular mayonnaise; 325 calories per serving with low-fat mayonnaise. Can also make 8 side-dish servings, at half the calories per serving.

Tuna Macaroni Niçoise

1 can (6½ or 7 oz.) water-packed solid white meat tuna,
  undrained
1½ cups cold tender-cooked small pasta shells or any leftover
  cooked macaroni, rinsed
½ small red onion, sliced into rings
Few leaves minced fresh oregano *or* pinch of dried
1 Tbs. minced fresh parsley (optional)
1 tsp. minced fresh thyme *or* pinch of dried (optional)
9 or 10 pitted ripe olives, sliced
1 Tbs. olive liquid (from jar of olives)
1 Tbs. olive or salad oil
1 Tbs. lemon juice or cider vinegar
1 large vine-ripened tomato
½ lb. fresh raw green beans (optional)
Salt and pepper

In a salad bowl, flake undrained tuna; add rinsed pasta and remaining ingredients, except tomato (and green beans, if desired). Cover; chill.

Just before serving, peel and dice tomato, diagonally slice green beans, add to salad. Mix well and season to taste

Note: If desired, 3 Tbs. of Italian salad dressing, regular or low-fat, may be used in place of the herbs, olive liquid, and olive oil; 40 additional calories per serving with regular salad dressing; 10 less calories per serving with low-fat dressing.

Makes 3 meal-size servings, 340 calories each (25 calories more per serving with herbs and green beans).

Cold Chicken and Spinach Pasta Salad

3 Tbs. minced basil
Garlic salt
½ cup plain low-fat yogurt
2 cups cooked fresh pasta, drained
1½ cups cubed cooked chicken
10 oz. leaf spinach, torn
2 Tbs. minced onion

Mix basil and garlic salt into yogurt. Toss with pasta. Refrigerate until chilled

Add chicken, spinach and onion; toss together. Refrigerate until serving time.

Makes 4 servings, 210 calories each.

Tangy Macaroni and Cheddar Cheese Salad

4 cups tender-cooked shell or elbow macaroni, drained
½ cup creamy cucumber salad dressing (regular or low-fat)
1 cup shredded sharp cheddar cheese
½ cup sliced celery
3 Tbs. minced onion
6 Tbs. chopped red or green sweet bell pepper
Salt and pepper
Lettuce or other greens
Paprika

In a large bowl, toss macaroni with creamy cucumber dressing. Let stand 10 minutes.

Add remaining ingredients and toss. Mound on serving platter, surrounded by crisp greens and sprinkled with a little paprika.

Makes 8 side-dish servings, 180 calories per serving with regular dressing; 140 calories per serving with low-fat dressing.

Cold Pasta Pesto with Ricotta

3 cups hot tender-cooked macaroni
½ cup ricotta cheese (regular or part-skim)
2 Tbs. lemon juice
2 to 3 Tbs. minced fresh parsley
¼ cup loosely packed fresh basil leaves or fresh spinach
1 small clove garlic
Salt and pepper to taste

While macaroni is cooking, combine remaining ingredients in blender or food processor, using steel blade. Process until completely smooth.

Drain macaroni, then return it to cooking pot. Stir in cheese mixture, until hot pasta is coated. Chill until serving time. If desired, serve on lettuce garnished with tomato wedges. (Macaroni may also be served hot.)

Makes 6 side-dish servings, 70 calories per serving with regular ricotta; 60 calories per serving with part-skim ricotta.

Pasta Primavera Riviera-Style

4 cups tender-cooked, hot spaghetti or linguine
1 cup pared, diced eggplant
1 cup unpared, sliced, small zucchini
1 medium onion, peeled and sliced
1 green bell pepper, seeded and sliced
1 large vine-ripened tomato, peeled and cubed
2 cups tomato juice
1 clove garlic, minced (optional)
Pinch of thyme and basil (optional)
Salt and pepper to taste
1 Tbs. grated cheese (optional)

While pasta cooks, simmer remaining ingredients (except cheese) in covered nonstick skillet for 10 minutes. Uncover and continue simmering, stirring often, until sauce thickens and vegetables are tender but still crisp, about 5 minutes. (If needed, add a little water.)

Drain hot pasta; top with sauce. Sprinkle with 1 Tbs. grated cheese, if desired.

Makes 4 meatless main-course servings, 220 calories each (grated cheese has approximately 25 calories per Tbs.).

Beef and Peppers with Pasta

3 cups tender-cooked high protein thin spaghetti
2 medium sweet bell peppers (1 red, 1 green)
1 Spanish onion
¾ lb. top round steak
2 tsp. olive oil
½ cup dry white wine
1 clove minced garlic (optional)
3 cups plain tomato juice
3 Tbs. fresh minced basil or oregano *or* 2 tsp. dried
Salt and pepper to taste
4 Tbs. grated sharp Romano cheese
3 Tbs. chopped curly parsley

Cook spaghetti in boiling salted water and set aside in a strainer to drain. Slice bell peppers and onion in half; then slice into spaghetti-thin strips.

Coat both sides of the beef lightly with the olive oil. Spray large nonstick skillet or electric frying pan with cooking spray. Cook the beef quickly on both sides over high heat, about 2 to 3 minutes per side. Transfer to a cutting board and set aside.

Stir wine, garlic (if desired), sliced onions and peppers into the skillet over high heat. Cook and stir until all the wine evaporates. Stir in tomato juice and basil. Simmer uncovered, until vegetables are tender but still crunchy and the tomato juice has evaporated into a thick sauce, about 3 to 4 minutes.

Meanwhile, slice the beef into thin strips. Stir beef and drained spaghetti into the sauce in skillet. Cook, stirring often, over low heat until heated through and the liquid is bubbling. Season to taste. Sprinkle with cheese and parsley. Serve from the skillet.

Makes 4 servings, 355 calories each.

Mexican Spaghetti

3 cups tender-cooked high-protein spaghetti
1 small onion, minced
1 clove garlic, minced
1 can (8 oz.) tomatoes, broken up
1 can (8 oz.) Spanish-style or seasoned tomato sauce
1 bell pepper, chopped
1 to 3 tsp. chili powder, to taste (optional)
4 Tbs. shredded extra-sharp cheddar cheese (optional)

Cook spaghetti according to package directions.

Combine remaining ingredients, except cheese. Cover tightly and simmer 8 to 10 minutes. Uncover; cook and stir until sauce is thick, an additional 6 to 8 minutes.

Divide cooked, drained spaghetti into 4 portions; spoon sauce over and sprinkle with cheese, if desired. Serve with a salad of crisp shredded iceberg lettuce, cucumber, celery, tomatoes and green pepper topped with Italian dressing.

Makes 4 servings, 200 calories each; cheddar cheese adds 30 calories per serving.

Baked Vegeroni and Cheese

4 cups tender-cooked macaroni
2 tomatoes, peeled, seeded and chopped
1 cup cut asparagus
½ cup shredded American cheese (regular or low-fat)
¼ cup mayonnaise (regular or low-fat)
Salt and pepper
3 Tbs. Italian-seasoned breadcrumbs

Combine all ingredients, except breadcrumbs. Spoon into a 3-qt. nonstick casserole which has been sprayed with cooking spray. Top with breadcrumbs.

Bake, uncovered, 40 minutes in a 375° oven.

Makes 6 servings, 235 calories per serving with regular ingredients; 175 calories per serving with low-fat ingredients.

Baked Macaroni and Ratatouille

1 cup pared, diced eggplant
1 cup unpared, diced zucchini
1 onion, peeled and minced
2 peeled tomatoes, diced *or* 1 can (8 oz.) tomatoes
1 clove garlic, peeled and minced
2 cups tomato juice
2 cups water or fat-skimmed broth
8 oz. uncooked high-protein elbow macaroni
Salt and pepper to taste
½ tsp. dried basil, oregano or mixed Italian herbs (optional)

Topping
4 Tbs. grated extra-sharp Romano or Parmesan cheese
2 Tbs. Italian-seasoned breadcrumbs

Preheat oven to 325°.

Stir all ingredients together except topping ingredients. Spoon into a nonstick baking dish which has been sprayed with cooking spray or wiped lightly with oil.

Combine topping ingredients; sprinkle over top. Cover and place the baking dish on a cookie sheet on the middle oven shelf. Bake 1 hour. Uncover; bake 10 to 15 minutes more, until liquid is absorbed and topping is brown.

Makes 6 main-course servings, 210 calories per serving with water; 220 calories per serving with broth.

Ratatouille Spaghetti Sauce

1 lb. eggplant, pared and minced
1 zucchini, chopped
2 cups peeled, crushed tomatoes, fresh or canned
1 cup chopped onion
2 or 3 cloves garlic, minced (optional)
1 can (10 oz.) chicken or beef broth, fat-skimmed, or water
½ cup dry red wine or water
½ cup water
1 can (6 oz.) tomato paste
2 Tbs. minced fresh parsley
1 Tbs. minced fresh basil leaves *or* 1 tsp. dried (optional)
1 tsp. fresh thyme leaves *or* pinch of dried (optional)
Salt and pepper to taste

Combine ingredients in a heavy Dutch oven; cover tightly. Simmer over low heat 2 hours or more, stirring occasionally, until sauce is thick (add water, if needed). Spoon sauce over hot, drained pasta. Leftover sauce can be stored in the refrigerator or freezer and reheated.

Makes 6 servings of sauce, 90 calories per serving with broth and wine; 75 calories per serving with water.

Hot Ham and Spinach Pasta Salad

1 package (8 oz.) spinach noodles
½ cup ricotta cheese (regular or part-skim)
½ cup plain low-fat yogurt
1 egg
Salt and pepper
1 package (10 oz.) frozen chopped spinach, defrosted
1 cup chopped cooked ham
¼ cup seasoned breadcrumbs

Preheat oven to 375°.

Cook noodles according to package directions; drain. Mix thoroughly with cheese, yogurt, egg and seasonings to taste.

Drain spinach; fold into pasta mixture along with ham. Place in a nonstick 2-qt. baking dish. Sprinkle with breadcrumbs.

Bake 30 minutes in a 375° oven.

Makes 8 servings, 210 calories per serving with regular ricotta; 205 calories per serving with part-skim ricotta.

Spaghetti with Ham and Mushroom Sauce

¾ lb. ready-to-eat ham steak
2 tsp. oil (optional)
2 Tbs. dry white wine
1 cup sliced mushrooms (fresh or canned)
½ cup chopped onion
1 cup plain tomato juice
½ cup chicken broth, fat-skimmed
1 Tbs. fresh basil or oregano *or* 1 tsp. dried
Salt or garlic salt and pepper to taste
4 cups hot tender-cooked high-protein spaghetti or linguine

Cut ham steak into 1-inch cubes. Heat the oil in a large nonstick skillet or electric frying pan (or spray with cooking spray). Add the ham cubes and cook over high heat, turning once, until lightly browned. Stir in wine and (drained) mushrooms (reserve the canning liquid). Cook and stir until wine evaporates and mushrooms start to brown. Stir in onion, tomato juice, (reserved mushroom liquid), broth and basil or oregano. Lower heat to medium. Cook uncovered, stirring often, until liquid evaporates to a thick sauce, about 6 to 7 minutes. Season to taste. Spoon over hot, drained, rinsed spaghetti.

Makes 4 servings, approximately 310 calories each.

Salsa Rustica and Spaghetti

3 cups tender-cooked high-protein spaghetti
¾ lb. fat-trimmed ground beef round
2 cups thinly sliced onion
1 cup shredded raw carrot or green bell pepper
2 cloves garlic, finely minced
4 Tbs. dry red wine or water or beef broth
½ cup tomato juice
4 cups peeled, fresh, ripe tomato wedges
4 Tbs. chopped fresh basil or oregano *or* 2 tsp. dried
Salt and pepper to taste
4 Tbs. grated sharp Romano cheese (optional)
4 Tbs. chopped parsley (optional)

Cook spaghetti and set aside in a strainer.

Spray a large nonstick skillet or electric frying pan with cooking spray or wipe lightly with oil. Spread the ground meat in a shallow layer. Cook over moderate heat until underside is browned. Break up into chunks; turn to brown evenly. Drain and discard fat.

Stir in onion, carrot or bell pepper, garlic and wine. Cook and stir over high heat until wine has evaporated. Stir in tomato juice, tomato wedges and seasonings. Simmer until most of the liquid has reduced.

Stir in drained spaghetti. Cook and stir until heated through. Sprinkle with cheese and fresh parsley, if desired. Serve from the skillet.

Makes 4 servings, 325 calories each; 355 calories each with optional ingredients.

Linguine with Chicken and Zucchini

6 oz. dry linguine
¾ lb. chicken or turkey cutlet
1 Tbs. butter or olive oil
1 zucchini, sliced
2 vine-ripened tomatoes, peeled and cubed
¼ cup minced chives or scallions
¼ cup chopped fresh parsley
¼ cup dry white wine
½ cup chicken broth, fat-skimmed
Pinch of nutmeg
2 Tbs. grated Parmesan cheese

Cook pasta in boiling salted water until tender.

Meanwhile, slice the poultry into thin strips. Spray a large nonstick skillet or electric frying pan with cooking spray. Add the butter or oil. Cook the poultry strips over moderate heat about 4 to 5 minutes, just until cooked through. Remove from the skillet and add the zucchini slices in a single layer. Cook over high heat until lightly browned, 1 to 2 minutes, then turn to brown the other side.

When pasta is cooked, drain well. Combine the hot drained pasta in the skillet with the browned poultry and zucchini. Add tomatoes, chives, parsley, wine, broth and nutmeg. Cook and stir until everything is heated through and most of the liquid has evaporated. Sprinkle with Parmesan cheese.

Makes 4 complete-meal servings, 155 calories each; alternative ingredients add 20 calories per serving.

Spaghetti with Seafood Sauce

2 cups tender-cooked high-protein spaghetti
1 tsp. oil (optional)
½ cup thinly sliced fresh mushrooms
1 cup chopped sweet onion
½ cup dry white wine
½ cup water
2 large vine-ripened tomatoes, peeled and diced
2 Tbs. minced fresh parsley
1 Tbs. chopped fresh thyme *or* ½ tsp. dried
1 cup (5 oz.) cooked flaked fish or crabmeat or drained, water-
    packed tuna
Salt and pepper to taste
1 Tbs. grated Parmesan cheese (optional)

Cook pasta in salted water. Meanwhile, heat oil in a nonstick skillet
or electric frying pan (or spray with cooking spray.) Brown mushrooms
over medium heat. Stir in onion and 2 Tbs. wine. Cook and stir until
onion begins to brown. Stir in remaining wine, ½ cup water, diced
tomatoes, parsley and thyme. Simmer uncovered about 6 to 8 minutes, until most of the liquid has evaporated. Stir in seafood. Cook
and stir until heated through. Season to taste. Serve over hot drained
pasta. Sprinkle with cheese, if desired.

Makes 2 servings, 295 calories each with fish or crab; 330 calories
each with tuna; cheese adds 10 calories per serving; oil adds 20 calories
per serving. (Double or triple the recipe for 4 or 6 servings.)

Molded Rice Salad

2½ cups water
2 Tbs. herb vinegar
2 chicken bouillon cubes
1 cup raw rice
½ cup unpeeled, diced cucumber
½ cup minced celery
½ cup chopped red bell pepper
2 Tbs. minced chive
Salt and pepper to taste
4 Tbs. mayonnaise (regular or low-fat)

Combine water, vinegar and bouillon cubes in a saucepan; heat to boiling. Stir in rice; cover and simmer 25 minutes, or until tender. Remove from heat, drain, if necessary, and stir in remaining ingredients. Spoon into a 1-qt. mold and chill for several hours. To serve, unmold on lettuce and garnish with additional vegetables. Serve with dressing.

Makes 6 servings, 195 calories per serving with regular mayonnaise; 155 calories per serving with low-fat mayonnaise.

Spanish Rice Salad

2 cups cold rice cooked in fat-skimmed chicken broth
4 tomatoes, quartered
1 cup chopped green bell pepper
1 cup chopped celery
¼ cup chopped onion
¼ cup chopped pimiento
3 Tbs. white wine
Pinch of cumin
2 tsp. mixed Italian seasoning
Salt and pepper to taste

Toss all ingredients together and serve.
Makes 8 servings, 80 calories each.

Rice and Sprout Salad

3 cups cooked brown rice
¼ cup bean sprouts
½ cup sliced scallions
½ cup chopped parsley
¼ cup chopped watercress
¼ cup chopped pimiento
3 Tbs. tarragon vinegar
3 Tbs. olive oil
Salt and pepper to taste

Toss all ingredients together. Chill thoroughly.
Makes 4 servings, 240 calories each.

Middle Eastern Rice Salad

4 Tbs. golden raisins
½ cup white wine
1 onion, peeled and chopped
1 clove garlic, minced
1½ cups cooked rice
4 tomatoes, chopped
4 Tbs. minced parsley
3 Tbs. creamy cucumber salad dressing (regular or low-fat)
2 Tbs. pine nuts (optional)

In a small saucepan, combine raisins, wine, onion and garlic. Simmer, covered, 15 minutes. Toss with remaining ingredients.

Makes 6 servings, 115 calories per serving with regular salad dressing, 105 calories per serving with low-fat dressing; pine nuts add 15 calories per serving.

Tabouli

½ cup beef broth, fat-skimmed
1 cup bulgur wheat
1 tomato, peeled, seeded and chopped
½ cup minced parsley
2 Tbs. snipped chives
¼ cup lemon juice
3 Tbs. olive oil
2 Tbs. minced fresh mint
Salt and pepper

Warm broth; add bulgur. Let stand 1 hour. Add tomato, parsley and chives.

Combine lemon juice, olive oil, mint and seasonings to taste. Stir into salad mixture.

Makes 6 servings, 175 calories each.

Tabouli-Style Rice Salad

1 cup unseasoned, cold cooked rice
3 cups diced vine-ripened tomatoes
½ cup chopped parsley
¼ cup chopped fresh mint
¼ cup thinly sliced scallions
3 Tbs. olive oil
3 Tbs. lemon juice
Salt and pepper to taste

Combine ingredients. Cover and chill several hours.
Makes 6 servings, 120 calories each.

Turkish Cold Rice Salad

2 cups cold cooked rice (plain or cooked with a bay leaf)
1 small red onion, minced
1 bell pepper, diced
2 Tbs. minced fresh parsley
6 or 8 pitted black olives
1 Tbs. raisins
Salt or garlic salt and pepper to taste

Dressing
2 Tbs. olive oil
3 Tbs. olive liquid (from jar of olives)
3 Tbs. lemon juice
2 tsp. fresh thyme *or* ¼ tsp. dried
A few bay leaves (optional)

Garnish
1 large vine-ripened tomato, cut in wedges
1 Tbs. pine nuts or slivered almonds

Combine salad ingredients. Toss with dressing ingredients. Marinate
in the refrigerator several hours.
Before serving, arrange on beds of lettuce and garnish with tomato
and pine nuts.
Makes 8 servings, approximately 100 calories each.

Salmon Rice Salad

1½ cups water
1½ cups instant rice
2 cans (6½ oz. each) salmon, drained, deboned and flaked
3 cups diagonally sliced celery
4 Tbs. pitted ripe olives, sliced
1 red bell pepper, seeded and diced
½ cup sliced scallions
¼ cup wine vinegar
¼ cup olive oil
Salt and pepper

Combine water and rice in a saucepan. Heat to boiling. Remove from heat; cover and allow to cool. Combine with remaining ingredients, except seasonings. Refrigerate.

Before serving, season to taste.

Makes 6 lunch-size servings, 325 calories each.

Turkeyaki Rice Salad

1 cup cooked, diced turkey white meat
3 Tbs. soy sauce
¼ tsp. powdered ginger
1 cup fresh (or frozen) peas
1 cup water
1 cup instant rice
1 cup diagonally sliced celery
½ cup sliced scallions
¼ cup diced red or green bell pepper
5 Tbs. mayonnaise (regular or low-fat)
½ cup plain low-fat yogurt
1 cup alfalfa sprouts (optional)

Mix turkey, soy sauce and ginger. Cover and chill. In a saucepan, bring peas and water to a boil. Remove from heat; stir in rice. Cover and allow to cool. Add celery, scallions, bell pepper, mayonnaise and yogurt; refrigerate.

At serving time, arrange rice salad on beds of lettuce; add turkey. Garnish with sprouts, if desired.

Makes 4 meal-size servings, 350 calories per serving with regular mayonnaise; 275 calories per serving with low-fat mayonnaise (sprouts add 10 calories per serving).

Chicken Pilaf Salad

3 cups cold cooked rice
1½ cups cut-up cooked chicken
1½ cups finely chopped celery
1 can (16 oz.) young tender sweet peas, drained
2 Tbs. diced red or green sweet bell pepper
1 cup mayonnaise (regular or low-fat)
1 can (8 oz.) juice-packed pineapple tidbits, undrained
Salt and pepper
3 Tbs. dry-roasted cashews, broken up

Mix rice with chicken and vegetables. Combine mayonnaise with undrained pineapple; toss with rice mixture. Season to taste. Chill.

Before serving, top with cashews.

Makes 6 servings, 510 calories per serving with regular mayonnaise; 350 calories per serving with low-fat mayonnaise.

Paella Salad

1 cup raw rice
2½ cups water
1 chicken bouillon cube
Pinch of saffron (optional)
1 cup cubed, cooked chicken
1 cup cooked, shelled shrimp
2 Tbs. diced pimiento
1 cup cooked artichoke hearts
1 can (10 oz.) clams, undrained
4 Tbs. olive oil
4 Tbs. minced fresh oregano or parsley
Salt and pepper to taste

Cook rice in water with bouillon cube and saffron, if desired. Drain, cool. Toss with remaining ingredients. Serve chilled.

Makes 6 lunch-size servings, under 300 calories each.

Seasoned Rice

1 can (10 oz.) chicken or beef broth, fat-skimmed
2 Tbs. minced onion *or* 2 tsp. flakes
¼ cup minced celery
⅓ cup raw rice
1 Tbs. minced fresh parsley

Combine broth, onion and celery in a saucepan; heat to boiling. Stir in rice. Cover and simmer over low heat until liquid is absorbed, about 20 minutes. Add parsley and fluff with a fork.

Makes 3 servings, under 100 calories each.

Speedy Seasoned Rice

1 cup boiling water
2 tsp. chicken or beef broth concentrate
2 tsp. onion flakes
Pinch of thyme or other herbs
1 cup instant rice

Heat water to boiling; remove from heat. Stir in broth concentrate until dissolved. Stir in remaining ingredients. Cover tightly and wait 5 minutes until liquid is absorbed.

Makes 4 servings, 90 calories each.

Layered Beef Bake

1 lb. lean beef round or flank steak
1 Tbs. chopped fresh oregano *or* 1 tsp. dried
Salt and pepper to taste
1 large green bell pepper, thinly sliced
1 cup thinly sliced onion
4 Tbs. raw rice
2 cloves garlic, minced
4 cups sliced tomatoes (fresh or canned)

Trim fat, if any from steak. Slice the raw steak, against the grain, into very thin strips. Put a layer of meat on the bottom of a nonstick casserole; sprinkle with seasonings.

Preheat oven to 400°.

Alternate thin layers of remaining ingredients, ending with a layer of sliced tomatoes. (If canned tomatoes are used, pour juice over casserole.) Cover tightly with lid or aluminum foil and place in oven. Check during baking; add a little water if dish begins to dry out. Bake 4 hours. Or combine ingredients in a crock pot and slow-cook according to manufacturer's directions.

Makes 4 servings, approximately 285 calories each (10 calories more per serving with flank steak).

Cheese-Taco Topping—Just before serving, sprinkle the top of the casserole with 2 Tbs. shredded extra-sharp cheddar and 8 crushed corn chips. Adds 35 calories per serving.

Baked Rice-Stuffed Tomatoes

3 firm, well-shaped tomatoes
1 cup cooked rice
¼ cup minced chives
2 Tbs. minced parsley
2 Tbs. minced fresh mint
Salt and pepper
2 Tbs. olive oil
½ cup tomato juice

Preheat oven to 350°.

Cut tomatoes in half across. Scoop out pulp. Discard seeds and chop pulp. Combine with rice, chives, parsley, mint, salt and pepper to taste and olive oil. Fill tomato shells with this mixture.

Place filled shells in a nonstick baking pan. Pour tomato juice around shells. Bake in 350° oven 20 minutes, basting occasionally.

Makes 6 servings, 100 calories each.

7

Fruitful Salad Ideas

Fruit is Mother Nature's sugar bowl, a container that balances flavor, fiber and nutrients with sweetness. When you want to add a touch of sweetness to salad, consider fruit instead of sugary dressings. Sugar adds nothing but calories and one-dimensional sweetness, but fruit adds taste, texture and eye appeal, too.

Some fruitful ideas:

- Diced eating oranges add color and contrast to green salad mixtures, and their sweet-sour acid accent makes them the ideal replacement for tasteless, off-season tomatoes.
- Firm-textured, thinly sliced apples can take the place of water chestnuts in Oriental salad mixtures.
- A bit of ripe banana blended into salad dressing mixtures adds creamy texture along with a touch of sweetness.
- Sour fruits can provide pickle-like tartness in salad mixtures. Consider fresh cranberries in a salad, for example.
- Immature fruit that has no hope of ever ripening can be salvaged as a salad ingredient. The tart taste and firm texture of underripe peaches can add an interesting bit of mystery to a salad.
- Exchange related fruits to create something new. How about making your Waldorf salad with pears instead of apples?
- If you like your coleslaw with a touch of sweetness, add crushed pineapple to the dressing—instead of sugar!

119

- Consider fruit as the container for salad: mound chicken salad on fresh pineapple wedge "boats," or pile curried seafood salad in cantaloupe halves.
- Leave the skins on fruit for color as well as fiber. Diced red apples have much more eye appeal than peeled.
- Explore culinary ideas borrowed from hot dishes that use fruit. If you like applesauce with roast pork, why not try a cold salad with leftover cooked pork and diced raw apples?

Spiced Spinach-Apple Salad

½ lb. fresh spinach leaves
1 tart red apple
½ cup toasted soy nuts *or* ¼ cup toasted sunflower seeds
  (optional)

Dressing
½ cup mayonnaise (regular or low-fat)
¼ cup apple or orange juice concentrate, defrosted

Wash and trim spinach; tear into bite-size pieces; dry and chill. Just before serving, core and slice unpared apple. Toss with spinach and nuts or seeds, if desired.

Mix mayonnaise and juice concentrate; serve with salad.

Makes 4 servings, 260 calories per serving with regular mayonnaise; 145 calories per serving with low-fat mayonnaise. (Soy nuts add 105 calories per serving; sunflower seeds add 50 calories per serving.)

Oriental Shrimp and Apple Salad

1 small red apple, unpared, diced
3 ribs celery, minced
½ cup cooked tiny shrimp
1 tsp. instant minced onion
2 tsp. lemon juice or vinegar
½ tsp. sugar or equivalent sugar substitute
1 Tbs. soy sauce

Combine all ingredients in a bowl and toss lightly.

Makes 1 serving, 190 calories with sugar; 185 calories with sugar substitute.

Apple Slaw

1 cup sliced celery
2 cups shredded cabbage
1 cup shredded carrots
2 large unpeeled red apples, diced
4 Tbs. raisins

Dressing
1 cup plain low-fat yogurt
¼ cup lemon juice
Salt and black pepper to taste
2 tsp. prepared mustard

Combine slaw ingredients. Beat together dressing ingredients until smooth; toss with slaw. (Excellent with all pork dishes.)
Makes 8 servings, 75 calories each.

Curried Apple-Pear Salad

1 yellow pear, unpared
1 red apple, unpared
2 ribs celery
1 Tbs. mayonnaise (regular or low-fat)
1 Tbs. low-fat yogurt
1 tsp. curry powder
Cinnamon (optional)

Dice fruit into ½-inch cubes. Discard celery leaves; mince celery; add to fruit. Stir in mayonnaise, yogurt and curry. Spoon into cups or arrange on lettuce and sprinkle with cinnamon, if desired.
Makes 4 servings, 70 calories per serving with regular mayonnaise; 55 calories per serving with low-fat mayonnaise.

Low-Fat Oven "Fried" Bananas

2 firm, yellow, ripe bananas, peeled
1 tsp. butter or margarine

Preheat oven to 450°.

Cut bananas in half lengthwise. Spray a small square nonstick cakepan with cooking spray. Add butter; put pan in the hot oven just long enough for butter to melt. Place bananas in the pan and tilt the pan so the bananas roll and become lightly coated with butter. Place the pan on the bottom oven shelf and bake 5 minutes, turning the bananas once, until just browned. Serve with salt and pepper as a starchy side dish, or sprinkled with cinnamon as a dessert.

Makes 4 servings, 60 calories each.

Cantaloupe and Grape Salad

1 cup cantaloupe balls
1 cup seedless green grapes
¼ cup mayonnaise (regular or low-fat)
¼ cup lemon yogurt
Cinnamon or nutmeg

In 4 parfait glasses (or glass serving bowl), layer cantaloupe, grapes and mixture of mayonnaise and yogurt. Sprinkle with cinnamon or nutmeg.

Makes 4 servings, 155 calories per serving with regular mayonnaise; 95 calories per serving with low-fat mayonnaise.

Grape and Carrot Salad

1 cup green grapes
3 cups grated carrots
1 Tbs. minced fresh oregano
3 Tbs. pineapple juice
1 Tbs. plain low-fat yogurt

Toss all ingredients together lightly. Chill.

Makes 6 servings, 40 calories each.

Bombay Orange Salad

Dressing
>¼ cup creamy cucumber or yogurt dressing (regular or low-fat)
>2 Tbs. orange juice or water
>Pinch of allspice
>½ tsp. curry powder

Salad
>½ head romaine lettuce, torn
>¼ cup chopped onion or sliced scallions (or more to taste)
>1 small red or green bell pepper, diced
>1 eating orange, peeled and diced

Stir dressing ingredients together; toss with salad ingredients.
Makes 4 servings, 105 calories per serving with regular dressing; 70 calories per serving with low-fat dressing.

Indian Spiced Orange and Peas Salad

>½ cup green peas, fresh or defrosted frozen
>½ cup mandarin orange segments, drained
>1 cup cottage cheese
>Pinch each or more, to taste, of ginger, cardamom, cumin, chili
> and salt

Mix ingredients. Serve on leaves of romaine lettuce.
Makes 2 servings, 155 calories each.

Spiced Orange-Spinach Salad

Dressing
>3 Tbs. bottled French dressing (regular or low-fat)
>Pinch of cinnamon or apple pie spice
>2 Tbs. orange juice

Salad
>4 cups torn raw spinach
>½ small red onion, sliced into rings
>1 eating orange, peeled, quartered and thinly sliced

Stir dressing ingredients together. Toss with salad ingredients.
Makes 2 servings, approximately 175 calories per serving with regular bottled dressing; 120 calories per serving with low-fat dressing.

Orange, Pear and Onion Salad

1 head iceberg lettuce
2 oranges
2 ripe pears
1 medium Spanish sweet onion

Shred lettuce and arrange on a platter. Peel and slice oranges into circles; remove pits. Core pears, but do not pare; slice into thin wedges. Peel onion; slice into circles; separate into rings. Arrange fruit and onion rings decoratively over lettuce. Serve immediately with Honey and Yogurt Dressing (page 51) if desired.

Makes 4 servings, 110 calories each (salad only); 120 calories with Honey and Yogurt Dressing.

Oriental Orange Salad

Dressing
¼ cup French dressing (regular or low-fat)
1 Tbs. soy sauce
Pinch each of cinnamon, ginger, nutmeg, and clove or a pinch of pumpkin pie spice

Salad
½ head crisp lettuce, shredded
¼ cup diagonally sliced scallions
¼ cup sliced fresh fennel or diagonally sliced celery
½ cup diced red or green bell pepper (optional)
1 eating orange, peeled and diced

Combine dressing ingredients, mix until smooth. Toss with salad ingredients.

Makes 4 servings, approximately 130 calories each with regular dressing; 95 calories each with low-fat dressing.

Roka-Pear Salad

2 cups cubed, unpeeled ripe pears
2 cups sliced celery

Dressing
½ cup plain low-fat yogurt
2 Tbs. mayonnaise (regular or low-fat)
1 oz. Roquefort or blue cheese, coarsely crumbled

Combine pears and celery. Blend yogurt and mayonnaise; stir in cheese. Toss with pear and celery mixture. Serve on crisp salad greens, if desired.

Makes 6 servings salad, 105 calories per serving with regular mayonnaise; 85 calories per serving with low-fat mayonnaise.

Pear and Spinach Salad

4 cups torn leaf spinach
2 ribs celery, sliced
1 cup fresh bean sprouts
2 ripe pears or apples
1 Tbs. lemon juice

Dressing
2 oz. blue cheese
4 Tbs. salad oil
1 Tbs. lemon juice
½ tsp. grated lemon peel (optional)
½ cup plain low-fat yogurt
Onion salt and lemon pepper to taste

Toss together spinach, celery and bean sprouts. Core pears (or apples) and slice into thin wedges. Coat the wedges with 1 Tbs. lemon juice. Arrange pears on top of greens on a serving platter.

Mash blue cheese with the salad oil and 1 Tbs. lemon juice. Blend in remaining ingredients. Serve over salad.

Makes 8 servings, 135 calories each.

Pineapple and Beet Salad

1 can (16 oz.) julienne-sliced beets, drained
2 Tbs. wine vinegar
1 Tbs. sugar
Pinch each of ground cloves and cinnamon
Salt to taste
½ cup juice-packed crushed pineapple, drained

Mix beets with a combination of the vinegar, sugar and seasonings; chill. Just before serving, mix in pineapple.

Makes 3 servings, 90 calories each.

Fruited Cottage Cheese

    1 eating apple, unpeeled, diced
    1 eating orange, peeled, seeded and diced
    2 Tbs. golden raisins
    ¼ tsp. apple pie or pumpkin pie spice
    2 tsp. vanilla extract
    12 oz. container cottage cheese (regular or low-fat)

Stir apple, orange, raisins, pie spice and vanilla together. Spoon over cottage cheese.

Makes 2 servings, 280 calories each with regular cottage cheese; 230 calories each with low-fat cottage cheese.

Fruit Salad Stuffed Apples

    6 large apples
    1 cup juice-packed fruit salad, drained (reserve juice)
    1 tsp. apple pie spice

Core apples, leaving the base solid. Do not peel. Place apples, open end up, in a nonstick baking dish. Mix fruit salad with spice. Spoon into the hollowed apples.

Preheat oven to 375°.

Pour reserved juice over and around the apples. Bake approximately 45 minutes, or until apples are just barely tender. Baste occasionally with pan juices.

Makes 6 servings, 100 calories each.

Fruit Slaw

    1 can (16 oz.) juice-packed fruit cocktail
    4 cups shredded cabbage

Dressing
    3 Tbs. plain low-fat yogurt
    1 tsp. prepared mustard
    Splash of Worcestershire sauce
    Pinch pumpkin pie spice
    Salt to taste

Drain fruit cocktail; reserve juices. In large bowl, toss drained fruit with cabbage.

In another bowl mix dressing ingredients with 1 Tbs. reserved juice. Toss dressing ingredients with salad ingredients.

Makes 8 servings, 35 calories each.

Waldorf Salad

3 unpeeled apples (preferably 1 red, 1 yellow, 1 green)
2 Tbs. lemon juice
2 cups sliced celery
¼ cup mayonnaise (regular or low-fat)
¼ cup lemon yogurt
Seasoned salt
Lettuce
¼ cup chopped walnuts

Core, but don't peel apples; cut in cubes. Toss apple cubes with lemon juice, coating completely. Mix with celery. Stir together mayonnaise and yogurt; add seasoned salt to taste. Combine apple mixture and mayonnaise mixture. Mound on beds of lettuce. Sprinkle with chopped nuts.

Makes 4 servings, 235 calories per serving with regular mayonnaise; 175 calories per serving with low-fat mayonnaise.

Fruited Waldorf Salad

1 cup sliced fresh strawberries
1 eating orange, peeled, seeded and diced
1 unpared yellow apple or ripe pear, diced
2 cups diced celery

Dressing
¼ cup plain low-fat yogurt
3 Tbs. mayonnaise (regular or low-fat)
2 Tbs. defrosted undiluted orange juice concentrate

Combine fruit and celery in a bowl. Stir dressing ingredients together; toss with salad mixture. Chill.

Makes 6 servings, 105 calories per serving with regular mayonnaise; 75 calories per serving with low-fat mayonnaise.

Turkey Pineapple Salad Bowl

½ cup diced, cooked turkey white meat
½ cup fresh or canned unsweetened pineapple chunks
4 ribs celery, thinly sliced
1 tsp. instant minced onion

Dressing
1 tsp. salad oil
2 tsp. vinegar
1 Tbs. soy sauce

Toss salad ingredients lightly. Combine dressing ingredients, and toss with salad. Serve in a bowl (or spoon over a hollowed-out fresh pineapple quarter, with leaves still attached, if desired).
Makes 1 serving salad, 255 calories.

Steak and Grapefruit Salad

½ cup chilled unsweetened grapefruit sections (fresh or canned)
½ tsp. sugar or equivalent sugar substitute
½ cup leftover lean broiled beef round steak (rare)
3 ribs celery, thinly sliced
1 tsp. instant minced onion
1 tsp. vinegar
1 Tbs. soy sauce

Toss grapefruit sections with sugar or sugar substitute. Slice steak into very thin strips. Combine all ingredients in a bowl; toss lightly.
Makes 1 serving, 220 calories.

8

Fast and Fancy Gelatin Salads

One way to add glamour to any salad mixture is to serve it "under glass" . . . beneath a windowpane of sweet or savory jelled juice. If you pack your mixture into a fancy mold, so much the better! What could be prettier than a jeweled crown of cool gelatin set with fruits or vegetables!

While commercial flavored gelatin mixes are popular and easy to use, their fake flavors and phony colors are no match for gelatins made from real fruit juice. Actually, real fruit gelatin is just about as easy to make, and it contains no artificial ingredients, not even the "artificial" sweetness of added sugar.

Here's how:

REAL FRUIT GELATIN WITH FRUIT JUICE: Sprinkle 1 Tbs., or 1 envelope, unflavored gelatin on 1 cup of fresh or canned fruit juice. Wait 1 minute, until gelatin has softened, then heat gently over low flame until gelatin melts. Remove from heat and stir in 1 additional cupful of fruit juice. Chill gelatin mixture until syrupy before folding in fruits or vegetables.

REAL FRUIT GELATIN FROM FRUIT JUICE CONCENTRATE: Sprinkle 1 Tbs. unflavored gelatin on ½ cup cold water. Wait 1 minute, then heat gently, until gelatin melts. Stir in 1 can (6 oz.) defrosted undiluted frozen fruit juice concentrate, and ¼ cup cold water.

CAUTION: Do *not* use fresh or frozen pineapple (fruit or juice) in gelatin mixtures. Pineapple contains an enzyme that digests the protein in gelatin and prevents it from jelling. However, the enzyme is destroyed by heat, so canned fruit or juice may be used. Fresh or frozen pineapple or pineapple juice that has been boiled may also be used.

Blender-Quick Gelatin Salad

2 envelopes unflavored gelatin
½ cup cold water
1½ cups boiling water
¼ cup cider vinegar
2 Tbs. lemon juice
1 tsp. salt or seasoned salt *or* to taste
1 Tbs. chopped fresh mixed herbs *or* ½ tsp. dried (optional)
1 can (6 oz.) unsweetened frozen cider or apple juice concentrate, slightly thawed, undiluted
3½ cups raw vegetables, or ½ cup each: diced bell pepper; sliced radishes, scallions, raw mushrooms, peeled cucumber; shredded carrot, raw shelled peas

In the freezer, chill a nonstick rectangular cakepan, a round-bottomed bowl, or a fancy 5-cup mold.

Sprinkle gelatin on cold water in blender container. Wait 1 minute for gelatin to soften, then add boiling water, cover and blend, until gelatin is thoroughly dissolved. Scrape sides with a rubber scraper. Add vinegar, lemon juice, seasonings and undiluted frozen juice. Cover and blend until juice melts and blends in. Refrigerate until mixture is partially set and syrupy.

Meanwhile, remove pan or mold from freezer and arrange vegetables in it in an attractive design. Pour syrupy gelatin mixture over vegetables. (If using a deep bowl or mold, alternate layers of vegetables and gelatin, ending with a layer of gelatin.) Refrigerate until thoroughly set.

To serve, cut in squares and arrange on beds of lettuce. If using a mold, unmold on a platter of lettuce. Garnish with parsley and cherry tomatoes, if desired.

Makes 8 servings, approximately 70 calories each.

Easy Aspic

3 cups plain tomato juice *or* 1½ cups plus 1½ cups Bloody Mary-
  seasoned tomato juice or tomato-vegetable juice
2 envelopes unflavored gelatin
¼ cup lemon or lime juice
1 cup shredded raw cabbage
1 cup chopped celery
1 cup chopped green bell pepper
4 to 8 Tbs. minced onion or scallions
1 clove garlic, minced

Empty 1¾ cups tomato juice into a small saucepan. Sprinkle on gelatin. Wait a few minutes, until gelatin softens, then heat gently until gelatin melts. Remove from heat and stir in remaining tomato juice and lemon juice. Chill until syrupy. Fold in vegetables. Chill until firm.

Makes 8 servings, approximately 40 calories each.

Molded Beet Salad

1 orange
1 can (8 oz.) julienne-style beets
4 Tbs. lemon juice
1 envelope unflavored gelatin
½ cup sliced celery
Salt and pepper

Peel, seed and dice orange, reserving any juice that collects. Set fruit aside.

Drain juice from beets. Add beet juice to orange juice. Set drained beets aside with diced orange.

Add lemon juice to orange and beet juices. Add enough water to make 1½ cups liquid, all together. Pour liquid into a saucepan. Sprinkle on gelatin; wait 1 minute for gelatin to soften. Then, heat and stir until gelatin granules are completely dissolved. Chill until beginning to set.

Mix drained beets, diced orange and celery. Season to taste. When gelatin is ready, fold in. Spoon mixture into a 4-cup nonstick mold; refrigerate several hours until completely set. Unmold to serve.

Makes 6 servings, 30 calories each.

Molded Red Cabbage Salad

1 envelope unflavored gelatin
1 cup unsweetened canned pineapple juice (see Caution on page 130)
1 cup shredded red cabbage
2 unpeeled cucumbers, diced
Salt or seasoned salt

Sprinkle gelatin over pineapple juice in a small saucepan. Wait 1 minute for gelatin to soften. Then, heat and stir until gelatin granules dissolve. Chill until beginning to set.

Meanwhile, shred cabbage and dice cucumber. Season to taste. When gelatin is ready, fold in vegetables. Spoon into a 1-qt. nonstick mold and refrigerate several hours until completely set. Unmold to serve.

Makes 6 servings, 40 calories each.

Molded Gazpacho

1 package (8-serving) lemon gelatin (regular or sugar-free)
1½ cups tomato juice
½ cup non-fat dry milk powder
½ cup water
2 Tbs. catsup
Salt
½ cup chopped celery
½ cup diced unpeeled cucumber
¼ cup minced green bell pepper

Combine gelatin and tomato juice in a small saucepan. Cook and stir over low heat until gelatin is dissolved. Chill until thick but not set. Whip until foamy.

Mix dry milk, water, catsup and salt to taste. Gradually add to whipped gelatin.

Fold in vegetables. Pour into a nonstick 4-cup mold. Chill several hours until completely firm.

Makes 6 servings, 150 calories per serving with regular gelatin; 55 calories per serving with sugar-free gelatin.

Vegetables Under Glass

2 envelopes unflavored gelatin
2½ cups cold water
4 Tbs. cider vinegar
1 Tbs. brandy (optional)
1 cup shredded carrot
1 cup diced tomatoes
1 cup sliced celery

Sprinkle gelatin over 1 cup cold water in a small saucepan. Wait 1 minute for gelatin to soften. Heat and stir until gelatin granules are completely dissolved. Stir in remaining cold water, vinegar and brandy, if desired. Chill until mixture begins to thicken.

Place each of the vegetables in a separate bowl. Mix ⅓ of the thickened gelatin into each. Spray a 4-cup ring mold with cooking spray, or wipe lightly with salad oil. Spoon half of each vegetable into ⅙ of the circle of the mold, making vertical sections of the vegetables. Refrigerate several hours or overnight, until gelatin is completely firm. Unmold onto lettuce and serve.

Makes 6 servings, approximately 30 calories each.

Molded Chicken Salad

1 envelope unflavored gelatin
1 cup cold water
⅓ cup plain low-fat yogurt
⅓ cup mayonnaise (regular or low-fat)
1½ Tbs. lemon juice
1 tsp. prepared mustard
2 cups cooked chicken white meat, diced
½ cup chopped celery
½ cup minced red or green bell pepper
2 scallions, sliced

In a small saucepan, sprinkle gelatin over the water. Allow to soften 1 minute; heat and stir until gelatin dissolves.

Pour gelatin mixtures, yogurt, mayonnaise, lemon juice and mustard into blender container. Blend smooth. Add to remaining ingredients and fold in. Spoon into a 4-cup mold, 4 individual molds, or a loaf pan. Chill until firm. Unmold to serve.

Makes 4 servings, 285 calories per serving with regular mayonnaise; 205 calories per serving with low-fat mayonnaise.

Molded Tuna

2 cans (6½ or 7 oz. each) water-packed tuna
1 envelope unflavored gelatin
½ cup fresh or bottled creamy cucumber dressing (regular or low-
    fat)
2 Tbs. minced celery
2 Tbs. minced chives
1 cup plain low-fat yogurt
2 Tbs. drained green olives, thinly sliced (optional)

Drain ¼ cup liquid from cans of tuna into a small saucepan. Sprinkle on the gelatin powder; let soften 1 minute. Heat and stir until gelatin dissolves. Set aside.

Drain and flake tuna. Combine with dressing, celery, chives and yogurt. Beat and mix until fairly smooth. Blend in gelatin mixture. Stir in olives, if desired.

Turn into a 1-qt. mold; chill several hours until firm. Unmold on a bed of crisp greens.

Makes 4 servings, 310 calories per serving with regular dressing; 230 calories per serving with low-fat dressing.

Cran-Banana Gelatin

1 package (4-servings) gelatin: strawberry, cherry or raspberry
    (regular or sugar-free)
1 cup boiling water
1 cup ice cubes and water
1 cup raw cranberries
2 ripe bananas, peeled and sliced

Combine gelatin and boiling water in blender; cover and blend until gelatin dissolves. Put ice cubes in a 1-cup measure and fill with tap water. Add to blender; cover and blend until ice dissolves. Add cranberries; cover and blend, just until coarsely chopped. Chill mixture until partly set. Layer with banana slices in 6 individual dessert cups.

Makes 6 servings, 95 calories per serving with regular gelatin; 45 calories per serving with sugar-free gelatin.

Molded Pineapple-Cottage Cheese Salad

2½ cups canned, crushed juice-packed pineapple (see Caution on
    page 130)
¾ cup hot water
1 package (4-servings) lemon gelatin (regular or sugar-free)
Juice of 1 lemon
2 cups cottage cheese
1 cup skim milk

Drain juice from pineapple, reserving fruit. Heat juice and water with
gelatin, stirring until gelatin is completely dissolved. Stir in lemon
juice. Cool until mixture mounds on spoon.

Beat cottage cheese, reserved pineapple and milk together; fold
into gelatin. Pour into 6-cup nonstick mold; chill several hours until
firm.

Makes 8 servings, 140 calories per serving with regular gelatin; 105
calories per serving with sugarless gelatin.

Strawberry Champagne Mold

1 package (4-servings) strawberry gelatin (regular or sugar-free)
1 cup boiling water
½ cup champagne or any white wine
Pinch of salt
½ cup ice cubes and water
1 cup fresh sliced strawberries
1 small ripe banana, thinly sliced
3 Tbs. flaked sweetened coconut

Dissolve gelatin in boiling water. Add champagne, salt, ice cubes and
water; stir until ice is melted. Refrigerate until partly set. Fold in
strawberries, banana and coconut. Pour into a 4-cup mold, 6 individual molds or a loaf pan. Chill until firm.

Makes 6 servings, 115 calories per serving with regular gelatin; 70
calories per serving with sugar-free gelatin.

Molded Peach Salad

1 envelope unflavored gelatin
1 cup peach nectar
1 cup orange sherbet
1 cup fresh peach slices

Sprinkle gelatin over nectar in a saucepan; allow to soften 1 minute, then heat and stir until all gelatin granules are dissolved. Mix sherbet in thoroughly. Refrigerate until partly set; stir in peach slices. Chill until thoroughly set. This salad may be set in a decorative 3-cup mold, a serving dish, or individual dessert cups or parfait glasses.

Makes 6 servings, 80 calories each.

9

Salad
Appetizers

Unfortunately, most appetizers are actually so rich and filling that they tend to kill both the appetite and appreciation for the foods that follow! Fatty and protein-rich party foods like nuts, cheeses and smoked meats all carry a weighty wallop of calories, so it's easy for the person of average appetite to put away more nourishment *before* the meal than he would normally eat *during!* Those with weight problems and boundless appetites will overdo on both and regret it, while those with bird-like eating habits may reach the dinner table unable to consume another morsel.

The smart solution is to keep it light where premeal nibbles are concerned. Nature has provided the perfect first course in the form of "crudités," the French word for raw vegetable munchies served with drinks before dinner. For casual entertaining, raw vegetable finger foods with dressings for dipping can take the place of the salad normally served with the meal.

Crudités Pronto

Slice or cut a variety of raw vegetables into spears, chips or dippers. (To make them fresh and crisp, soak them in ice water, then drain.) Arrange attractively on trays, with an eye toward color and contrast, around bowls of well-seasoned dips and dressings. For a shortcut dip

137

that requires no work at all, simply transfer any favorite commercial salad dressing from the bottle into a bowl (add some parsley for garnish). Or stir packets of any favorite salad dressing mix into plain yogurt or sour cream.

Vegetable Nachos Con Queso

12 oz. cottage cheese (regular or low-fat)
3 oz. extra-sharp cheddar cheese
1 Tbs. fresh oregano *or* ½ tsp. dried
1 to 2 tsp. cumin seeds *or* ½ to 1 tsp. ground cumin
1 clove garlic, minced
2 tsp. prepared mustard
1 tsp. chili powder or more to taste
4 Tbs. minced cilantro or fresh parsley

Combine ingredients in blender or food processor (using the steel blade); blend smooth. Spoon into a small crock or container and refrigerate until serving. Surround with raw vegetable chips and dippers.

Makes about 1⅔ cups dip, 15 calories per Tbs.

Vegetable Bundles with Cucumber Dip

Raw vegetables: carrots, zucchini, summer squash, celery,
    cucumbers, etc.
1 large unwaxed cucumber
½ cup plain low-fat yogurt
4 oz. farmer cheese
4 Tbs. mayonnaise (regular or low-fat)
1 Tbs. minced chives or scallions
2 Tbs. minced fresh parsley or mint
1 Tbs. chopped fresh dill *or* 1 tsp. dried
Salt and pepper to taste

Cut fresh raw vegetables into 3-inch sticks.

Slice unwaxed, unpared cucumber into half-inch slices. Use a sharp pointed knife to hollow out the centers. Reserve the cucumber pulp to add to the dip.

Divide the vegetable sticks into bundles and insert them into raw green cucumber "napkin rings."

Combine cucumber pulp with remaining dip ingredients in a blender or food processor and blend smooth. Refrigerate until serving. Put the dip in a bowl and surround with vegetable stick bundles and other raw vegetable dippers (whole cherry tomatoes, radishes, raw mushroom slices, etc.).

Makes about 2 cups dip, approximately 15 calories per Tbs.

Bell Pepper Dip

1 very large well-shaped green bell pepper
4 Tbs. minced red pepper (either sweet bell pepper or canned
    pimiento)
8 oz. cottage cheese
1½ oz. extra sharp cheddar cheese, diced
2 tsp. prepared mustard (mild or spicy)
1 to 2 tsp. Tabasco sauce to taste (optional)

Slit off the top of the green pepper to form a cup. Discard seeds and membranes. Chop the edible part of the pepper top and add it to the minced red pepper. Set aside.

Combine remaining ingredients in blender or food processor (using the steel blade) and blend smooth. Fold in minced pepper. Pile the mixture into the pepper cup. Refrigerate until serving. To serve, surround with thin vegetable scoopers (or corn chips).

Calories: 20 per Tbs. (cheese mixture only).

Spicy Coriander Dip

1 green bell pepper
1 cup plain low-fat yogurt
¼ cup dill pickle relish
1 tsp. ground coriander
1 tsp. mixed pumpkin pie spice

Cut top from bell pepper; discard seeds and membranes. Chop the top (remove stem), reserving bottom.

Combine remaining ingredients and add chopped bell pepper. Fill hollowed pepper with the mixture. Refrigerate until serving. Serve with raw vegetable dippers.

Makes approximately 1¼ cups dip, 10 calories per Tbs.

Parsley-Garlic Spread or Dip

1 cup fresh parsley
1 Tbs. fresh basil *or* 1 tsp. dried
1 clove peeled garlic
Salt or butter-flavored salt or butter flavoring
3 Tbs. grated extra sharp Romano cheese
¾ cup part-skim ricotta cheese

Combine ingredients in blender or food processor (using the steel blade); blend smooth. Thin with a little milk, if desired. Use as a dip or spread.

Makes approximately 1 cup, 25 calories per Tbs.

Parsley-Pesto Sauce—Follow preceding directions; thin with a little boiling water. Toss the parsley sauce with 2 cups hot drained noodles or green spaghetti. Makes 2 servings, 390 calories each.

Fresh Herb Dilly Dip

½ cup mayonnaise (regular or low-fat)
½ cup fresh or bottled Green Goddess dressing (regular or low-fat)
1 cup cottage cheese
4 Tbs. snipped fresh dill
4 Tbs. snipped chives
2 Tbs. snipped parsley
2 Tbs. snipped chervil (optional)
1 Tbs. snipped basil
Pinch of cayenne pepper

Combine all ingredients in container of blender or food processor, using the metal blade. Cover, process smooth. Refrigerate in storage-serving container.

Makes approximately 2¼ cups dip, 30 calories per Tbs. with regular mayonnaise and dressing; 15 calories per Tbs. with low-fat alternatives.

Middle-Eastern Low-Fat Hummus Bean Dip

1 can (15 or 16 oz.) chickpeas (1¾ cups)
1 to 2 Tbs. salad oil or liquid from the canned chickpeas
1 to 3 Tbs. fresh lemon juice or to taste
2 large or 3 small cloves fresh garlic
Salt to taste
Minced fresh parsley

Drain chickpeas, reserving liquid. Combine chickpeas with remaining ingredients in blender or food processor, adding only 1 Tbs. oil or chickpea liquid. Cover and process at high speed until completely smooth. (Add more oil or liquid, if desired.) Refrigerate in covered container or crock until serving time. Serve with vegetable dippers, or with toasted pita bread (torn into dippers), sesame crackers or breadsticks.

Makes 1¼ cups, 30 calories per Tbs. with oil; 25 calories per Tbs. with chickpea liquid.

Tahini Hummus—Substitute 3 to 4 Tbs. tahini (ground sesame seed paste) for the salad oil; 30 calories per Tbs.

Indian Bean Dip

1 can (15 or 16 oz.) chickpeas (1¾ cups)
1 or 2 Tbs. salad oil or liquid from chickpeas
1 Tbs. lemon or lime juice
2 to 3 cloves garlic, peeled
¼ tsp. cinnamon
1 Tbs. cumin seeds
1 tsp. curry powder or more to taste
Salt and pepper to taste

Combine chickpeas with remaining ingredients in blender or food processor, adding only 1 Tbs. oil or chickpea liquid. Cover and process at high speed until completely smooth. (Add more oil or liquid, if desired.) Refrigerate in covered crock or serving container.

Makes 1¼ cups, 30 calories per Tbs. with oil; 20 calories per Tbs. with chickpea liquid.

Tahini-Style Bean Dip—Substitute 2 to 3 Tbs. tahini (ground sesame seed paste) or peanut butter for the salad oil; 30 calories per Tbs. with tahini; 35 calories per Tbs. with peanut butter.

Yogurt Cucumber Dip

1 cucumber, peeled
1 cup plain low-fat yogurt, drained
2 Tbs. white vinegar or lemon juice
Salt and pepper to taste
2 Tbs. fresh dill weed *or* 1 tsp. dried

Slice cucumber into spears. With a sharp knife, discard seeds and mince the cucumber finely. Combine with all other ingredients and chill several hours before serving. Store in refrigerator. Serve with raw vegetables or chips.

Makes about 1½ cups, approximately 7 calories per Tbs.

Pineapple Cheese Ball

1 cup juice-packed crushed pineapple
2 packages (16 oz.) cream or Neufchâtel or farmer cheese
¼ cup minced bell pepper
3 Tbs. chopped chives or scallions
½ cup salted dry-roasted sunflower seeds

Drain pineapple, pressing out all moisture. Discard juice. Combine pineapple with remaining ingredients, except sunflower seeds, and blend well. Shape mixture into a ball and roll in sunflower seeds until well coated.

Makes 32 servings, 65 calories per serving with cream cheese; 55 calories per serving with Neufchâtel; 35 calories per serving with farmer cheese.

Mixed Cheese Ball

2 oz. Swiss cheese
1 package (8 oz.) cream cheese (regular or low-fat)
1 Tbs. grated sharp Romano cheese
4 Tbs. blue cheese salad dressing (regular or low-fat)
¼ cup chopped walnuts

Cut room-temperature cheeses into 1-inch cubes. Place cheeses and salad dressing in bowl of food processor with steel blade; process until light and creamy. Chill.

Shape into ball. Cover with walnuts. (If desired serve with apple wedges.)

Makes about 1¼ cups spread, 80 calories per Tbs. with regular ingredients; 50 calories per Tbs. with low-fat ingredients.

Italian Tuna Pâté

1 can (6½ oz.) water-packed solid white meat tuna, well drained
1 package (7½ oz.) farmer cheese
Butter-flavored salt to taste (optional)

Break tuna into flakes. Combine it with farmer cheese in the container of a food processor (using the steel blade). Process 2 to 3 minutes, until buttery smooth. (This stiff mixture may also be prepared in a blender with a powerful motor.) Season to taste. Spoon into a container, and store in the refrigerator. Pâté gets firm when chilled. Serve with crackers, thin rounds of Italian bread or breadsticks.

Makes 1⅓ cups, 25 calories per Tbs.

Cottage-Tuna Party Pâté

¾ cup cottage cheese
1 package (3 oz.) cream cheese (regular or low-fat)
¼ cup chili sauce
¼ cup minced fresh parsley
1 Tbs. minced scallions or onion
1 large can (13 oz.) water-packed tuna, drained.

Combine ingredients in a food processor, using the steel blade (or in a blender with a strong motor). Process until smooth. Pack into a container and refrigerate until firm. Serve with crackers or celery sticks.

Makes 3½ cups, 20 calories per Tbs. with regular cream cheese; 15 calories per Tbs. with low-fat cream cheese.

Vegetable and Liver Pâté

1 Tbs. butter or margarine or diet margarine
1 lb. chicken livers
6 Tbs. minced onion
½ lb. fresh mushrooms, chopped
½ cup minced parsley
1 tsp. poultry seasoning
Salt and pepper to taste
1 Tbs. cognac
1 Tbs. mayonnaise (regular or low-fat)

Melt butter or margarine in a nonstick skillet. Add chicken livers and onion. Cook, stirring occasionally, until livers are browned but not dry. Add mushrooms to pan, cook an additional 2 minutes.

Place chicken liver mixture and remaining ingredients in food processor, using metal blade. Process until almost smooth. Pack into a small round bowl; refrigerate.

Use as a spread directly from bowl, or unmold onto a serving platter.

Makes approximately 2 cups, 30 calories per Tbs. with regular ingredients; 25 calories per Tbs. with low-fat ingredients.

Polynesian Pineapple and Shrimp Cocktails

1 lb. cooked, shelled large shrimp
1 sweet bell pepper, diced
2 cups juice-packed pineapple tidbits, drained (reserve juice)
Lettuce
¼ cup pineapple juice (from can)
1 cup creamy French salad dressing (regular or low-fat)
¼ cup soy sauce
1 Tbs. grated fresh ginger root *or* 1 tsp. ground ginger
Parsley
Lime wedges

Arrange shrimp, bell pepper and drained pineapple on lettuce in 8 stemmed cocktail cups. Combine remaining ingredients except parsley and lime; mix well. Pour over shrimp. Garnish with the parsley and lime.

Makes 8 servings, 205 calories per serving with regular dressing; 175 calories per serving with low-fat dressing.

Shellfish-Topped Cucumber Hors D'Oeuvres

2 medium cucumbers, unpared
1 cup drained cooked crabmeat or minced lobster
2 Tbs. mayonnaise (regular or low-fat)
2 tsp. lemon juice
2 tsp. spicy mustard
Salt and pepper to taste
1 Tbs. minced parsley or chives (optional)

Slice cucumbers thickly. Combine remaining ingredients and mix well; spoon onto cucumber slices. Serve chilled.

Makes about 16, 20 calories each with regular mayonnaise; 15 calories each with low-fat mayonnaise.

Cucumber Tuna Hors D'Oeuvres—Substitute drained water-packed tuna for crabmeat; 5 additional calories each.

Shrimp and Cucumber Cocktails

1 cucumber
Salt (optional)
½ lb. deveined cooked shrimp

Cocktail sauce
1 cup chili sauce or catsup
2 Tbs. lemon juice
3 Tbs. drained prepared horseradish or more to taste

Wash cucumber and cut off the ends. (Don't peel it unless wax-coated.) Slice it wafer thin (sprinkle with salt, if desired). Line the inside of 6 small glass bowls or shrimp cocktail dishes with cucumber slices arranged into flower petals. Pile with cold cooked peeled shrimp.

Combine chili sauce or catsup with lemon juice and horseradish to taste. Spoon over cocktails.

Makes 6 servings, approximately 100 calories each.

Baked Mushrooms

½ lb. fresh whole mushrooms
4 Tbs. grated Parmesan cheese
4 Tbs. Italian-seasoned breadcrumbs
Onion or garlic salt and pepper (optional)

Preheat oven to 475°.

Separate the mushroom stems from the caps. Wash caps and stems; do not dry. Combine the cheese, crumbs and desired seasonings. Roll the mushroom caps in the cheese-crumb mixture.

Spray a shallow nonstick baking pan with cooking spray, or wipe lightly with oil. Arrange the caps in a single layer on the baking tray, cups facing up. Chop the stems; combine them with the remaining cheese and crumbs. Spoon this mixture into the caps. Bake uncovered, in a very hot 475° oven 8 to 10 minutes, until crisp.

Makes 6 servings, 45 calories each.

Fresh Cheese Spreads

Fresh cheeses—pot, cottage, ricotta, farmer—are generally leaner and less fattening than aged or hard cheeses. Their soft, creamy taste and texture make them the perfect base for blender cheese spreads, which combine dairy flavor with home-grown herbs or other fresh ingredients. Small amounts of very sharp cheeses, grated, can be combined with fresh cheeses for flavor without lots of butterfat or calories. Here are some ideas to try:

Italian Part-Skim Crock Cheese

2 oz. very sharp Romano cheese, grated
1 cup part-skim ricotta cheese
2 Tbs. minced fresh basil or parsley
2 Tbs. minced fresh Italian parsley (optional)
1 clove garlic, peeled (optional)
Salt and pepper to taste.

Combine ingredients in blender or food processor, using the steel blade. Process until completely smooth. Spoon into crock or container and store in refrigerator (cheese firms as it chills).

Approximately 25 calories per Tbs.

Speedy Mexican Crock Cheese—Substitute extra-sharp shredded cheddar cheese for the Romano. Omit basil. Add 2 tsp. onion flakes, 1 tsp. dried oregano, 1 tsp. whole cumin seeds and 1 tsp. chili powder.

Homemade Low-Fat Creamed Cheese

8 oz. unsalted fresh farmer cheese
Butter salt or butter-flavored granules or butter flavoring

Break up the farmer cheese in the blender or food processor container (using the steel blade). Process on high speed until graininess disappears and cheese has the consistency of whipped cream, about 2 to 3 minutes. Beat in the butter flavoring, a little at a time, to taste. Transfer to a covered container; store in the refrigerator (cheese becomes firm when cold). Use as cream cheese.

Only 21 calories per Tbs. (regular cream cheese has 52 calories per Tbs.).

Mexican Cream Cheese

1 package (8 oz.) cream cheese (regular or low-fat)
1 or 2 hot red cherry peppers (fresh or canned)
1 Tbs. fresh oregano *or* 1 tsp. dried
1 clove peeled garlic
1 Tbs. cumin seeds

Combine ingredients in food processor, using the steel blade (or in a blender with a strong motor). Process until smooth. Pack into a crock or container. Refrigerate until serving time. Serve with corn chips, celery scoopers, or thin crackers.

Makes 1 cup, 55 calories per Tbs. with regular cream cheese; 25 calories per Tbs. with low-fat cheese.

Feta Cheese Spread

8 oz. feta cheese
8 oz. low-fat pot cheese (uncreamed cottage cheese)

Dice or crumble feta. Combine with pot cheese in blender. Blend smooth. Store in refrigerator.

Makes 2 cups, 25 calories per Tbs.

Low-Fat Olive Cottage Cheese Spread

12 oz. low-fat cottage cheese
¼ tsp. dry mustard *or* ½ tsp. prepared
Pinch of chili powder *or* ¼ tsp. Tabasco sauce
½ cup stuffed green olives

Combine ingredients, except olives, in a blender or food processor, using steel blade. Cover and process until cheese is completely smooth. Add olives and process quick with on-off motions, until olives are either coarsely chopped or finely minced, whichever you prefer. Spoon into a cheese crock or container and store in the refrigerator; cheese will be firmer when chilled. Garnish with a few thinly sliced stuffed olives, if you like.
Makes 1¼ cups, 15 calories per Tbs.

Easy Cheesy Italian Spread

2 oz. grated sharp Romano cheese
1½ cups pot cheese (uncreamed cottage cheese)
1 small clove garlic, chopped
2 Tbs. minced onion *or* 2 tsp. onion flakes
2 Tbs. fresh minced parsley
1 Tbs. fresh minced oregano *or* 1 tsp. dried
1 Tbs. fresh minced basil *or* 1 tsp. dried
Butter flavoring and salt and pepper to taste

Combine cheeses in blender or food processor using steel blade; process until smooth. Stir in remaining ingredients. Refrigerate.
Makes about 1½ cups, approximately 20 calories per Tbs.

Easy Cheesy Greek Spread

1 cup pot cheese (uncreamed cottage cheese)
3 Tbs. plain low-fat yogurt
2 tsp. lemon juice
1 small clove garlic, peeled
⅛ tsp. nutmeg
Butter flavoring and salt and pepper to taste
2 oz. crumbled feta cheese
3 Tbs. fresh chopped parsley
1 Tbs. fresh mint or marjoram, minced, *or* 1 tsp. dried
2 tsp. fresh oregano or basil, minced, *or* ½ tsp. dried (optional)

Combine pot cheese, yogurt, lemon juice, garlic, nutmeg, butter flavoring and salt and pepper in blender or food processor, using steel blade; process until smooth. Stir in remaining ingredients. Refrigerate.

Makes about 1½ cups, approximately 15 calories per Tbs.

Easy, Cheesy Texas Spread

2 oz. extra-sharp, aged cheddar cheese
1½ cups pot cheese (uncreamed cottage cheese)
1 clove garlic, minced
2 Tbs. minced onion *or* 2 tsp. onion flakes
2 Tbs. fresh minced parsley
1 Tbs. fresh minced oregano *or* 1 tsp. dried
2 tsp. whole cumin seeds *or* 1 tsp. ground cumin
1 tsp. chili powder
Butter flavor to taste (optional)

Combine cheeses in blender or food processor, using steel blade; process until smooth. Stir in remaining ingredients. Refrigerate.

Makes about 1½ cups, approximately 20 calories per Tbs.

10

Salad Soups

Soup or Salad?
Why Not Have Both!

When a waiter asks you, "Soup or salad?" you have to make a choice. However, when *you're* the cook, you can combine the best of both—and serve "salad soup"!

What *is* salad soup?

Perhaps the best-known example is gazpacho, the spicy Spanish blend of tomatoes with other vegetables that is usually seasoned with vinegar and oil (sort of salad-plus-dressing, all blended together!). Cold cucumber soup, a puree of raw cucumber with sour cream or yogurt and herbs, is another popular example of a salad you drink. What makes it drinkable is the blender, and what makes it a soup is the soupspoon.

However, soup needn't be cold to qualify as a "salad soup." The latest trend is "crisp soup": steamy combinations of flavorful broth and garden vegetables simmered only till crunchy-tender—cooked quickly instead of simmered! (Given the popularity of salads and stir-fry vegetables, the idea of quick-cooking soup was inevitable, an example of East meets West, so to speak.) Crunchy, quick-cooking soups have lots of advantages over the traditional garden variety of slowly simmered soups, particularly if you have little time to pot-watch. The vegetables retain their taste and texture as well as their vitamin content.

Whether you serve your "salad soup" chilled from the blender or steamy hot from the stockpot, I'm sure you'll enjoy these drinkable variations on the salad theme. I hope they'll inspire you to invent your own creations, using favorite ingredients.

Gazpacho

4 large tomatoes, chopped
1 cucumber, chopped
1 onion, minced
1 green bell pepper, seeded and diced
6 pitted ripe olives, sliced
1 clove garlic, minced
1 cup tomato juice
1 Tbs. red wine vinegar
3 Tbs. olive oil
Salt and pepper
Lettuce

Mix together all the ingredients, except the lettuce, and season to taste. Chill several hours (mixture will thicken). Spoon into lettuce lined bowls to serve.

Makes 8 appetizer servings, 90 calories each.

Iceberg Gazpacho

3 medium vine-ripened tomatoes
¼ cup corn oil
¼ lb. mushrooms, sliced
½ cup sliced scallions
1 large green bell pepper, seeded and chopped
1 clove garlic, minced
1 cup water
⅓ cup tarragon vinegar
½ tsp. paprika
½ tsp. celery seed
Salt and pepper to taste
Iceberg lettuce, cut into small cubes

Chop tomatoes, reserving juice. Heat oil in a large skillet; add mush-rooms and saute until tender. Combine with all remaining ingredients except lettuce. Refrigerate several hours.

To serve, spoon into individual bowls. Top with lettuce cubes.

Makes 6 servings, 120 calories each.

Cold Cucumber Soup

    1 cucumber
    1 cup plain low-fat yogurt
    1 tsp. lemon or lime juice
    Salt and pepper
    1 Tbs. minced onion (optional)
    Minced parsley or mint (optional)

Peel cucumber, then quarter lengthwise. Cut away and discard seeds. Cut cucumber into chunks. Combine in blender with yogurt and lemon juice. Cover and blend until smooth. Season to taste. Serve in chilled bowls set in larger bowls of crushed ice. Garnish with a few thin unpeeled slices of cucumber, if desired, or minced onion, parsley or mint. Or serve with ice cubes in glass mugs.

Makes 2 servings, 90 calories each.

Summer Re-Run Salad Soup

    Dressed tossed salad, chilled
    Plain or spicy tomato juice, chilled

Here's a way to salvage the tossed salad that remains after everyone has taken a portion. Transfer the remaining salad mixture to a plastic bag or covered bowl and store it in the refrigerator. Next day, com-bine the chilled salad mixture with an equal amount of cold tomato juice in the blender; process until smooth. Taste for seasonings; add additional herbs or lemon juice, if desired. Spoon into bowls and garnish with thin slices of lemon or cucumber.

Each cupful has under 150 calories, the exact number depending on the amount of oil remaining from the salad dressing.

Cold Garden Salad Soup

¾ cup shredded carrots
¾ cup chopped tomatoes
¾ cup chopped cucumber
¾ cup chopped green bell pepper
½ cup shredded zucchini
½ cup chopped celery
½ cup chopped onion
1 clove garlic, minced
2 cups tomato juice
4 Tbs. corn oil
2 Tbs. red wine vinegar
1 Tbs. lemon juice
1 Tbs. minced oregano *or* 1 tsp. dried
1 Tbs. minced basil *or* 1 tsp. dried

Reserve ¼ cup each of carrots, tomatoes, cucumber, bell pepper to use for garnish. Stir remaining vegetables into tomato juice, along with remaining ingredients. Refrigerate until serving time. Serve soup from a large bowl. Let guests help themselves to garnishes from small individual cups.

Makes 10 servings, 75 calories each.

Blender Easy Instant Cold Salad Soup

Torn salad greens (available at supermarket produce counter in cellophane bags)
Plain or spicy tomato juice or tomato-vegetable juice, chilled
Fresh or bottled Italian salad dressing (regular or low-fat)
Minced fresh or dried onion or garlic (optional)
Fresh or dried herbs (optional)

Wash salad vegetables and combine with juice in covered blender, varying the proportions to suit your preference. Cover and blend until smooth. Add 1 Tbs. salad dressing per serving (or to taste). Mix. Add remaining ingredients to taste. Mix again. Serve chilled.

Each serving has approximately 135 calories with regular salad dressing; 80 calories with low-fat dressing.

Cold Papaya or Melon Soup

3 ripe papayas *or* 2 medium cantaloupes
1 cup unsweetened pineapple juice
1 Tbs. lime juice
Mint leaves

Remove the peel and seeds, and dice papayas (or cantaloupes). Combine with pineapple juice and lime juice in the blender or food processor; blend until smooth. (Add more pineapple juice if a thinner consistency is desired.) Garnish with mint leaves.
Makes 6 servings, 85 calories each.

Cold Yogurt Spinach Soup

1 package (10 oz.) frozen chopped spinach
1 can (10½ oz.) chicken broth, undiluted, fat-skimmed
16 oz. plain low-fat yogurt
Minced fresh dill or chives or parsley (optional)

Allow spinach to defrost until it can be broken up. Combine it with broth and yogurt in blender container. Cover and blend until smooth. Serve immediately or refrigerate to allow flavors to blend. Top each serving with minced fresh herbs, if desired.
Makes 6 servings, 70 calories each.

Basic Hot "Crisp Soup"

4 cups liquid (some possibilities: tomato juice, homemade or
    canned fat-skimmed beef or poultry broth, water or any
    combination of these)
1 tsp. dried herbs (some possibilities: oregano, basil, thyme
    marjoram, savory or herb combinations)
½ cup each of 4 vegetables (some possibilities: onions, carrots,
    celery, bell pepper, unpared zucchini, parsnips, green beans,
    mushrooms)

Combine liquid and herbs in a nonstick pan; heat to boiling.
Meanwhile, slice vegetables wafer-thin in the food processor, using the slicing disk (or, if you prefer, vegetables may be coarsely shredded). Add vegetables to simmering liquid; simmer uncovered, 6 to 10 minutes, depending on vegetables used.
Makes 4 servings, under 100 calories each.

Quick Hot "Crisp Soup"

1 can (10½ oz.) condensed chicken or beef broth, fat-skimmed
Water
1 package (10 oz.) any frozen mixed vegetables

Combine broth with an equal amount of water in a saucepan and heat to boiling. Add frozen vegetables. Cook uncovered, only until vegetables are barely tender (consult package directions and deduct a half-minute; avoid overcooking).
Makes 2 servings, under 125 calories each.

With Noodles—Combine broth and water and heat to boiling. Stir in ½ cup of fine uncooked noodles. Simmer 2 minutes. Stir in frozen vegetables. Simmer covered, until vegetables are barely tender but still crisp and noodles are tender. Calories: 195 per serving.

Easy Cabbage "Crisp Soup"

4 cups (1 qt.) tomato juice
1 can (10½ oz.) beef broth, fat-skimmed, undiluted
1 onion, chopped
1 tsp. dried basil or oregano
2 cups packaged coleslaw vegetables or shredded cabbage
Juice of 1 lemon
1 or 2 tsp. sugar or fructose or sugar substitute to taste (optional)
3 Tbs. minced parsley

Heat tomato juice and beef broth to boiling. Add onion and basil; simmer 5 minutes. Add coleslaw vegetables and simmer 6 or 8 minutes, uncovered. Stir in lemon juice and sugar (or substitute), if desired. Sprinkle with parsley.
Makes 4 servings, approximately 90 calories each.

Spicy Cabbage Soup—Add a dash of Tabasco and Worcestershire sauces to taste, or a pinch of red cayenne pepper. Or replace half of the plain tomato juice with spicy Bloody Mary-seasoned tomato juice.

Meatball and Cabbage Soup—Using a melon baller, shape ½ lb. lean ground beef round into 9 small meatballs. Season the meat with herbs, onion or garlic powder, if desired. Add the meatballs to the soup along with the cabbage. Makes 3 meal-size servings, under 200 calories each.

Homemade Poultry Stock for Soup

Meaty bones left over from a roast turkey *or* 1 lb. raw turkey or
   chicken necks
2 to 3 qts. cold water
2 or 3 onions, peeled and quartered
1 or 2 carrots, unpeeled, sliced
3 to 4 Tbs. minced fresh parsley
1 or 2 bay leaves
2 or 3 ribs of celery, with leaves
1 or 2 cloves garlic, peeled and mashed (optional)
2 to 4 Tbs. salt (optional)
2 to 3 tsp. MSG (optional)

Combine meaty bones and water in a soup kettle and heat to boiling.
Skim foam; add remaining ingredients. Cover and simmer over low
heat 2 to 3 hours, until bones are slightly soft and meat is easily
removable. Pour soup through a colander.

Chill strained broth until fat rises to the surface. Skim and discard
fat. Divide fat-skimmed broth among jars, leaving 1-inch headroom
for expansion; label and freeze.

Remove meat particles; discard skin and bones. Package meat in
meal-size portions; label and freeze.

Each cup fat-skimmed broth, approximately 50 calories; each cup
of meat, approximately 265 calories.

Low Sodium—Omit salt, MSG and celery. Use the smaller amount
of water and the larger amounts of other ingredients. If salt substitute
is used, add it at the table, not to the soup kettle.

Quick-Cooking Chicken Noodle Soup with Vegetables

2½ cups chicken broth, fat-skimmed
½ cup water
1 cup thinly sliced unpared carrots
½ cup minced onion (optional)
½ cup thinly sliced celery
1 oz. fine uncooked noodles
3 bay leaves
Salt and pepper to taste
½ cup cooked diced chicken or turkey

Combine ingredients, except poultry; simmer 10 minutes. Add poultry and heat through. Remove bay leaves before serving.
Makes 2 servings, 215 calories each.

Mexicali Chili Soup

½ lb. fat-trimmed lean ground beef round or raw ground turkey
4 cups (1 qt.) tomato juice
1 can (10½ oz.) condensed beef broth, fat-skimmed, undiluted
1 large onion, chopped
1 green bell pepper, chopped
1 or 2 ribs celery, diagonally sliced
1 package (10 oz.) frozen corn kernels
1 Tbs. vinegar
1 tsp. dried oregano *or* 1 Tbs. fresh
1 tsp. cumin seeds *or* ½ tsp. ground cumin
Hot pepper or Tabasco sauce to taste
4 Tbs. shredded sharp cheddar cheese (optional)

Spread ground meat in the bottom of a nonstick pot which has been sprayed with cooking spray or lightly wiped with oil. Brown over moderate heat. Break meat into chunks; turn the chunks to brown evenly. Drain and discard any melted fat.

Add remaining ingredients, except shredded cheese; heat to boiling. Simmer uncovered, 8 to 10 minutes. Ladle into bowls and sprinkle with cheese, if desired.

Makes 4 meal-size servings, 225 calories each (cheese adds 30 calories per serving).

Primavera Chicken Soup

1½ cups chicken broth, fat-skimmed
2 small or 1 large ribs celery, very thinly sliced
¼ cup chopped sweet onion
½ cup sliced mushrooms
2 Tbs. minced parsley
Minced fresh sage or thyme leaves (optional)
Soy sauce to taste (omit if broth is salty)
½ cup diced cooked chicken white meat (optional)

Heat broth to boiling. Dice up ingredients and add them to the boiling broth in the order listed. (By the time you get to the last ingredient, the soup will be nearly ready.) Simmer an additional 2 or 3 minutes, if desired, until vegetables are just barely tender. Serve immediately.

Makes 2 servings, 45 calories each (chicken adds 60 calories per serving).

Creamed Primavera Chicken Soup—After soup is cooked, remove the pan from the heat and stir in 1 Tbs. whipped part-skim ricotta cheese, until soup is blended and creamy. For a smooth "bisque," combine hot soup and ricotta in the blender and blend smooth; serve immediately. Ricotta cheese adds approximately 15 calories per serving.

Mini-Caloried Minute Minestrone

1 can (10½ oz.) beef broth, fat-skimmed
1 can (12 oz.) tomato or tomato-vegetable juice
4 cups shredded cabbage or packaged coleslaw vegetables
1 medium onion, chopped
1 package (10 oz.) frozen sliced green beans
1 can (16 oz.) stewed tomatoes
Salt or garlic salt and pepper to taste
6 Tbs. grated sharp Romano cheese
1½ tsp. dried oregano or basil or Italian mixed herbs

Combine all ingredients and heat to boiling. Simmer 3 to 5 minutes.
Makes 6 servings, 85 calories each.

Spinach, Mushroom and Tomato Soup

3 cups beef broth, fat-skimmed
2 cups torn spinach leaves
1 cup sliced fresh mushrooms
2 tomatoes, peeled, seeded and diced
¼ cup snipped chives
⅛ tsp. dried tarragon
1 cup milk (regular or skim)
2 Tbs. all-purpose flour
Salt and pepper

Simmer together 5 minutes the broth, spinach, mushrooms, tomatoes, chives and tarragon. Mix milk and flour until smooth; stir into simmering soup until thickened. Cook 5 minutes more; season to taste.

Makes 6 servings, 70 calories per serving with regular milk; 55 calories per serving with skim milk.

Variation—The entire mixture may be pureed in a blender or food processor, if desired. Puree after cooking.

French Mixed Vegetable Soup

1 large onion
2 carrots
3 potatoes
2 ribs celery, including leaves
2 Tbs. snipped parsley
5 cups water
Salt and pepper

Peel and slice the onion. Pare the carrots and potatoes; cut them in chunks. Cut the celery in large pieces. Combine all the vegetables in a large pot with the water and seasonings to taste. Cover and simmer 1 hour.

Makes 6 servings, 70 calories each.

Pureed Vegetable Soup—After cooking, force soup and vegetables through a sieve, or place in a blender or food processor and process until smooth.

Cream-Style—After cooking, blend in ½ cup of milk (skim or regular); reheat just to boiling. Makes 7 servings, 65 calories per serving with skim milk; 70 calories per serving with regular milk.

11

Breakfast Salads

Salad for breakfast? Even the most committed rabbit-food fans are likely to wriggle their noses at the thought of lettuce or coleslaw first thing in the morning, although there's really no harm in it! Nevertheless, most of us *do* eat some form of salad for breakfast on occasion. Only we call it "mixed fruit." These same combinations served at a later meal—or on lettuce—would be called "fruit salad" (or maybe "fruit cocktail" or "fruit compote," depending on whether it was served before or after dinner). Whatever you call it, fresh fruit is healthy and delicious and deserves to be enjoyed more often.

In my book, breakfast is as good a time as any!

What about fruit juice? While it's possible to match the vitamin value of whole fruit by drinking juice, juice is not really a substitute for fruit. Juice contains virtually all of the calories and sugar of fruit but little of its appetite-appeasing (and regularity-producing) pulp and fiber. Many fruit juices have more calories than Coke. And, like soda pop, the sugar calories from fruit juice are absorbed quickly, thus flooding the blood. Then your blood sugar drops off sharply, resulting in that shaky, hungry feeling a few hours later.

Wide swings in blood sugar are less likely to happen when you start your day with whole fruits instead of just juice because the natural food fiber found in the flesh of the fruit slows down the absorption of the fruit's natural sugar. If you combine your breakfast fruit salad with grains (breads or cereals) or lean protein foods like cottage cheese or

161

eggs, the hunger-allaying ability of breakfast is extended.

If you prefer to drink your breakfast fruit rather than eat it, your blender or food processor can turn whole fruit (or combinations) into thick shakes that will be much more appealing and satisfying than any thin juice from a can or carton. Fruit salad mixtures taste terrific with eggs, cereals, toast, cream or cottage cheese, too.

Whole Orange Juice

Juice oranges, peeled and seeded
Ice water

Slice oranges on a tray (to catch the juice). Put the slices in a blender or food processor (using the steel blade) and add ¼-cup cold water for each orange. Cover and process until liquefied, thick and pulpy. Refrigerate until serving time. Shake before serving.

Each orange has approximately 65 calories.

Whole Tomato Juice—Slip off the peels from soft, vine-ripened tomatoes. Process the peeled tomatoes in the blender or food processor with a few ice cubes. Serve immediately. Each tomato approximately 35 calories.

Fresh Fruit Nectar

Ripe pulp of fresh fruit, such as cantaloupe, mango, nectarine,
    papaya, peach, pear
Ice water

Use only very ripe, well flavored, soft-textured fruits, alone or in combination. Remove peel and seeds or pits. Combine the soft pulp with an equal amount of cold water in the blender or food processor (using the steel blade); blend smooth. Thin with additional ice water, if desired. Serve over ice cubes, garnished with mint (or additional ice cubes or slices of fresh fruit, if desired).

Calories per whole fruit:

Cantaloupe 160
Mango   150
Nectarine   90
Papaya   120
Peach   50
Pear   100

Fruit Salad in a Drink

1 peeled banana
1 cup grapefruit juice
1 cup orange juice
1 cup skim milk
2 Tbs. honey

Combine all ingredients in blender; blend 1 minute. Chill.
Makes 1 qt., 130 calories per cup.

Tutti-Frutti Shake

1 can (8 oz.) juice-packed fruit cocktail, chilled
1 cup fresh skim milk
⅓ cup nonfat dry milk
1 cup ice cubes
1 Tbs. sugar or equivalent sugar substitute
½ tsp. vanilla extract
Dash of salt or butter-flavored salt

Combine in covered blender; blend until smooth. (Try this with other canned fruits, too.)
Makes 2 servings, 175 calories per serving with sugar; 155 calories per serving with sugar substitute.

A banana eggnog whipped up in the blender can serve as a speedy eye-opener that sends you out with some lean protein under your belt.

Banana Nog

1 very ripe banana, peeled
1 egg
1 cup cold fresh nonfat milk
1 tsp. vanilla
Dash of cinnamon or nutmeg

For a very cold banana nog or milkshake, store the unpeeled banana overnight in the refrigerator. Peel, and slice into the blender.
Add remaining ingredients. Cover and blend until frothy. Serve immediately. 275 calories.

Banana Yogurt Nog—Substitute ¾ cup plain low-fat yogurt for the milk. Under 300 calories each.

Banana Blender Breakfast

2 cups skim milk
1 cup plain or vanilla low-fat yogurt *or* add 2 tsp. vanilla extract
1 large egg
Nutmeg
1 very ripe banana, peeled and cut into chunks
1 can (6 oz.) frozen concentrated orange juice, undiluted

Combine ingredients in a blender; cover and blend at high speed. Pour over ice cubes to serve.

Makes 4 1-cup servings, 220 calories per serving with plain yogurt; 225 calories per serving with vanilla yogurt.

More Ways to Enjoy Fruit at Breakfast Time

- Garnish cold cereal liberally with fresh fruit.
- Fill your cereal bowl with more fruit and less cereal—try half and half, an equal amount of fruit and cereal.
- Serve mixed fruits with cereal—how about strawberries and blueberries!
- Make pancakes or crepes in a nonstick skillet with no fat added. Fill them with cottage cheese and roll them up. Use pureed fresh fruit in place of syrup.
- Use crushed or sliced fruit instead of jelly or jam on bread, rolls or toast.
- Fill or garnish omelets with sliced fruit.
- With fresh fruit on hand, you always have time for breakfast, even if you don't! If you can't eat breakfast at home, toss an apple or an orange into your handbag or attaché case to eat on the way. Or save it for an early coffee break to eat instead of pastry.

Breakfast Waldorf Salad

1 red eating apple, unpared, diced
2 Tbs. raisins or minced prunes
3 Tbs. plain or vanilla low-fat yogurt
1 Tbs. broken walnuts *or* 2 Tbs. granola or bran or other dry cereal (optional)
Cinnamon or apple pie spice (optional)

Stir fruit and yogurt together and sprinkle with nuts or cereal and spice, if desired.

Makes 1 serving, approximately 165 calories (nut or cereal topping adds 60 calories or less).

"Cheese Danish" Breakfast Salad

    1 container (12 oz.) California-style cottage cheese (regular or
       low-fat)
    1 can (8 oz.) juice-packed crushed pineapple, drained
    Pinch of ground cinnamon
    ½ tsp. vanilla extract
    1 or 2 tsp. honey (optional)
    Fresh fruit garnish

Stir cottage cheese and drained pineapple together; add cinnamon, vanilla and honey, if desired. Store in the refrigerator.

For each serving, put 2 scoops (½ cup) of the cheese mixture in a bowl and surround it with ½ cup sliced or diced raw fresh apples, berries, orange sections, or other fruit. (Top with crushed cereal crumbs, if desired.)

Makes 1 serving of the cheese-pineapple mixture, approximately 420 calories per serving with regular cottage cheese; 380 calories per serving with low-fat cottage cheese (honey adds 21 calories per tsp.); ½ cup of apples adds 37 calories per serving; ½ cup strawberries adds 28 calories per serving; ¼ cup oranges adds 44 calories per serving.

Cantaloupe with Orange Cheese Filling

    ½ medium vine-ripened cantaloupe
    Few drops vanilla extract
    1 Tbs. frozen undiluted orange or other fruit juice concentrate,
       defrosted
    ½ cup cottage cheese (regular or low-fat)

Scoop and discard seeds from melon. Stir vanilla and juice concentrate into cottage cheese; mound this mixture into the cavity of the melon. (Garnish with berries, if desired.)

Makes 1 serving, 215 calories with regular cottage cheese; 195 calories with low-fat cottage cheese. (Garnish adds calories.)

Sundae Breakfast

2 tsp. honey
½ cup pureed fresh strawberries or blueberries or peaches
½ cup California-style cottage cheese (regular or low-fat) or part-skim ricotta
Fresh fruit garnish

Add honey to pureed fruit in the blender or food processor, or mash until crushed (reserve a few berries or slices of peach for garnish). Scoop chilled cheese into tulip-shaped sundae glasses, spoon pureed fruit over each scoop. Top with a few berries or slices of fresh fruit.

Makes 1 serving, 175 calories each with regular cottage cheese and strawberries; 20 calories less with low-fat cheese; 70 calories more with part-skim ricotta; 15 calories more with blueberries; 5 calories more with peaches.

Bagels, Cream Cheese 'n' Berries

1 toasted bagel (regular or whole wheat), split
4 Tbs. cream cheese (regular or low-fat) or Neufchâtel cheese or Farmer Cheese Breadspread (see recipe page 168)
½ tsp. honey (optional)
¼ cup fresh blueberries or raspberries or thinly sliced strawberries

Spread bagel halves with cheese. Stir honey (if desired) into berries. Arrange the berries on top of the cheese.

Each half-bagel, with cheese and berries: 205 calories with regular cream cheese and blueberries; 55 calories less with low-fat cream cheese; 25 calories less with Neufchâtel; 70 calories less with Farmer Cheese Breadspread; 5 calories less with raspberries; 5 calories less with strawberries. (Honey adds 5 calories.)

Cream Cheese and Strawberry Breakfast Sandwiches

2 slices toasted wheat or white bread (regular or high-fiber)
3 Tbs. cream cheese (regular or low-fat) or Neufchâtel cheese or
  Farmer Cheese Breadspread (see recipe p. 168)
¼ cup sliced fresh strawberries
4 whole strawberries for garnish (optional)
Cinnamon and brown sugar (optional)

Spread both slices of toast with cheese. Arrange thinly sliced strawberries on cheese (reserving a few for garnish). Sprinkle lightly with
cinnamon and brown sugar, if desired. Close sandwich and slice it
diagonally into quarters. If desired, spear a whole berry with a frilled
toothpick; insert into each quarter.

Makes 1 sandwich, 285 calories with regular wheat bread, regular
cream cheese; 30 calories more with regular white bread; 20 calories
less with high-fiber bread; 80 calories less with low-fat cream cheese;
40 calories less with Neufchâtel; 105 calories less with Farmer Cheese
Breadspread. (Brown sugar adds 15 calories per tsp. Whole-berry garnish adds 14 calories per serving.)

Fruit 'n' Cheese Pita Pockets

Small pita breads, lightly toasted
3 or 4 Tbs. cottage cheese (plain or with pineapple)
3 or 4 Tbs. whole blueberries or raspberries or sliced strawberries
Cinnamon or apple pie spice
Few drops of honey or vanilla extract (optional)

Slice the pita breads into half moons, so each half opens to form a
pocket. Mix the remaining ingredients; spoon the mixture into the
two pockets.

Each filled pocket, 145 calories with plain cottage cheese and blueberries; 20 calories more with pineapple cheese; 5 calories less with
raspberries; 10 calories less with strawberries (¼ tsp. honey adds 5
calories).

Orange-Raisin Pita Pockets—Remove the skin and seeds from a
small eating orange and dice. Stir in 2 tsp. raisins. Substitute this
fruit mixture for the berries in the preceding recipe. Substitute
pumpkin pie spice for the apple spice. Calories: 190 per pocket.

Farmer Cheese Breadspread

8 oz. salt-free fresh soft farmer cheese or dry curd cottage cheese
Butter flavoring or buds or butter salt to taste

Be sure to use *fresh* farmer cheese, which is similar in texture to cream cheese or cottage cheese. Crumble it into a food processor using the steel blade, or into the container of your blender. Cover and process until completely smooth and creamy. Add butter flavoring or butter salt to taste. Scoop cheese into a covered container and store in the refrigerator (spread firms as it chills).
Makes 1 cup, 20 calories per Tbs.

Fruit Spread—Sweeten and flavor Farmer Cheese Breadspread with 2 or 3 Tbs. defrosted undiluted fruit juice concentrate. (Orange juice concentrate is 30 calories per Tbs; apple juice concentrate, 30 calories per Tbs.; pineapple juice concentrate, 32 calories per Tbs.)

Fresh Fruit and Cheese Omelet for One

1 tsp. oil (optional)
2 large eggs, beaten
¾ oz. part-skim or low-cal "diet" cheese, in julienne strips
¼ unpeeled eating apple, thinly sliced
6 or 7 seedless green grapes, halved
Pinch of cinnamon
Salt and pepper

In an Omelet Pan or Skillet (with a nonstick finish)
Spray the pan well with cooking spray, or use 1 tsp. oil. Heat pan over moderate flame. Add the beaten eggs. When underside of egg is partially set, gently lift the egg mixture with a spatula so uncooked portion can run underneath. Arrange cheese on the right side of the mixture, fruit on the left. Sprinkle cheese with cinnamon. When cheese begins to melt, use a flexible plastic spatula to gently fold cheese half over fruit half. Leave the omelet in the pan. Cover the pan with a heavy china plate and turn off the heat. Leave pan covered about 2 or 3 minutes to warm the fruit through. Season to taste.

In a Double-Sided Hinged Omelet Pan (with a nonstick finish)
Spray well with cooking spray or put 1 tsp. oil in each side. Heat the pan over moderate flame. Pour the egg equally into each side of the pan. Cook undisturbed, until slightly set underneath, then use a

heatproof plastic scraper or flexible spatula to lift the egg slightly so uncooked portion can run underneath. Sprinkle julienne strips of cheese on the egg mixture in the right side of the omelet pan and sprinkle lightly with cinnamon. Arrange thinly sliced fruit over the egg mixture in the other half. When cheese begins to melt, close the cheese-filled side of the pan over the fruit. Turn off the heat and allow the omelet to remain in the closed pan for 2 or 3 minutes to heat the fruit through. Season to taste and serve (with soy-seasoned cooked brown rice, if desired, or whole grain toast).

For a Two-Person Omelet—Double the ingredients and use a 10-inch nonstick skillet or frying pan with a cover (or wipe lightly with oil). When the omelet is ready, cut it in half. Or several single omelets can be made in a small nonstick omelet pan and transferred to a larger covered skillet or kept in a warm oven or briefly reheated in a microwave oven.

Other Fruit Fillings—Substitute thinly sliced banana, strawberries, unpared pears, apricots, or pineapple.

Each omelet, approximately 230 calories.

Frittata Florentine

2 tsp. olive oil
2 Tbs. minced onion
1 small clove garlic, minced
1 package (10 oz.) frozen chopped spinach, defrosted
½ tsp. dried thyme
¼ tsp. ground nutmeg
4 eggs
Salt and pepper
¼ cup grated mozzarella cheese (regular or low-fat)

Heat oil in a large nonstick skillet. Add onion and garlic; saute 2 minutes. Add spinach; cook and stir until most of the moisture evaporates. Stir in thyme and nutmeg.

Fork-beat eggs with salt and pepper to taste. Pour over vegetables in pan. Cover and cook over low heat 10 to 12 minutes without disturbing, or until eggs are set. Uncover and sprinkle cheese over egg mixture. Replace cover and cook 2 to 3 minutes more until cheese is melted. Let stand 2 minutes before cutting into wedges and serving from the skillet.

Makes 4 servings, 140 calories per serving.

12

Salad for Lunch

When the noon whistle blows, think "salad for lunch"—instead of, in addition to, or as part of a sandwich! Midday is as good a time as any to add some greenery to your daily diet. For many, it may be the most convenient time.

In many restaurants, company cafeterias and school lunchrooms, the salad bowl is rapidly displacing the sandwich plate in popularity. Meal-size salads and serve-yourself salad bars are an increasingly familiar part of the eat-out menu. If time for food shopping and space in your refrigerator are in short supply, and you routinely eat out at lunchtime, ordering salad for lunch may be your easiest access to fresh ingredients.

If you brownbag your lunch, there's no reason why your desk top meal can't be an appealing picnic! Thoughtful planning and creative thinking (plus insulated containers) widen the possibilities for salad lunches that travel. Even if sandwiches are the simplest solution to workaday lunches, the fillings can borrow inspiration from "Green Cuisine."

For lunching at home, tossing together a meal-size salad is every bit as easy as assembling a sandwich, and can include many of the same ingredients: cold meats, canned tuna or seafood, lean cheeses and the like. Lunchtime salads are an ideal way to recycle cold leftovers into a satisfying and nourishing meal that provides the vitality you need to carry you through a busy afternoon.

Lettuce Rolls

Large outer leaves of crisp iceberg lettuce
Tuna, chicken, shrimp or egg salad or thinly sliced sandwich
    meats or cheese

Crisp the leaves in chilled water, then pat dry with paper towels. For each serving, spread 1 large leaf with ½ cup sandwich filling, or 2 to 3 oz. thinly sliced sandwich meat or cheese (lightly spread with mustard, catsup or dressing, if desired). Add salt and pepper to taste; roll up tightly. Keep chilled until lunchtime. Eat with fingers.

Each lettuce leaf contains less than 5 calories.

Cheddar Fruit Salad

1 cup red or black grapes, seeded and halved
1 cup green grapes, halved
1 red delicious apple, unpared and cubed
1 golden delicious apple, unpared and cubed
¼ lb. sharp cheddar cheese, cubed
2 cups plain low-fat yogurt
4 lettuce leaves

Combine fruit and cheese with yogurt; mix gently until blended. Mound on lettuce.

Makes 4 lunch-size servings, 275 calories each.

Raw Italian Spinach Salad with Horseradish Dressing

1 lb. raw spinach, torn
3 Tbs. mayonnaise (regular or low-fat)
1 Tbs. prepared horseradish or to taste
Salt and pepper to taste

Tear spinach into bite-size pieces, discarding stems. Rinse in cold water. Drain but do not dry. Stir in remaining ingredients, until well coated. Refrigerate until serving time.

Makes 4 servings, 105 calories per serving with regular mayonnaise; 60 calories per serving with low-fat mayonnaise.

Quick Tossed Salad with Italian Cheese Dressing

1 small head lettuce
2 or 3 scallions, sliced
2 Tbs. minced fresh parsley (optional)
1 cup cherry tomatoes

Dressing
2 Tbs. mayonnaise (regular or low-fat)
1 Tbs. lemon juice or vinegar
2 Tbs. cold water
1 Tbs. grated Parmesan cheese
1 Tbs. fresh oregano *or* 1 tsp. dried
Salt or garlic salt to taste

Tear lettuce into bite-size pieces; combine with scallions and parsley, if desired, in ice-cold water to freshen the vegetables. Drain well.

Combine dressing ingredients. Toss with salad greens. Divide among 4 salad bowls; top with cherry tomatoes.

Makes 4 servings, 90 calories each with regular mayonnaise; 60 calories each with low-fat mayonnaise.

Instant Low-Fat Italian Salad Dressing—Combine 1 packet (.8 oz.) Italian-style regular salad dressing mix with 2 Tbs. olive oil, ⅓ cup white vinegar or red wine vinegar or cider vinegar, ¼ cup dry red wine and ⅓ cup water. Cover and shake well before pouring over salad. Makes 1 cup, 20 calories per Tbs.

Sombrero Mexican Salad

1 medium head crisp iceberg lettuce, coarsely shredded
1 small onion, sliced into rings
2 bell peppers (1 red, 1 green) diced
1 cup diced jicama root or cucumber
2 tomatoes, diced
½ tsp. ground cumin or chili powder
1 cup fresh or bottled Italian herb dressing (regular or low-fat)
8 tsp. dry roasted sunflower seeds

Toss together the lettuce, onion, bell pepper, jicama and tomatoes.

To make the dressing, stir cumin (or chili powder) into the salad dressing. Pour over the salad. Sprinkle with sunflower seeds.

Makes 8 servings, 215 calories per serving with regular dressing; 115 calories per serving with low-fat dressing.

Mexican Slaw

1 medium head very crisp, firm, iceberg lettuce
1 small onion
1 unpared cucumber
4 or 5 radishes
1 hot pepper
1 vine-ripened tomato, peeled and cubed

Dressing
½ cup Italian salad dressing (regular or low-fat)
2 tsp. cumin seeds *or* 1 tsp. ground cumin
1 Tbs. grated sharp cheese

Shred lettuce by hand or in food processor. (To shred in processor, cut the head of lettuce in half, and remove the core. Slice each half into wedges to fit the feeding tube of a food processor. Shred the wedges, emptying the container into a bowl as it becomes crowded.) Shred onion, cucumber, radishes and pepper. Rinse in cold water and drain. Combine the rinsed vegetables with the tomato.

Stir together Italian dressing and cumin. Toss with salad ingredients. Top with cheese.

Makes 8 servings, 110 calories per serving with regular dressing; 60 calories per serving with low-fat dressing.

Veggies in a Pocket

½ cup chopped unpeeled cucumber
½ cup chopped carrot
½ cup chopped cauliflower
1 tomato, chopped
¼ cup creamy cucumber salad dressing (regular or low-fat)
4 3-inch pita breads
4 tsp. toasted sesame seeds

Toss chopped vegetables with salad dressing. Fill each pita pocket with the mixture. Sprinkle each with a teaspoon of the toasted sesame seeds.

Makes 4 servings, 185 calories per serving with regular dressing; 155 calories per serving with low-fat dressing.

Hamburger Pita Pocket

3 oz. lean ground beef patty
Shake of cinnamon and nutmeg
Garlic salt and pepper to taste
Lemon juice (optional)
3-inch pita bread, split
2 Tbs. chopped fresh mint or oregano
Onion, pickle and tomato slices
2 Tbs. plain low-fat yogurt

Shape beef into a patty; season with cinnamon, nutmeg, garlic, salt and pepper, and broil 2 or 3 minutes each side, depending on thickness, until medium rare. Baste with lemon juice, if desired. Slice around the outside of the pita bread so it splits open and insert beef patty. Garnish with mint or oregano, onion, pickle, tomato and yogurt.

Makes 1 serving, under 230 calories.

Veggie French Bread Pizzas

1 French or Italian roll or small hero or submarine roll
¾ cup crushed tomatoes (fresh or canned)
½ small bell pepper, diced
1 small onion, thinly sliced
2 oz. (2 slices) low-fat turkey or beef salami
Salt or garlic salt to taste
Pepper or hot pepper to taste
Minced fresh or dried oregano or basil
2 or 3 mushrooms, sliced
1 oz. mozzarella cheese (regular or part-skim), shredded

Preheat oven to 400°.

Slit roll lengthwise, as if to make a sandwich. Pull out the bready center, leaving just the crisp shells. Discard, or save to make bread crumbs. Place the 2 bread shells on a nonstick pan.

Fill each shell with half of the remaining ingredients, sprinkling on the shredded cheese last. Bake, uncovered, about 15 minutes.

Makes 2 meal-size servings, approximately 215 calories per serving with regular mozzarella cheese; 210 calories per serving with part-skim mozzarella.

Tex-Mex Pizza Breads

1 cup lean raw hamburger
1 cup crushed tomatoes
1 small onion, minced
½ small bell pepper, minced
2 tsp. vinegar or lime juice or lemon juice
1 to 2 tsp. chili powder or more, to taste
Salt or garlic salt to taste
1 French or Italian roll
1 oz. extra-sharp cheddar (or 2 oz. diet cheese), shredded or finely
  chopped

Preheat oven to 450°.

Spray a nonstick skillet with cooking spray. Spread the meat in the skillet; brown over moderate heat with no fat added, breaking into chunks to brown evenly. Drain and discard fat.

Stir in tomatoes, onion, pepper, vinegar, chili powder and salt. Simmer 6 to 8 minutes uncovered, stirring often, until most of the liquid has evaporated and mixture is thick.

Slit rolls in half lengthwise and pull out the bready center. Discard, or save to make bread crumbs. Arrange the shells on a baking tray. Spoon hamburger mixture into the hollow. Top with cheese. Place in tray in hot oven just until bread is crisp and cheese is melted.

Makes 2 servings, under 280 calories each.

Middle-Eastern Hero

5-inch Italian or French roll
2 oz. thinly sliced lean roast beef or lamb
Salt or garlic salt and pepper to taste
¼ cup thinly sliced new pickles
1 thin slice of onion
3 slices vine-ripened tomato
2 Tbs. fresh chopped *or* 1 tsp. dried mint or oregano
2 Tbs. plain low-fat yogurt

Split roll; pull out and discard bready center. Add sliced meat and sprinkle with (garlic) salt and pepper. Add sliced pickles, onion and tomato. Sprinkle with mint, spread with yogurt.

Makes 1 serving, approximately 300 calories.

French Beef and Mushroom Salad

3½ oz. sliced leftover broiled lean steak (approximately ½ cup)
½ cup sliced raw mushrooms
5 or 6 radishes, sliced
2 scallions, sliced
2 cups torn romaine lettuce or raw spinach
2 Tbs. French dressing (regular or low-fat)
Salt or garlic salt and freshly ground pepper to taste

Toss all ingredients together lightly.

Makes 1 serving, 470 calories with regular salad dressing; under 400 calories with low-fat dressing.

Meal-Size Reuben Salad

2 cups shredded cabbage or packaged coleslaw mix
1 to 2 Tbs. minced onion (optional)
½ cup thinly sliced cucumbers or new green pickles
½ oz. diced Swiss cheese or Swiss-style part-skim cheese
2 oz. lean cooked corned beef round, sliced into julienne strips or
    bite-size cubes

Dressing
1 Tbs. mayonnaise (regular or low-fat)
1 Tbs. pickle juice (from jar) *or* 1 tsp. vinegar and 2 tsp. water
1 Tbs. plain low-fat yogurt
1 tsp. prepared mustard (mild or spicy)

If packaged coleslaw is used, soak it in ice water and drain well, to freshen it. Put all salad ingredients in a plastic bag, close top tightly and shake well; transfer to a salad bowl. Or arrange vegetables in a bowl, with cheese and meat on top. Blend dressing ingredients and pour over salad.

Makes 1 serving, 290 calories with regular cheese and mayonnaise; 200 calories with part-skim cheese and low-fat mayonnaise.

Apple Reuben Salad Bowl

1 cup chopped unpeeled red apple
1 cup shredded cabbage or packaged coleslaw mix
2 slices (2 oz.) lean corned beef round, shredded
½ oz. shredded Swiss cheese

Dressing
1 Tbs. mayonnaise (regular or low-fat)
1 Tbs. plain or lemon low-fat yogurt
½ tsp. dry mustard

Toss salad ingredients lightly. Combine dressing ingredients and toss with salad.

Makes 1 serving, 415 calories with regular mayonnaise and plain yogurt; 60 calories less with low-fat mayonnaise; 5 calories more with lemon yogurt.

Steak and Potato Salad Bowl

1 cup leftover broiled round steak or rare roast beef round, lean only, thinly sliced
1 cup sliced, cooked pared potatoes
½ cup thinly sliced mushrooms
1½ Tbs. wine vinegar
1½ Tbs. dry red wine
1 tsp. catsup
½ tsp. prepared mustard
1 Tbs. fresh minced parsley (optional)
5 Tbs. plain low-fat yogurt
Salt and freshly ground pepper

Combine all ingredients, except yogurt, salt and pepper, in a non-metallic bowl. Cover and refrigerate. Just before serving, add yogurt and mix well. Season to taste and serve on lettuce leaves.

Makes 2 servings, 225 calories each.

Ham and Egg Salad

1 cup cooked diced ham
2 hard-cooked eggs, peeled and cut in chunks
1 cup celery slices

Dressing
 ⅓ cup creamy cucumber salad dressing (regular or low-fat)
 1 tsp. prepared mustard
 Coarse-ground pepper

Mix ham, eggs and celery. Combine salad dressing and mustard; toss gently with salad. Sprinkle lightly with coarse-ground pepper.

If desired, serve on a bed of mixed salad greens, garnished with cherry tomatoes and parsley sprigs.

Makes 2 meal-size servings, 410 calories per serving with regular salad dressing; 305 calories per serving with low-fat dressing.

Ham, Cheese and Apple Salad

 1 cup diced unpeeled apple
 1 cup thinly sliced celery
 2 oz. (2 thick slices) lean boiled ham
 ½ oz. shredded extra-sharp cheddar cheese

Dressing
 2 tsp. lemon juice
 1 Tbs. mayonnaise (regular or low-fat)

Toss salad ingredients lightly. Combine dressing ingredients and toss with salad.

Makes 1 serving, 350 calories with regular mayonnaise; 290 calories with low-fat mayonnaise.

Sprout and Ham Salad

 2 cups bean sprouts
 ¼ cup minced chives
 ½ cup minced celery
 1 cup diced cooked ham
 ⅓ cup mixed herb dressing.

Toss together ingredients; chill thoroughly.

Makes 2 lunch-size servings, 410 calories each.

Macaroni, Ham and Cheese Salad

1 cup uncooked elbow macaroni
1 cup chopped cooked ham
½ cup cheddar cheese or low-fat cheese, cubed
½ cup chopped green bell pepper
½ cup chopped celery
¼ cup chopped parsley
¼ cup pickle relish, drained
½ cup mayonnaise (regular or low-fat)
Salt and pepper to taste
Paprika (optional)

Cook macaroni according to package directions until tender. Rinse and drain. Combine with remaining ingredients. Cover and chill.

Makes 6 servings, 320 calories per serving with regular cheese and mayonnaise; 215 calories per serving with low-fat cheese and mayonnaise.

Peachy Chicken Salad

1½ cups sliced peaches
2 Tbs. lemon juice
2 cups cubed cooked chicken
½ cup sliced celery
¼ cup diced green bell pepper

Dressing
¼ cup low-fat lemon yogurt
¼ cup mayonnaise (regular or low-fat)
¼ tsp. poultry seasoning
Salt and pepper to taste

Mix peaches with lemon juice to coat evenly. Toss peaches with remaining salad ingredients.

Combine dressing ingredients; mix with salad.

Makes 4 servings, 265 calories per serving with regular mayonnaise; 205 calories per serving with low-fat mayonnaise.

Variation—Replace chicken with cooked ham cubes or julienne slices. Or use turkey or pastrami.

California-Style Chicken Salad

2 cups cooked, cubed white-meat chicken
¾ cup sliced scallions
1 cup sliced fresh raw mushrooms
¼ cup sliced black olives
Lettuce

Dressing
3 Tbs. Russian dressing (regular or low-fat)
3 Tbs. plain low-fat yogurt
1 Tbs. dill pickle relish
2 tsp. prepared mustard

Toss together salad ingredients. Arrange on beds of lettuce.
Thoroughly combine dressing ingredients. Spoon over salad.
Makes 4 servings, 180 calories per serving with regular dressing;
165 calories per serving with low-fat dressing.

Chicken-Stuffed Tomatoes

3 cups chopped cooked chicken or turkey
4 Tbs. bottled Italian salad dressing (regular or low-fat)
4 Tbs. mayonnaise (regular or low-fat)
½ cup chopped celery
3 Tbs. sliced scallions
6 tomatoes
Salt and pepper

Combine chicken, salad dressing and mayonnaise; cover, chill.
At serving time, toss with celery and scallions. Place each tomato
stem end down; cut almost through in 6 wedges. Open to flower-like
shape and sprinkle inside with salt and pepper. Spoon on salad mixture. Serve on crisp greens, if desired, garnished with parsley sprigs.
Makes 6 servings, 285 calories per serving with regular ingredients;
210 calories per serving with low-fat alternatives.

Chicken or Turkey Salad or Spread

1 cup minced chicken or turkey meat
1 rib celery, minced
2 tsp. grated onion *or* ½ tsp. dried
1 Tbs. minced parsley
Pinch of dried sage or thyme or poultry seasoning
2 Tbs. mayonnaise (regular or low-fat)
Dash of Tabasco sauce (optional)
Salt and pepper to taste (optional)

Mix ingredients together until well blended. Refrigerate until serving time.

Makes 2 servings, 240 calories each with regular mayonnaise; 190 calories each with low-fat mayonnaise; or filling for 3 sandwiches 160 calories each with regular mayonnaise; 125 calories each with low-fat mayonnaise (filling only).

Pâté—For a smooth pâté, combine ingredients in blender or food processor, using the metal blade, and process with on-off motions. Refrigerate.

Zucchini Shrimp Boats

2 large zucchini
½ lb. shrimp, cooked and cleaned
1 can (8 oz.) water chestnuts, drained
¼ cup mayonnaise (regular or low-fat)
¼ cup French salad dressing (regular or low-fat)

Cut zucchini in half lengthwise; scoop out seeds and discard. Set aside zucchini shells. Chop shrimp and water chestnuts together. Mix mayonnaise and French dressing; stir in shrimp and water chestnuts. Pile the shrimp mixture into the hollowed-out zucchini.

Makes 4 "boats," 290 calories each with regular ingredients; 195 calories each with low-fat ingredients.

Apple Crabmeat Salad

1 cup unpeeled, cubed apple
3 oz. canned crabmeat, rinsed and drained
1 cup unpeeled, cubed raw zucchini or cucumber

Dressing
   1 Tbs. low-fat lemon yogurt
   1 Tbs. mayonnaise (regular or low-fat)
   ¼ tsp. curry powder

Toss salad ingredients lightly. Combine dressing ingredients and toss with salad.

   Makes 1 serving, 275 calories with regular mayonnaise; 215 calories with low-fat mayonnaise.

Tuna Salad or Sandwich Filling

   1 large or 2 small ribs celery
   1 can (6½ or 7 oz.) water-packed solid white meat tuna
   2 Tbs. mayonnaise (regular or low-fat)
   1 to 2 tsp. lemon juice (optional)
   Salt or seasoned salt and pepper to taste

Mince celery fine. Drain tuna well and flake. Combine with all other ingredients. Mix well for chunky salad, or mash together with a fork for finer texture. Refrigerate.

   Makes enough for 3 salad servings, or filling for 4 sandwiches. Each salad, 155 calories with regular mayonnaise (115 calories with low-fat mayonnaise); each sandwich filling, 115 calories with regular mayonnaise (85 calories with low-fat mayonnaise).

Tuna Yogurt Salad—Substitute 2 Tbs. plain low-fat yogurt (9 calories per Tbs.) for 2 Tbs. mayonnaise (100 calories per Tbs., regular; 40 calories per Tbs., low-fat). Or use 1 Tbs. of each.

Crabmeat—Substitute 1 can (6½ oz.) crabmeat for the tuna. Proceed as above after picking over crabmeat flakes; 25 calories less each salad; 35 calories less each sandwich filling.

Salmon—Substitute 1 can (approximately 7 oz.) salmon for tuna. Proceed as above, discarding salmon bones and skin; 70 calories more each salad; 55 calories more each sandwich filling.

Chicken or Turkey—Substitute 1 cup minced cooked chicken or turkey. Omit lemon juice. Prepare as for tuna salad. Calories approximately the same as tuna.

Food Processor—Cut celery into 1-inch pieces. Mince fine using the steel blade. For chunky salad, replace steel with plastic blade, add remaining ingredients. Process just until blended with quick on-off pulses. For a smooth texture, use the steel blade.

Dieter's Tuna Sandwich Spread

1 can (6½ or 7 oz.) water-packed white meat tuna
1 large rib celery, trimmed and minced
1 Tbs. mayonnaise (regular or low-fat)
1 Tbs. plain low-fat yogurt
Salt or celery-seasoned salt and pepper to taste
Lemon or lime juice to taste (optional)

Drain the canned tuna well by pressing the lid against the contents while inverting the can over the sink. Before removing the tuna from the can, use a sharp pointed knife to cut through the tuna, breaking up the flakes. Empty the tuna into a bowl and mix in remaining ingredients with a fork. Cover and refrigerate.

Makes enough filling for 4 sandwiches, approximately 95 calories each with regular mayonnaise; 80 calories each with low-fat mayonnaise.

Food Processor—Mince celery fine using the steel blade. Remove celery and steel blade from the processor. Replace with plastic blade. Combine minced celery with remaining ingredients and blend with short on-off motions just until mixed.

Tuna Mandarin Salad

½ cup (3½ oz.) water-packed tuna
1 cup diagonally sliced celery
1 scallion, sliced
1 cup diced apple
1 seedless orange, peeled and cut in chunks
1 Tbs. mayonnaise (regular or low-fat)

Toss all ingredients together lightly.

Makes 1 serving, 370 calories with regular mayonnaise; 60 calories less with low-fat mayonnaise.

Variation—Cooked chicken or turkey cubes, marinated in 1 Tbs. soy sauce, may be substituted for tuna.

Chinese Tuna-Cucumber Salad

1 can (6½ or 7 oz.) water-packed solid white meat tuna
2 cucumbers, diced
2 Tbs. cider vinegar
1 Tbs. sherry wine
2 tsp. oil

Drain tuna; flake into a bowl. Mix with cucumber.

Combine remaining ingredients; toss with tuna and cucumber. Serve cold.

Makes 4 servings, 105 calories each.

Tuna Veronique

1 can (6½ or 7 oz.) water-packed tuna, drained and flaked
1 cup seedless green grapes
½ cup sliced celery
¼ cup sliced stuffed green olives
⅓ cup mayonnaise (regular or low-fat)
2 Tbs. lemon juice
Salt to taste
Dash of cayenne pepper (optional)
¼ cup slivered almonds, toasted (optional)

Combine all ingredients except almonds. Sprinkle almonds on top. Serve on crisp greens, if desired.

Makes 2 servings, 295 calories per serving with regular mayonnaise; 235 calories per serving with low-fat mayonnaise; almonds add 85 calories per serving.

Strawberry Lunch Punch

2 cups fresh or frozen unsweetened strawberries
1 cup strawberry low-fat frozen yogurt
2 cups skim milk

Combine in blender container; blend until smooth.

Makes 3 lunch-size servings, 170 calories each; or 6 snack-size servings, 85 calories each.

Yogurt Lunch Punch

1 container (8 oz.) any fruit-flavored low-fat yogurt
1 can (8 oz.) any juice-packed fruit or fruit salad
Ice cubes

Combine yogurt and undrained fruit in blender; add 3 or 4 ice cubes. Process until smooth.

Makes 1 meal-size serving, 365 calories.

13

Main-Course and Meal-Size Salads

You say you could live on salad? To be "meal-size" in nutrition and appetite satisfaction, your salad plate should also include some rib-sticking, protein-rich foods that are filling and slow to digest. Cooked lean meats, poultry and seafood are the obvious choices, but not the only ones. Eggs, low-fat cheeses and other dairy foods, nuts and beans are also rich in body-building proteins and make nutritious contributions to your salad meals.

Protein ingredients can go *on* your salad as well as in it—as dressings or toppings. An all-vegetable salad becomes protein-rich when it's topped with a dressing based on cottage cheese, ricotta, yogurt or other dairy foods. And any salad gains protein power when it's garnished with shredded hard-cooked egg, grated cheese, toasted nuts or seeds.

Eating your meat and vegetables together in the form of a salad is particularly appealing in the summer when hot meals lose their appeal and the prospect of heating up the kitchen to cook dinner has little charm. In winter, however, the opposite is true. No matter how nutritionally worthy, a chilly salad can be cold comfort to come home to! For that reason, this section also includes a number of quick and easy hot dishes that are main-course variations on the "Green Cuisine" theme: more vegetables and less meat, yet nutrition rich.

187

COLD SALADS

Greek Salad

2 cups shredded lettuce
2 Tbs. minced onion
1 cup cherry tomatoes, whole or halved
¼ cucumber, thinly sliced
3 pitted black olives, thinly sliced
2 Tbs. fresh chopped mint or marjoram *or* 2 tsp. dried
2 Tbs. yogurt, creamy cucumber or Italian dressing (regular or
   low-fat)
1 Tbs. plain low-fat yogurt
Salt or garlic salt and pepper to taste
1 tsp. lemon juice (optional)
1 oz. feta cheese, crumbled

Combine vegetable ingredients; toss lightly with mint or marjoram, salad dressing, yogurt, seasonings and lemon juice, if desired; top with crumbled feta cheese.

Makes 1 meal-size serving, approximately 355 calories with regular dressing, 275 calories with low-fat dressing; or 2 side-dish salads, one half calories of meal-size serving.

Garden Salad with Pesto Sauce

½ cup sliced onion
½ cup sliced celery
1 tomato, seeded and chopped
½ cup sliced carrots
2 cups shredded cabbage
2 zucchini, sliced
1 cup (8 oz.) corn kernels, drained (defrosted, cooked or canned)

Sauce
¼ cup ricotta cheese (regular or part-skim)
1 clove garlic, minced
1 tsp. dried basil
½ tsp. dried marjoram
Salt and pepper to taste

Toss together salad ingredients. Thoroughly mix pesto sauce ingredients. Serve sauce spooned over salad.

Makes 6 servings, 80 calories per serving with regular ricotta; 75 calories per serving with part-skim ricotta.

Beef Salad

Dressing

    1 clove garlic, minced
    ½ cup olive oil
    ¼ cup dry red wine
    1 egg
    ½ tsp. salt
    ¼ tsp. pepper
    ½ tsp. dry mustard
    2 Tbs. Parmesan cheese (optional)

Salad

    ½ cup bite-size wheat cereal squares
    1 large head romaine lettuce *or* 1 bag raw spinach
    2 cups cooked lean leftover roast beef or steak, cut in strips
    ½ cup diced Swiss or low-fat cheese
    ½ cup radish slices
    10 cherry tomatoes
    6 Tbs. French dressing (regular or low-fat homemade or bottled)

To make the dressing, add garlic to olive oil; let stand several hours or overnight.

Preheat oven to 375°. Place cereal squares in a single layer on a baking tin; toast for 5 minutes. Meanwhile, add wine, egg, seasonings and cheese, if desired, to oil mixture. Shake or stir thoroughly.

In a large salad bowl, break up lettuce or spinach into bite-size pieces. Add beef, cheese, radishes and tomatoes.

Toss with dressing. Sprinkle with wheat cereal squares. Serve immediately.

Makes 6 servings, 160 calories each with Swiss cheese and regular French dressing; 145 calories each with low-fat cheese and dressing.

Steak and Squash Salad

Dressing
   1 tsp. (or envelope) beef bouillon powder
   ¼ cup boiling water
   3 Tbs. red wine vinegar
   ¼ cup mayonnaise (regular or low-fat)
   2 tsp. brown mustard
   2 Tbs. minced fresh parsley
   2 Tbs. fresh tarragon *or* 1 tsp. dried (optional)
   Salt and pepper to taste

Salad
   2 cups cooked, thinly sliced, rare flank steak or rare roast beef
      (about ⅔ lb.), chilled
   1 medium zucchini, sliced lengthwise in strips then cut into
      2-inch pieces
   1 medium yellow squash, sliced lengthwise then cut into 2-inch
      pieces
   1 sweet red or green bell pepper, cut in rings or strips
   1 red onion, thinly sliced
   4 cups torn lettuce

Dissolve bouillon in boiling water. Stir in remaining dressing ingredients until smooth. Refrigerate until ready to use.
   Arrange salad ingredients on beds of lettuce; pour on dressing.
   Makes 4 main-course servings, 255 calories each; or 10 side-dish servings, 100 calories each. With low-fat mayonnaise, 200 calories per main-course serving and 75 calories per side-dish serving.

Spiced Corned Beef Salad Bowls

   1½ cups torn lettuce
   ½ cup shredded cabbage (red or green)
   1 to 2 Tbs. chopped onion (optional)
   ½ cup sliced cucumber or green pepper or halved cherry tomatoes
   2 Tbs. salad dressing (coleslaw, Russian, Thousand Island
      recommended—regular or low-fat)
   2 oz. lean cooked corned beef round, sliced into julienne strips or
      bite-size cubes (see following recipe)
   ½ tsp. caraway seeds (optional)
   2 Tbs. ryebread or cheese croutons (optional)

Toss vegetables with salad dressing; arrange corned beef on top. Sprinkle with caraway and croutons, if desired.

Makes 1 serving, 115 calories without the dressing. Dressing adds 60 to 160 calories depending on choice; caraway seeds add 10 calories; croutons add about 15 calories.

Spiced Corned Beef

Corned beef, round or brisket (about 3 lbs.)
Water to cover
4 to 6 cloves garlic, mashed
4 to 6 bay leaves
2 to 3 Tbs. mixed pickling spices

Unwrap and drain the corned beef. Trim and discard surface fat.

Place the meat in a heavy pot just large enough to hold it. Cover it completely with water. Heat to boiling. Skim foam. Add remaining ingredients. Lower heat to just barely simmering. Cover tightly and simmer until just tender, about 3 to 3½ hours depending on thickness. (Do not overcook; meat should not be falling apart.) When done, turn off heat and allow meat to cool in cooking liquid. Remove meat from cooking liquid; wrap and refrigerate. Slice very thin to serve on cold platter, or slice into julienne strips or cubes to add to salads.

Each 3½-oz. serving: round, 135 calories; brisket, 285 calories.

Note: Do not be put off by the quantities of garlic and spices. Keep in mind that the flavor will be diluted by a large amount of water, and that corned beef is very dense and relatively resistant to penetration. The flavor of corned beef prepared in this manner is actually quite mild, though not nearly so bland as most commercial corned beef prepared by simmering in plain water.

Hot Corned Beef and Cabbage—Slice cabbage into 4 or 6 wedges, cutting through the core so that the leaves remain attached to it. Simmer the wedges in the strained corned beef cooking broth just until tender, about 10 minutes depending on size of the wedges. Each 3½ oz. serving cooked cabbage, 20 calories.

Italian Ham and Macaroni Salad

Lettuce
2 cups high-protein tender-cooked cold macaroni
3 Tbs. sliced scallions
1 cup raw broccoli florets
¼ cup minced fresh parsley (preferably Italian)
1 raw carrot, shredded
2 vine-ripened tomatoes, in wedges
2 cups diced, fat-trimmed, lean smoked ham or turkey ham or
   turkey salami
1 red or green bell pepper, diced

Line 4 plates or meal-size salad bowls with lettuce. Mix macaroni with following dressing or use 1-cup low-fat Creamy Italian (page 40) or Creamy Italian Cheese dressing (page 42). Stir in scallions, broccoli, parsley and carrot. Divide among plates. Top with tomatoes, diced ham and bell pepper.

Makes 4 meal-size servings, 270 calories each. With turkey ham, 60 calories less per serving; with turkey salami, 15 calories less per serving.

Dressing

4 Tbs. mayonnaise (regular or low-fat)
4 Tbs. bottled Italian dressing (regular or low-fat)
4 Tbs. plain low-fat yogurt
2 Tbs. water
Pinch of nutmeg
1½ Tbs. grated extra-sharp Romano cheese
3 Tbs. minced fresh basil or oregano *or* 1 tsp. dried Italian herbs

Combine ingredients and beat or stir smooth.

Makes enough for 4 meal-size salads, 200 calories per serving (15 calories per Tbs.) with regular ingredients; 90 calories per serving (5 per Tbs.) with low-fat ingredients.

Ham and Turkey Chef's Salad

½ cup diced, cooked white meat turkey
½ cup diced, cooked ham
4 cups torn lettuce or mixed salad vegetables

Dressing
2 Tbs. mayonnaise (regular or low-fat)
2 Tbs. plain low-fat yogurt
2 Tbs. water
1 Tbs. grated Parmesan cheese

Mix dressing ingredients thoroughly; toss with salad ingredients.

Makes 2 servings, 270 calories per serving with regular mayonnaise; 210 calories per serving with low-fat mayonnaise.

Hawaiian Chicken or Turkey Salad Bowl

1 medium cantaloupe or papaya or mango, well ripened
2 cups leftover roast chicken or turkey meat, in thin strips
1 package (10 oz.) frozen whole green beans, defrosted
1 green bell pepper, seeded and cut in thin strips
1 red bell pepper, seeded and cut in thin strips
1 cup vine-ripened cherry tomatoes
1 small purple onion, thinly sliced (optional)
2 Tbs. minced flat Italian parsley
4 Tbs. broken walnut meats or toasted almonds

Dressing
¼ cup salad oil
½ cup unsweetened pineapple juice
2 Tbs. lemon juice
1 tsp. grated lemon peel (optional)
Few drops walnut flavoring (optional)
Salt and pepper to taste

Be sure the melon, papaya or mango is ripe and sweet. Cut the flesh into bite-size cubes, or shape with a melon baller. Combine with remaining salad ingredients.

Combine dressing ingredients in a jar; cover and shake up. Pour over the salad just before serving.

Makes 4 meal-size servings, under 400 calories each; or 10 side-dish servings, 160 calories each.

Curried Ham and Chicken Salad

½ cup diced, cooked white meat chicken
½ cup diced, cooked ham
1 unpeeled apple, diced
1 eating orange, peeled, cut in chunks
2 cups sliced celery

Dressing
2 Tbs. mayonnaise (regular or low-fat)
2 Tbs. plain or lemon low-fat yogurt
1 tsp. curry powder

Mix dressing ingredients thoroughly; toss with salad ingredients.

Makes 2 servings, 330 calories per serving with regular mayonnaise; 270 calories per serving with low-fat mayonnaise (5 calories more per serving with lemon yogurt).

Chicken and Egg Salad

1 cup diced, cooked white meat chicken
4 hard-cooked eggs, peeled and cut in chunks
2 Tbs. minced fresh dill

Dressing
⅓ cup mayonnaise (regular or low-fat)
⅓ cup low-fat lemon yogurt
1 envelope chicken bouillon granules
Pinch of red cayenne pepper

Gently mix chicken, eggs and dill.

Stir together mayonnaise, yogurt, bouillon granules and cayenne pepper until bouillon granules are completely dissolved. Combine dressing with salad ingredients.

Makes 4 servings, 290 calories per serving with regular mayonnaise; 210 calories per serving with low-fat mayonnaise.

Moroccan Chicken Salad

¾ lb. cooked chicken cutlets (1 skinned boned chicken breast),
    cubed
½ cup chopped Spanish onion
Pinch of instant garlic (optional)
¼ cup chopped fresh parsley
2 Tbs. raisins (optional)
Salt or butter salt and pepper to taste
½ tsp. each of ground turmeric, cinnamon, ginger
Juice of ½ lemon
3 Tbs. mayonnaise (regular or low-fat)
2 Tbs. sliced almonds (optional)

Toss chicken with onion, garlic (if desired), parsley, raisins (if desired), seasonings, spices, lemon juice and mayonnaise. Refrigerate several hours. Before serving, sprinkle with almonds, if desired.

Makes 3 main-course servings, 230 calories per serving with regular mayonnaise; 170 calories per serving with low-fat mayonnaise; optional ingredients add 45 calories per serving.

Continental Fruited Turkey Salad

1 cup orange sections
2 cups diced cooked turkey
½ cup sliced celery
½ cup seedless green grapes
¼ cup minced parsley

Dressing
¼ cup mayonnaise (regular or low-fat)
¼ cup Italian salad dressing (regular or low-fat)
½ tsp. curry powder

Combine orange sections, turkey, celery, grapes and parsley. Cover and refrigerate 1 hour.

Thoroughly mix dressing ingredients; toss with salad. Serve in lettuce cups or hollowed-out orange shells, if desired.

Makes 4 servings, 355 calories per serving with regular ingredients; 245 calories per serving with low-fat ingredients.

Salmon and Spinach Salad

4 cups spinach leaves
1 can (16 oz.) salmon, drained
1 zucchini, shredded
½ cup minced fresh parsley
2 Tbs. snipped fresh dill

Dressing
½ cup low-fat lemon yogurt
2 Tbs. white wine
Celery salt and pepper to taste
Pinch cayenne pepper

Arrange spinach leaves on platter. Bone and flake salmon; mix with zucchini, parsley and dill. Mound on spinach.
Combine dressing ingredients; pour over salmon mixture.
Makes 4 servings, 295 calories each.

Meal-Size Salmon Salad

4 cups torn lettuce
1 cup minced parsley
1 avocado, pitted, peeled and diced
1 lb. cooked salmon, boned and flaked
½ cup sliced mushrooms
¼ cup capers (optional)

Dressing
3 Tbs. salad oil
4 Tbs. red wine vinegar
1 clove garlic, minced
¼ tsp. paprika

Toss together salad ingredients. Shake dressing ingredients in a jar. Pour dressing over salad; toss again to coat salad ingredients.
Makes 4 meal-size servings, approximately 380 calories each.

Sole Salad à la Bonne Femme

1½ lbs. cooked fillet of sole or flounder
1 can (2 oz.) sliced mushrooms (including liquid)
2 oz. Swiss cheese, shredded
⅓ cup mayonnaise (regular or low-fat)
¼ cup sherry
½ tsp. prepared mustard
1 Tbs. minced fresh parsley *or* 1 tsp. dried parsley flakes
Pinch of red cayenne pepper
Pinch of nutmeg
Salt and pepper
Paprika

Flake fish and gently mix with mushrooms and cheese. Stir together mayonnaise, sherry, mustard, parsley, cayenne pepper, nutmeg, salt and pepper to taste. Combine with fish and mushroom mixture. Mound on plate; sprinkle with paprika. (If desired, garnish with lettuce and parsley sprigs.)

Makes 6 servings, 230 calories per serving with regular mayonnaise; 175 calories per serving with low-fat mayonnaise.

Western Tuna-Bean Salad

3 to 4 cups torn salad greens
2 small navel oranges, peeled and cut in half cartwheels
2 cans (6½ or 7 oz. each) water-packed tuna, drained and flaked
1 cup canned red kidney beans, drained
3 Tbs. sliced green onions

Dressing
2 Tbs. orange juice
2 Tbs. fresh squeezed lemon juice
2 Tbs. salad oil
Grated peel of 1 fresh lemon
¼ tsp. seasoned salt
¼ tsp. paprika

Combine salad ingredients and chill.

Combine dressing ingredients in jar and shake well.

To serve, shake up dressing and pour over salad mixture; toss well.

Makes 4 servings, approximately 380 calories each.

Minted Tuna and Sweet Pea Salad

2 cans (6½ or 7 oz. each) water-packed white meat tuna
1 package (10 oz.) frozen green peas, defrosted
1 red apple, unpeeled, diced (optional)
1 small red onion, sliced into rings

Dressing
    ½ cup mayonnaise (regular or low-fat)
    ½ cup low-fat lemon yogurt
    2 Tbs. minced fresh mint leaves
    Fresh parsley sprigs

Drain and flake tuna. Mix with remaining salad ingredients.
    Combine mayonnaise, yogurt and mint. Stir gently into salad. Garnish with sprigs of fresh parsley.
    Makes 4 servings, 410 calories each with regular mayonnaise; 295 calories each with low-fat mayonnaise; apple adds 20 calories per serving.

Lower-Fat Salade Niçoise

2 cans (6½ or 7 oz.) water-packed solid white tuna, flaked
1 cup diced cooked potatoes
2 cups green beans, raw or lightly cooked or thawed without
    cooking
2 anchovy fillets, minced (optional)
1 head Boston or Bibb lettuce
3 tomatoes, in wedges
3 hard-cooked eggs, in wedges
4 Tbs. sliced pitted black olives
4 Tbs. minced fresh parsley

Dressing
    1 raw egg or egg yolk
    2 Tbs. vinegar
    1 Tbs. olive or salad oil
    4 Tbs. liquid from olive jar
    1 tsp. garlic salt
    ¼ tsp. pepper
    Pinch of sugar (optional)
    Prepared mustard
    ¼ tsp. dried tarragon *or* generous pinch of fresh

Toss together tuna, potatoes, green beans and anchovies, if desired. Shake dressing ingredients in a covered jar; then toss with the salad mixture. Refrigerate at least 1 hour to blend flavors.

At serving time, line a salad bowl with the lettuce and mound marinated mixture in center. Surround with alternating wedges of tomato and egg. Sprinkle on olives and parsley.

Makes 4 servings, 340 calories each.

Hurry-Up Niçoise—Combine shredded lettuce, diced leftover cooked potatoes, canned beans and drained tuna with Italian salad dressing and a dash of Worcestershire sauce. Garnish with fresh tomato and hard-cooked egg wedges.

Curried Tuna Salad

> 2 cans (6½ or 7 oz.) water-packed white meat tuna, drained and flaked
> 1 onion, sliced
> 1 apple, cored and diced
> 1 green bell pepper, seeded and diced
> 4 Tbs. golden raisins
> Toasted almonds, sliced (optional)

Dressing
> 6 Tbs. Green Goddess dressing
> 1 Tbs. curry powder
> ½ tsp. ground ginger

Toss together salad ingredients. Mix dressing ingredients thoroughly. Serve with dressing spooned over salad mixture. May be garnished with sliced, toasted almonds, if desired.

Makes 4 servings, 240 calories each; with almond garnish, add 45 calories per Tbs.

HOT SALADS

Zucchini Flan

3 medium zucchini, unpared, sliced
2 Tbs. chopped onion
¾ cup milk
2 eggs
¼ tsp. grated nutmeg
Salt and pepper to taste
¼ cup grated Swiss cheese

Preheat oven to 350°.

In a nonstick 2-qt. casserole, which has been sprayed with cooking spray, make a layer of the zucchini slices. Sprinkle with onion. Fork-blend milk, eggs and seasonings; pour over the vegetables. Sprinkle with grated cheese. Bake in a 350° oven 40 minutes, or until set.

Makes 6 servings, 80 calories each.

Lower-Fat Version—Substitute skim milk for regular milk; use ½ cup no-cholesterol egg substitute in place of the eggs; sprinkle with 2 oz. grated low-fat cheese instead of Swiss. Calories: 55 per serving.

Taco-Style Macaroni and Meatballs

1 large onion
1 bell pepper
1 tsp. cumin seeds *or* ¾ tsp. ground cumin
¼ cup bottled Italian salad dressing (regular or low-fat)
2 slices dry bread
1 lb. fat-trimmed lean ground beef round
1 egg
1 can (10½ oz.) beef broth, fat-skimmed
1 can (6 oz.) tomato paste
½ lb. (uncooked) high-protein macaroni
½ head crisp lettuce, shredded
6 Tbs. shredded extra-sharp cheddar cheese

Coarsely chop the onion and bell pepper. Stir in the cumin and the salad dressing, mixing well. Use half of this mixture in the meatballs, and half in the sauce.

Meatballs: Soak the bread in warm water, then squeeze out. Combine the bread, ground meat and egg. Add half the onion mixture; mix well. Shape into 16 meatballs.

Sauce: Stir broth, tomato paste, 1¼ cups cold water and remaining onion mixture in a nonstick saucepan. Heat to boiling. Add the meatballs. Lower to a simmer; simmer uncovered, until the sauce is thick, about 20 minutes.

Meanwhile, cook macaroni in rapidly boiling water, according to package directions. Drain and serve with sauce and meatballs. Top each serving with shredded lettuce and cheddar cheese.

Makes 8 servings, 315 calories per serving with regular salad dressing; 285 calories per serving with low-fat dressing.

Easy Meatballs Primavera

1 package (10 oz.) frozen mixed Italian or Oriental vegetables or broccoli florets
½ lb. lean fat-trimmed ground beef round
4 Tbs. Italian-seasoned breadcrumbs
1 cup tomato juice
Salt or garlic salt and pepper
1 can (8 oz.) stewed tomatoes
½ cup minced onion or celery

Defrost frozen vegetables.

Combine beef with breadcrumbs, and ¼ cup tomato juice, salt and pepper to taste. Toss lightly. Shape into 8 small meatballs. Spray a nonstick skillet or saucepan with cooking spray. Arrange the meatballs in a single layer. Place pan over moderate heat. Cook meatballs with no fat added until underside is browned; turn to brown evenly. Drain and discard any fat.

Stir in remaining ingredients. Cook uncovered, about 10 minutes, or until sauce is thick.

Makes 2 servings, 365 calories each.

Some serving suggestions: hot tender-cooked macaroni (80 calories per ½ cup); big tossed salad with low-fat Italian salad dressing; breadsticks (20 calories each 4-inch stick); cold broccoli (20 calories per ½ cup); light (low alcohol) red wine (20 calories per oz.); dark continental blend or espresso-style coffee and fresh fruit dessert.

Crocked Garden Goulash

1 lb. lean beef round or flank steak
2 or 3 bay leaves (optional)
2 small or 1 large bell peppers, thinly sliced
1 cup mushrooms (fresh or canned), thinly sliced
1 cup thinly sliced onion
4 oz. thin uncooked noodles, broken up
4 Tbs. dry red wine (optional)
4 cups sliced tomatoes
½ cup plain low-fat yogurt (optional)
Paprika (optional)
4 Tbs. minced fresh parsley (optional)

Slice raw fat-trimmed steak into thin strips. Layer ingredients in a casserole or crock pot, meat on the bottom, then layers of bay leaves (if desired), bell pepper, mushrooms, onion, noodles, wine (if desired) and tomatoes. Cover and bake at 300° for 4 hours (or slow-cook in small family-size crock pot according to manufacturer's directions). If desired, just before serving, spoon dollops of yogurt on top; may also be sprinkled with paprika and minced fresh parsley.

Makes 4 servings, 375 calories each (optional ingredients add approximately 5 calories per serving).

Japanese Ground Roundsteak with Hibachi-Style Vegetables

1 lb. fat-trimmed ground beef round
3 Tbs. soy sauce
1 clove garlic, peeled and minced *or* ¼ tsp. instant garlic
1 sweet Spanish onion, sliced
1 zucchini, sliced
¼ lb. mushrooms, sliced
1 Tbs. regular oil and vinegar salad dressing

Spray a shallow nonstick pan with cooking spray, or wipe lightly with oil. Gently shape the ground beef into 4 patties, but don't press or compact the meat because this will cause it to toughen and dry.

Sprinkle the top of the patties with a little soy sauce and garlic. Pierce the patties repeatedly with a fork to force some of the garlic and soy sauce inside the ground beef. Place the patties garlic-side down on the broiling pan and sprinkle the other side with additional soy sauce. Place under the broiler about 5 inches from heat source. Broil until topside is brown, 3 to 4 minutes. Turn the meat.

Toss the vegetables with salad dressing, coating well. Add them to the broiling pan, stirring lightly to coat them with the pan juices. Spread them in a shallow layer. Return the pan to the broiler and broil an additional 3 to 4 minutes, just until vegetables are tender and patties are done. (For very rare meat, reduce cooking time 1 minute for each side. For medium or well done meat, increase cooking time 1 or 2 minutes for each side. Or move broiling tray closer or further from heat source. Be careful not to overcook.)

Makes 4 servings, 205 calories each.

Primavera Meat Loaf

4 slices dry bread, preferably high-fiber or whole wheat
1 lb. lean ground beef round
½ lb. lean ground veal
½ lb. lean ground pork
2 onions, minced
1 green bell pepper, minced
1 red bell pepper, minced
2 eggs *or* 4 egg whites
2 Tbs. lemon or lime juice
1 Tbs. chopped fresh basil or oregano *or* 1 tsp. dried
Salt and pepper to taste
1 clove garlic, minced (optional)
1 cup plain tomato juice

Preheat oven to 325°.

Process bread into crumbs in blender or food processor (or put dry bread in a plastic bag and roll over it with a rolling pin until crushed into crumbs). Reserve 2 Tbs. for the top of the meat loaf. Combine remaining crumbs with other ingredients, except tomato juice. Add just enough tomato juice to moisten (about ⅓ cup). Toss lightly to mix well. Shape into a loaf on top of a shallow nonstick baking pan that has been sprayed with cooking spray. (Or pack mixture into a loaf pan to shape it; then invert the pan on a larger baking pan. Lift off loaf pan; meat loaf will hold its shape.) Sprinkle meat loaf with remaining reserved bread crumbs (decorate with a few pepper rings if desired). Bake uncovered in a 325° oven for 1 hour. Baste occasionally with reserved tomato juice.

Makes 8 servings, 240 calories each (225 calories each if using egg whites).

Hungarian Beef and Peppers

1 lb. lean beef top round steak, cut in 1-inch cubes
1 onion, thinly sliced *or* ½ cup minced celery
1 cup beef broth, fat-skimmed
2 green bell peppers, seeded and sliced
3 vine-ripened tomatoes, peeled and diced
2 tsp. paprika
1 tsp. caraway seeds
Salt and pepper to taste

Spray a nonstick skillet with cooking spray. Brown the beef cubes, with no fat added, over moderate heat. Turn to brown evenly. Drain and discard any fat.

Stir in 2 Tbs. water and the sliced onion. Cook and stir until water evaporates and onions begin to brown. Stir in broth (or 1 cup boiling water and 1 tsp. or cube of bouillon) and remaining ingredients. Cover and simmer 50 to 60 minutes, until meat is tender. Uncover and continue to simmer until most of the liquid has evaporated. Serve with hot cooked noodles, 100 calories per half cup, if desired.

Makes 4 servings, under 215 calories each (without noodles).

Veal and Peppers, Italian-Style—Substitute lean veal for beef. Omit the paprika and caraway seed; substitute 1 Tbs. chopped fresh *or* ½ tsp. dried oregano. If desired, add a pinch of red pepper flakes and 1 Tbs. of grated sharp Romano cheese (28 calories).

Stir-Fried Crunchy "Beef Stew"

¾ lb. lean fat-trimmed top beef round steak, cut into julienne
   strips
2 tsp. oil (optional)
3 Tbs. soy sauce
1 cup fat-skimmed beef broth
½ tsp. MSG (optional)
½ tsp. ground ginger (optional)
Pinch of instant garlic (optional)
1 Spanish onion
4 ribs celery
1 small red or green bell pepper
1 cup sliced fresh mushrooms
¼ cup dry sherry
2 tsp. cornstarch

Brown meat in a nonstick heavy Dutch oven or large skillet (or electric frying pan) which has been sprayed with cooking spray or wiped lightly with oil; stir to brown evenly. Drain and discard any fat. Add soy sauce, broth, MSG, ginger and garlic, if desired. Cover tightly and simmer until meat is tender, about 1½ hours.

Peel onion and cut in half; slice thinly. Diagonally slice celery. Remove seeds from bell pepper and cut into 1-inch squares or thin slices. Add onion, celery, and bell pepper to the pot; cover and simmer 5 minutes. Stir in mushrooms. Cover and cook 2 minutes. Combine sherry and cornstarch in a covered jar and shake up. Stir into the pan. Cook and stir until sauce is thick.

Makes 4 servings, 170 calories each; 190 calories each with oil.

20-Minute Hamburger Stew

¾ lb. lean hamburger (fat-trimmed ground round)
2 tsp. oil (optional)
1 large onion
4 carrots
2 potatoes, halved
3 ribs celery
1 cup boiling water or fat-skimmed beef broth
2 tsp. beef broth extract or flavoring or bouillon
2 bay leaves
¼ tsp. dried thyme
Salt or garlic salt and pepper to taste
¼ cup dry red wine or water
2 Tbs. flour

Shape meat into tiny meatballs. Arrange in a single layer in a nonstick skillet or electric frying pan which has been well sprayed with cooking spray or wiped with oil. Brown meatballs over moderate heat; turn to brown evenly. Drain and discard any fat.

While meat is browning, slice vegetables wafer-thin using a steel-bladed slicer, or the slicing disk of a food processor.

Stir onions into skillet and cook 1 minute. Add boiling water and broth extract. Add remaining vegetables, bay leaves, thyme, salt and pepper to taste. Cover and cook over low heat about 15 minutes, until vegetables are tender. Combine wine (or water) and flour in a covered jar. Shake well and stir into the skillet. Cook and stir, uncovered, until sauce is thick, about 4 minutes.

Makes 4 servings, 225 calories each with water; 255 calories each with optional ingredients.

Skillet Steak with Crunchy Vegetables

2 tsp. salad oil
¾ lb. flank steak
1 cup sliced sweet onions
1 clove garlic
¼ cup sherry wine
1¼ cups (10 oz.) beef broth, fat-skimmed
1 tsp. MSG (optional)
4 ribs celery
1½ cups sliced red or green bell peppers
2 cups fresh broccoli florets
2 tsp. cornstarch or arrowroot
1 to 2 Tbs. soy sauce

Spray a large nonstick skillet or electric frying pan with cooking spray. Add the oil. Brown the steak quickly on both sides over high heat; remove to a cutting board.

Stir onions, garlic and wine into the skillet; cook and stir over high heat until most of the wine evaporates.

Stir beef broth, and MSG, if desired, into skillet. Add celery, bell pepper and broccoli. Lower heat and simmer uncovered, until vegetables are tender but still crisp, about 6 or 7 minutes.

Meanwhile, slice steak against the grain into thin strips. (It will be very rare, almost raw, inside.) Stir the steak slices into the skillet; allow to simmer uncovered, until cooked to desired doneness (medium-rare pink is best), about 3 to 4 minutes.

Combine cornstarch with 1 or 2 Tbs. soy sauce and mix into a paste. Stir into the skillet, cook 1 or 2 minutes until mixture simmers and forms a transparent glaze.

Makes 4 servings, approximately 230 calories each.

Pork Chops with Tomatoes and Wine

4 lean center-cut pork chops (approximately 1¼ lb.), trimmed of
  fat
1 onion, thinly sliced
2 vine-ripened tomatoes *or* 8-oz. can, peeled and diced
¼ cup dry white wine
2 Tbs. chopped fresh basil *or* ¼ tsp. dried (optional)
1 clove garlic, minced (optional)
Salt or garlic salt and pepper to taste

Spray a nonstick skillet well with cooking spray. Arrange the chops
in a single layer. Cook over moderate heat with no fat added, until
the underside begins to brown. Turn the chops and brown the other
side. Remove the chops from the skillet. (Drain fat, if any, from pan.)

Spread the onion in the bottom of the pan. Add the tomatoes,
wine, basil and garlic (if desired), salt and pepper. Arrange the chops
on top of the vegetables. Cover the skillet and cook over low heat
until chops are tender, about 45 to 50 minutes. (Add a little water, if
needed.) To serve, spoon the skillet sauce over the chops.

Makes 4 servings, under 300 calories each.

Skewered Ham and Turkey

4 onions, peeled and quartered
1 can (16 oz.) pineapple chunks (in juice or light syrup)
3 Tbs. soy sauce
Pinch of ground ginger
Pinch of ground cinnamon
1 lb. ready-to-serve smoked hamsteak, cut in 1-inch cubes
1 lb. raw turkey breast cutlets
2 green bell peppers, seeded and cut into squares
2 red bell peppers, seeded and cut into squares
2 tsp. salad oil

Preheat grill or broiler. Separate onions into "leaves." Drain pineapple and reserve ¼ cup of the juice. Combine reserved pineapple juice
with soy sauce, ginger and cinnamon. Thread cubes of ham and turkey
with pineapple chunks, pepper and onion on metal skewers. Brush
liberally with soy-pineapple juice mixture; brush lightly with oil. Broil
or barbecue about 5 minutes each side, brushing with any remaining
soy mixture each time skewers are turned.

Makes 8 servings, 225 calories each.

Speedy Chop Suey

1 skinned boned chicken breast (½ lb. chicken cutlets)
¾ cup canned or reconstituted chicken broth, fat-skimmed
1 package (10 oz.) frozen mixed Oriental vegetables, thawed
1 tsp. cornstarch
1 Tbs. soy sauce

Dice chicken into bite-size cubes.

Spray a large nonstick skillet or electric frying pan with cooking spray (or wipe lightly with oil).

Arrange chicken in a single layer. Cook uncovered over moderate heat just until underside is brown. Turn chicken cubes; brown other side. Stir in broth and defrosted vegetables. Cook uncovered, over moderate heat, stirring occasionally, until most of the liquid has evaporated.

Combine cornstarch and soy sauce. Stir into the simmering skillet. Cook and stir until sauce simmers and thickens.

Makes 2 servings, 250 calories each.

Hot Chinese Chicken Salad

2 skinned, boned, raw chicken breasts, diced in bite-size cubes
2 Tbs. soy sauce
1 Tbs. white wine
1 large clove garlic *or* ¼ tsp. instant
¼ tsp. ground ginger
Pinch of pepper
2 red or green bell peppers or 1 of each, diced
½ cup thinly sliced onion
1 cup chicken broth, fat-skimmed
1 tsp. cornstarch
½ head iceberg lettuce
4 Tbs. dry roasted peanuts, broken up (optional)

Combine chicken cubes with soy, wine, garlic, ginger and pepper. Marinate at least 15 minutes (if longer, place in refrigerator).

Spray a large nonstick skillet or electric frypan with cooking spray for no-fat frying. Remove each chicken cube from the marinating mixture, allowing the marinade to drip back in the bowl; then arrange in a single layer in the skillet with no fat added. Brown the cubes over high heat, turning to brown evenly. Remove them from the skillet and set aside.

In the same skillet, combine the peppers, onion and chicken broth. Cover and simmer 3 minutes. Uncover, add the chicken cubes. Cook and stir until heated through.

Stir the cornstarch into the reserved marinade and mix smooth (add a few tsp. of cold water, if needed). Stir the cornstarch mixture into the skillet over low heat, until mixture simmers, thickens and turns into a clear glaze. With a serrated knife, dice the lettuce into bite-size cubes; stir into the skillet, just until heated through. Garnish with peanuts, if desired.

Makes 4 meal-size servings, 190 calories each (peanuts add 40 calories per serving).

Sweet 'n' Sour Hot Chinese Chicken Salad for Two

1 Tbs. oil (optional)
½ lb. chicken cutlets (1 skinned boned chicken breast), cubed
½ large sweet onion, sliced, *or* 1 cup diagonally sliced celery
1 red or green bell pepper, cut in squares
½ cup chicken broth, fat-skimmed
½ tsp. five-spice powder
1 clove garlic, minced (optional)
1 can (8 oz.) pineapple chunks, packed in light syrup or juice
2 Tbs. soy sauce
1 Tbs. vinegar
1 tsp. cornstarch

Heat oil in a nonstick skillet or electric frying pan (or spray it with cooking spray). Add the raw chicken cubes in a shallow layer. Brown slowly, turning to brown evenly on all sides. Remove the chicken cubes and set aside.

Combine onion, bell pepper, broth, five-spice powder and garlic (if desired) in the pan. Cover and cook 2 minutes; uncover and continue to cook, stirring often, until nearly all the liquid evaporates. Add drained pineapple to the pan, reserving juice. Stir in browned chicken cubes. Cook and stir until heated through.

Combine pineapple juice, soy sauce, vinegar, and cornstarch in a cup and mix well. Stir pineapple juice mixture into the pan. Cook and stir over high heat until mixture simmers, thickens and clears.

Makes 2 servings, 210 calories each; oil adds 60 calories per serving.

Cantonese Stir-Fried Chicken

2 Tbs. salad oil *or* 1 Tbs. salad oil and cooking spray for no-fat
   frying
2 boned, skinned raw chicken breasts, cut in bite-size cubes
1 large onion, halved and sliced
½ cup dry white wine
1 cup water or chicken broth, fat-skimmed
2 cups broccoli florets
1 red or green bell pepper, halved and sliced
¼ cup thinly sliced radishes, preferably white radishes (optional)
1 tsp. ground ginger
¼ tsp. allspice
½ cup sliced mushrooms (optional)
1 cup fresh or canned drained bean sprouts
1½ tsp. cornstarch
¼ cup soy sauce

Arrange chicken in a shallow layer in a large nonstick skillet or electric frying pan that has been sprayed with cooking spray, or use
1 Tbs. oil. Place pan over medium heat. Cook undisturbed until
underside is browned. Turn and brown other side. Remove chicken
from the skillet and set aside.

Stir onion and 1 Tbs. oil (or 2 Tbs. water) into the skillet. Cook
and stir (until water evaporates). Add wine, water, broccoli, bell
pepper, radishes (if desired), ginger and allspice. Cover and simmer
4–5 minutes.

Uncover and stir in mushrooms (if desired), bean sprouts and
chicken cubes. Cook and stir uncovered 1 minute. Combine cornstarch with soy sauce and blend until smooth. Stir into simmering
skillet, until sauce thickens and clears and vegetables are glazed with
sauce. Serve from the skillet (or spoon over rice).

Makes 4 servings 265 calories each (optional ingredients add 10
calories per serving).

Chicken and Sweet Peppers Pronto

2 frying chicken breasts, split
1 onion, thinly sliced
2 red bell peppers, thinly sliced
½ cup Italian salad dressing (regular or low-fat)
1 cup water

Preheat oven to 425°.

Arrange chicken skin-side up in a shallow nonstick baking pan which has been sprayed with cooking spray or lightly wiped with oil. Bake uncovered, in a 425° oven for 20 to 25 minutes, until skin is crisp and brown. Drain and discard fat accumulated in pan.

Put onion and pepper slices under chicken. Combine salad dressing and water; pour over chicken. Lower heat to 325°. Bake uncovered, until chicken is tender, about 20 to 25 minutes, basting occasionally. If liquid evaporates, add a little water, or partially cover the baking pan with foil.

Makes 4 servings, 390 calories per serving, with regular salad dressing; 285 calories per serving with low-fat dressing.

Pineapple Pepper Chicken Curry

2 frying chicken breasts, split, *or* 2 lbs. cut-up chicken
1 Tbs. soy sauce
1 Tbs. lemon juice
¼ tsp. ground cinnamon (optional)
3 Tbs. flour
1 can (8 oz.) juice-packed pineapple chunks
1 Tbs. curry powder or more to taste
2 sweet red bell peppers, thinly sliced

Combine chicken with soy sauce, lemon juice and cinnamon (if desired) in a nonmetallic bowl. Marinate for at least 30 minutes (if longer, place in refrigerator).

Preheat oven to 425°.

Remove chicken from marinade; shake with flour in a heavy plastic bag until lightly coated. Then, arrange chicken skin-side up in a single layer in a nonstick baking pan which has been sprayed with cooking spray or lightly wiped with oil. Bake uncovered in 425° oven for 20 minutes, until chicken skin is crisp and brown. Discard any melted fat from the pan.

Drain pineapple, reserving juice. Combine drained juice with curry powder and pour over chicken. Cover the pan tightly with foil. Lower heat to 350°; bake 20 minutes. Add pineapple chunks and bell pepper to the pan; cover and bake 15 minutes more. Uncover; bake an additional 5 minutes.

Makes 4 servings, 270 calories per serving.

Mediterranean BBQ Chicken and Vegetables on Skewers

    1 lb. chicken cutlets or fillets (2 breasts, skinned and boned)
    8 small or 4 large mushrooms
    1 large or 2 small zucchini or yellow squash
    1 bell pepper, cut into squares
    2 onions, quartered (optional)
    1 cup tomato juice
    ½ tsp. dried basil or oregano
    Pinch of dried thyme
    Salt and pepper to taste
    1 Tbs. salad oil (preferably olive oil)

Slice skinless, boneless chicken meat into ¾-inch cubes. Cut mushrooms in half if they are large. Cut small zucchini in thick (half-inch) slices; if using large zucchini, quarter it lengthwise, then cut into 1-inch lengths. Alternate chicken and all vegetables on metal skewers. To make basting sauce: combine remaining ingredients except oil.

Place skewers on a shallow, nonstick, unperforated foil-lined broiler pan, which has been well-sprayed with cooking spray. Pour tomato juice mixture over skewers. Brush food lightly with oil. Broil 15 minutes on shelf closest to heat source. Turn and baste 3 times to cook evenly.

Makes 4 servings, 145 calories each; onions add 20 calories per serving.

Red Pepper Chicken Pilaf

    4 frying chicken thighs
    2 sweet onions, halved and sliced
    4 ribs celery, finely minced
    2 cups chicken broth, fat-skimmed
    1 cup raw brown rice
    1 Tbs. curry powder or more to taste
    1 tsp. cumin seeds
    Salt and pepper to taste
    2 red or green sweet bell peppers, diced
    ¾ cup peas, fresh or frozen and defrosted
    1 cup thinly sliced mushrooms

Spray a nonstick large frying pan or electric skillet with cooking spray, or wipe lightly with oil. Place chicken skin-side down in a single layer.

Add 2 Tbs. water. Cook over high heat until chicken browns, turn to brown evenly. Remove chicken, discard melted fat.

Add onions and 2 Tbs. water to the pan; cook and stir until the onion is soft. Add celery, broth, ½ cup water, rice and seasonings. Return chicken to pan, skin-side up. Cover tightly and simmer over low heat until chicken and rice are tender, about 45 minutes. Stir in remaining ingredients. Cover and cook 5 minutes more.

Makes 4 complete-meal servings, 460 calories each.

Hawaiian Baked Fish

1 lb. fish fillets or steaks, fresh or frozen and defrosted
¾ cup minced onion
1 cup minced celery
1 Tbs. butter or margarine
1½ tsp. curry powder or more, to taste
¾ cup (6-oz. can) unsweetened pineapple juice
Salt and pepper

Preheat oven to 350°.

Spray a nonstick baking dish well with cooking spray. Arrange the fish in a single layer.

Combine onion, celery, and butter (or margarine) in a small nonstick skillet. Cook and stir 5 minutes. Stir in curry and pineapple juice. Season to taste. Heat to boiling, then pour over the fish fillets.

Bake uncovered in a 350° oven about 15 to 20 minutes or until fish flakes easily.

Makes 4 servings, approximately 160 calories each.

Baked Fish Italiano

1 lb. fish fillets or steaks
¼ cup chopped green bell pepper
¼ cup chopped red bell pepper
¼ cup Italian salad dressing (regular or low-fat)

Defrost fish if frozen. Preheat oven to 450°.

Spray a nonstick baking dish well with cooking spray. Arrange fish fillets in a single layer. Stir bell peppers into salad dressing. Spoon evenly over fish. Bake uncovered in a 450° oven 10 to 12 minutes until fish flakes easily.

Makes 4 servings, 175 calories each with flounder or sole, and regular salad dressing; 125 calories per serving with low-fat dressing.

Fish fillets too fragile to barbecue on a wire rack can be cooked on the grill this way:

Foiled Fish

2 to 3 thin slices onion
Bay leaf (optional)
4 oz. fish fillet (flounder, fluke, sole, etc.)
3 slices peeled, vine-ripened tomatoes
Pinch of dried oregano or savory or dill weed
Minced garlic (optional)
Salt and pepper to taste
1 Tbs. lemon juice

Make one packet for each serving.

Preheat covered barbecue. Lay a square of aluminum foil on the counter, shiny-side up. Spray it lightly with no-fat cooking spray. Put sliced onion and broken-up bay leaf (if desired) in the center of the foil. Lay fish fillet on top of the onion. Arrange the sliced tomato over the fish. Sprinkle lightly with oregano, savory or dill weed, garlic (if desired), salt and pepper. Add lemon juice. Fold the foil loosely over the fish and crimp the edges to contain the liquid. Place on a rack in a preheated covered barbecue. Cook undisturbed about 12 to 15 minutes (depending on thickness of the fish), then open the foil. Continue to cook with the foil open until fish flakes easily. Remove from the foil and spoon the cooking sauce over the fish (discard bay leaf).

Makes 1 serving, approximately 120 calories.

Skewered Scallops

1 lb. ocean scallops, or cod, scrod, hake, pollock, swordfish, etc.
½ cup bottled Italian-style salad dressing (regular or low-fat)
2 bell peppers *or* 1 zucchini
2 small onions
12 cherry tomatoes

Combine scallops and salad dressing in a nonmetallic bowl or plastic bag. Marinate 15 minutes at room temperature or longer in the refrigerator.

Preheat barbecue. Remove seeds and tops from peppers and cut into 1-inch squares (or slice unpeeled zucchini). Peel and quarter onions and separate into leaves.

Alternate scallops and all vegetables on metal skewers. Brush with marinade. Broil or barbecue 3 to 4 inches from heat source, turning often and brushing with remaining marinade.

Makes 4 servings, under 300 calories per serving with scallops and regular salad dressing; under 200 calories per serving with scallops and low-fat salad dressing.

Seafood Omelet with Mediterranean Mushroom Sauce

    2 large eggs
    1 tsp. oil (optional)
    ¼ cup cooked crabmeat or flaked fish
    Salt or seasoned salt and pepper to taste
    Dash of Worcestershire sauce
    ¾ cup plain (or spiced) tomato juice
    1 can (2 oz.) mushroom stems and pieces, undrained
    2 Tbs. minced onion
    3 Tbs. minced bell pepper

Beat eggs until light. Heat oil in a small nonstick omelet pan (or spray with cooking spray until slick). Heat over moderate flame. Add beaten eggs. Cook undisturbed for 1 minute, then use a heat-resistant rubber spatula to lift egg mixture, permitting uncooked egg to run underneath. When nearly set, put crabmeat (or flaked fish) in the center of the omelet and season to taste with salt, pepper and a dash of Worcestershire. Carefully fold omelet over on itself, enclosing seafood, then turn onto a heated plate. Cover to keep warm.

Combine remaining ingredients in the same skillet. Raise heat to high. Cook and stir until tomato juice rapidly boils down into a sauce. Spoon over omelet.

Makes 1 serving, 125 calories; oil adds 40 calories.

Note: You may double the ingredients to make an omelet for 2, in a large omelet pan. To serve divide in half. For more than 2 servings, make omelets separately.

Seafood Creole

1 Tbs. oil (optional)
1 cup minced sweet (Spanish) onion
1 clove garlic, minced
1 Tbs. water or dry white wine
¾ cup tomato juice
2 cups diced, peeled tomatoes (vine-ripened or canned)
¾ cup minced celery
2 Tbs. minced bell pepper
1 Tbs. minced fresh parsley
1 Tbs. minced fresh sage or thyme *or* ½ tsp. dried
1 bay leaf
1 lb. frozen flounder or other fish fillets, defrosted
2 tsp. cornstarch
3 Tbs. cold water
Dash of hot pepper sauce *or* pinch of cayenne pepper

Heat oil in a nonstick skillet or electric skillet (or spray with cooking spray). Spread the onion and garlic in a shallow layer. Add water (or wine). Cook over low heat just until onion begins to brown. Stir in tomato juice, tomatoes, celery, bell pepper, parsley, sage or thyme and bay leaf. Cover tightly and simmer 10 minutes.

Meanwhile, cut fish into bite-size chunks. Arrange fish chunks on top of tomato mixture. Cover and simmer 5 minutes. Uncover and simmer just until fish is opaque and flakes easily.

Stir cornstarch into cold water until blended, then gently stir into the tomato mixture; season with a dash of hot pepper sauce or cayenne. Serve over cooked rice.

Makes 4 servings, 150 calories each. White rice adds 110 calories per ½ cup serving; oil adds 30 calories per serving.

14

Just Desserts

Anyone who has ever saved his fruit cup for the end of the meal knows that in one form at least salad can stand in for dessert (and that fruit can forestall caloric hari-kari!). In this section, the spirit of "Green Cuisine" reaches its sweet conclusion. Here you'll find some "grand finales" that focus on fruit as their main ingredient, with lesser amounts of the flour, fat and sugar that conspire to make conventional desserts so fattening.

Italian Ambrosia

    8 oz. ricotta cheese (regular or part-skim)
    ½ cup raisins
    1 tsp. grated orange peel (optional)
    2 oranges, peeled, cut in cubes and drained
    2 Tbs. flaked coconut

Combine ingredients; refrigerate for several hours. Serve from large serving bowl, or divide among individual parfait glasses or dessert cups.

Makes 4 servings, 195 calories per serving with regular ricotta; 175 calories per serving with part-skim ricotta.

Frosty Fruit

1 package (8 oz.) cream cheese (regular or low-fat)
4 cups low-fat strawberry yogurt
½ cup mayonnaise (regular or low-fat)
2 cans (1 lb. each) juice-packed fruit cocktail

Beat together cream cheese, yogurt and mayonnaise until well blended. Fold in fruit. Pour into 9-inch square nonstick pan. Freeze firm.

When ready to serve, remove from freezer and place in refrigerator for 15 minutes. Cut into 9 squares. (Garnish with mint leaves, if desired.)

Makes 9 servings, 305 calories per serving with regular cream cheese and mayonnaise; 205 calories per serving with low-fat alternatives.

Raw Fruit Pie

1 can (6 oz.) frozen apple juice concentrate
1 envelope plain gelatin
¾ cup cold water
2 to 3 cups raw fruit (bananas, berries, plums, any fruit *except* raw papaya or pineapple)
Ready-to-fill graham cracker pie crust

Defrost apple juice just enough to remove it from the can.

Sprinkle gelatin on cold water. Wait 1 minute, then heat gently, just until gelatin dissolves. Remove from heat and stir in undiluted apple juice, until melted. Refrigerate just until syrupy.

Meanwhile, arrange fruit attractively in pie crust. When apple gelatin is slightly thick, spoon it gently over fruit, using only as much as you need to entrap fruit in a see-through glaze (about ½ to ⅔ the full amount). Chill until set; store in the refrigerator.

Makes 8 servings, approximately 170 calories each (depends on ingredients chosen).

Blueberry-Topped Cheese Tarts

1 milk lunch cracker or other large nonsweet cracker or graham cracker
1 Tbs. Farmer Cheese Breadspread (see recipe page 168)
2 Tbs. fresh raw blueberries

Spread cracker with Farmer Cheese Breadspread. Arrange as many blueberries as will fit in concentric circles on the cheese. Serve immediately, or refrigerate until serving time.

Or, simply serve crackers, a crock of Farmer Cheese Breadspread and a bowl of chilled fresh blueberries and let snackers create their own fresh fruit tarts.

Makes 1 serving, approximately 90 calories.

Kid-Pleasing Cheese and Blueberry Sandwiches

 2 slices whole wheat bread
 1 oz. Farmer Cheese Breadspread (see page 168)
 ¼ cup fresh blueberries

If desired, toast bread. Apply Breadspread to one slice of bread. Press blueberries, in a single layer, into Breadspread. Top with second slice of bread or toast.

Each sandwich, 185 calories.

Variation—Try the sandwiches with thinly sliced strawberries or other fresh fruit.

Chocolate Fruit Fondue

 1 container (6 oz.) frozen orange or other fruit juice concentrate, thawed
 1 container (15 oz.) part-skim ricotta cheese
 5 Tbs. plain cocoa powder
 2 Tbs. orange or other fruit liqueur
 2 tsp. vanilla extract
 Pinch of salt or butter-flavored salt
 Fresh fruit for dipping: apples, oranges, pears, banana chunks, etc.

Combine undiluted orange juice with the ricotta in a blender or food processor, using the steel blade; process until smooth. Add cocoa, liqueur, vanilla and salt; blend until smooth. Chill mixture for several hours in the refrigerator.

Surround the bowl of chocolate dipping sauce with wedges or slices of fruit. (You can prevent the fresh fruit from browning by first rolling it in a little fresh orange or lemon juice before assembling the dessert tray.) Provide toothpicks or fondue forks.

Makes 2½ cups of dipping sauce, 21 calories per Tbs.

Layered Peachy Orange Cheese Mold

3 envelopes plain gelatin
1 can (6 oz.) frozen orange juice concentrate, defrosted
4 cups (1 qt.) boiling water
2 tsp. vanilla extract
6 Tbs. honey or fructose or equivalent sugar substitute
1 tsp. grated orange rind
1 package (8 oz.) cream cheese (regular or low-fat)
3 cups cubed peeled peaches or unpeeled nectarines

Stir gelatin into defrosted, undiluted orange juice concentrate. Wait 1 minute until it softens, then stir in boiling water, until completely blended. Pour half of this mixture into a blender. Add the vanilla, honey or other sweetener, orange rind and cream cheese, cut into cubes. Cover and blend until smooth. Pour the cream cheese mixture into a 5- or 6-cup mold, or a loaf pan, that has been sprayed with nonstick cooking spray. Refrigerate until set.

Leave remaining orange juice mixture standing at room temperature. When cream cheese mixture is firm, combine cubed peaches (or nectarines) with remaining orange juice mixture. Pour into mold on top of cream cheese mixture. Refrigerate several hours. Invert to unmold. (If using a ring mold, fill the center with additional sliced peaches, berries or other diced fresh fruit, if desired.)

Makes 10 servings, 190 calories per serving with regular cream cheese; 145 calories per serving with low-fat cheese (40 calories less per serving with sugar substitute).

Speedy Raspberry Crème Parfait

½ cup low-fat cottage cheese
½ cup fresh raspberries, sweetened with 2 tsp. honey or fructose or equivalent sugar substitute
¼ cup plain or vanilla low-fat yogurt
2 Tbs. pressurized whipped cream or light cream in aerosol can

Spoon ingredients into 2 parfait glasses or dessert cups in the order given and top with whipped cream. Refrigerate until serving time. If the parfaits will be refrigerated for some time before serving, top with whipped cream just before serving.

Makes 2 servings, approximately 130 calories each (20 calories less per serving with sugar substitute).

Pineapple Cheese Cookie Filling or Spread

½ cup juice-packed crushed pineapple
8 oz. farmer cheese
1 tsp. vanilla extract
2 Tbs. honey or fructose or equivalent sugar substitute (optional)
Cinnamon

Press out moisture from pineapple, combine pineapple with remaining ingredients except cinnamon in blender or food processor, using the steel blade. Blend until smooth.

Use as a spread for graham crackers or thin vanilla wafers, topped with raw apple wedges, whole strawberries or other fresh fruit. These taste like miniature cheesecakes.

Makes enough spread for 16 crackers, 25 calories each, spread only; if using honey or fructose, 35 calories each.

Winter Fruit and Cheese Dessert

1 cup diced mixed dried fruit
2 cups low-fat pot cheese or low-fat uncreamed cottage cheese
2 Tbs. orange liqueur
2 tsp. grated lemon or orange peel (optional)
Pinch of cinnamon or nutmeg

Mix ingredients well, then pack into 4 custard cups (or other round-bottom cups). Cover and refrigerate several hours. Unmold. (Garnish with orange wedges, if desired.)

Makes 4 servings, under 170 calories each, dessert only.

Cottage Cheese with Raisins—For each cup of low-fat cottage cheese, stir in 5 Tbs. raisins, ½ tsp. vanilla extract, pinch of cinnamon. Mix well. (If necessary, sweeten to taste.) Makes 1 serving, 300 calories each.

Curried Cheese Spread

8 oz. Neufchâtel cheese or low-fat cream cheese
½ tsp. pumpkin pie spice
1 tsp. curry powder or more to taste
Salt or butter-flavored salt (optional)
6 Tbs. diced dried fruit

Combine cheese, spices and salt (if desired) in food processor using the steel blade or in blender or electric mixer bowl. Beat until fluffy. Fold in fruit. Refrigerate. Serve as spread for saltines or thin wheat crackers.

Makes approximately 1⅓ cups spread, 30 calories per Tbs. with Neufchâtel, 25 calories per Tbs. with low-fat cream cheese.

Fruit-Filled Sandwich Cookies

Arrowroot biscuits or thin vanilla or lemon wafers
Farmer Cheese Breadspread (see page 168)
Fresh sliced strawberries, whole blueberries, etc.

Spread each cookie with 2 tsp. Farmer Cheese Breadspread. Arrange the berries in a single layer on a plate. Gently press one of the cookies into the berries, cheese-side-down, to pick up the fruit. Top with the other cookie, cheese-side-down, to make a fruit-filled sandwich cookie.

Each sandwich, approximately 70 calories.

Fruit Juice Gelatin

1 can (6 oz.) any frozen fruit juice concentrate *except* pineapple
1 envelope plain gelatin
1¼ cups water
Pinch of cinnamon (optional)

Partially defrost juice concentrate, just enough so the contents will slip easily from the can. Meanwhile, sprinkle gelatin over ¼ cup cold water. Wait a few minutes until gelatin softens then add 1 cup boiling water and stir until gelatin granules are thoroughly dissolved. Add cinnamon, if desired, and partially defrosted undiluted juice concentrate; stir until juice concentrate melts. Refrigerate until set.

Makes 4 servings, approximately 95 calories each.

Fruit Under Glass

1 can (6 oz.) any frozen fruit juice concentrate *except* pineapple
1 envelope plain gelatin
1¼ cups water
Pinch of cinnamon (optional)
1 ripe banana, sliced
1 ripe peach, peeled and sliced
½ cup blueberries or sliced strawberries
1 large or 2 small unpeeled purple plums, thinly sliced.

Partially defrost juice, just enough to remove it from the can.

Sprinkle gelatin over ¼ cup of cold water. Wait a few minutes until gelatin softens. Meanwhile, heat remaining 1 cup water to boiling; stir into softened gelatin mixture until gelatin completely dissolves. Add partially defrosted juice and cinnamon, if desired; stir until juice melts. Refrigerate mixture until syrupy.

Spoon a little of the partially set gelatin in a shallow glass pie plate, covering the bottom. Arrange fruit attractively over gelatin layer. (For an interesting arrangement, slice the banana lengthwise.) Spoon the remaining gelatin over the fruit, covering it completely. Refrigerate until firm.

Makes 8 servings, approximately 70 calories each.

Orange-Glazed Fresh Strawberries

1 can (6 oz.) frozen orange juice concentrate
1 pt. ripe strawberries

Defrost orange juice concentrate but do not dilute. Wash and hull berries but leave them whole. Mix berries with the orange juice concentrate. Refrigerate until serving time.

Makes 4 servings, 120 calories each.

Banana Strawberry Trifle

4 oz. sponge cake (1 layer) cut in 1-inch cubes
2 Tbs. orange liqueur
1 package (4-serving) strawberry or raspberry gelatin (regular or
  low-calorie)
1 cup boiling water
½ cup cold water
¾ cup sliced fresh strawberries
1 ripe banana, sliced
1 package (4-serving) vanilla instant pudding
2 cups skim milk

Arrange cake cubes in the bottom of a clear glass serving bowl. Prick
with a fork; sprinkle with liqueur.

Dissolve gelatin in boiling water. Mix in cold water, then strawberries. Chill until syrupy. Spoon over cake layer. Chill until firm.

Arrange banana slices over gelatin. Prepare pudding mix with milk
according to package directions. Pour over banana layer. Chill until
firm. (Garnish with several whole strawberries, if desired.) Serve directly from bowl.

Makes 12 servings, 120 calories per serving with regular gelatin; 95
calories per serving with low-calorie gelatin.

French Strawberry Cheese Parfaits

1 cup low-fat cottage cheese
½ cup part-skim ricotta
Pinch of salt
2 pts. fresh strawberries *or* 1 pt. fresh strawberries and 10 oz.
  frozen unsweetened strawberries
¼ cup honey or fructose or equivalent sugar substitute
1 cup whipped cream from aerosol can (light, if available)
½ cup low-fat vanilla yogurt

Beat cottage cheese, ricotta and salt with an electric mixer. Spoon
into a glass bowl or 8 individual dessert cups or parfait glasses.

Wash, hull and slice 1 pt. berries and set aside. Wash and hull
remaining berries (or defrost, if frozen) and puree in the blender.
Combine pureed berries and sliced berries, and sweeten to taste.
Spoon berry mixture over cheese mixture.

Spray whipped cream into a 1-cup measure. Empty into a bowl and
gently fold together with yogurt.

Top dessert with yogurt mixture. Garnish with a few whole berries, if desired. Chill until serving time.

Makes 8 servings, 110 calories each. (Approximately 30 calories less per serving with alternative lower-calorie ingredients.)

Orange-Strawberry Blender Mousse

1 can (6 oz.) frozen orange juice concentrate
2 envelopes unflavored gelatin
2 cups boiling water
3 cups frozen whole unsweetened strawberries

Allow the orange juice concentrate to defrost. Do not dilute. Combine the juice concentrate with the gelatin in the bottom of a blender container. Wait 2 minutes until the gelatin softens, then add the boiling water. Cover and blend on high speed, scraping once or twice, until all gelatin granules are dissolved. With blender running, add frozen whole berries through the small opening, a few at a time, until blended.

Pour into a glass bowl, or 8 individual glass dessert cups, and refrigerate until set. Dessert will set in less than an hour, and form its own foamy "whipped" topping. (Garnish with fresh fruit if desired.)

Makes 8 servings, 70 calories each.

Note: You can substitute any 6 oz. can of frozen fruit concentrate *except* pineapple.

Prune Apple Molded Salad

1 package (3 oz.) lemon gelatin (regular or sugar-free)
1 cup boiling water
½ cup pitted prunes, chopped
1 apple (preferably red-skinned), cored and chopped
¼ cup cubed Swiss cheese

Dissolve gelatin in boiling water. Chill until mixture mounds on a spoon.

Fold in prunes, apple and cheese. Pour into a 3-cup mold and chill until set. Unmold onto shredded lettuce.

Makes 4 servings, 155 calories each with regular gelatin; 85 calories each with sugar-free gelatin.

Ginger Peachy Bananas

2 very ripe bananas
2 crisp ginger cookies
2 very ripe large peaches

Peel bananas and cut into bite-size chunks. Divide among 4 parfait glasses or dessert cups. Put the cookies in a plastic bag and crush with a meat mallet or other heavy object (or process into crumbs in a food processor or blender). Sprinkle the crumbs over the bananas. Peel the peach and mash it by hand or coarsely chop it in the blender or food processor. Spoon over the bananas.

Makes 4 servings, 95 calories each.

Pineapple-Apricot Spread

1 can (6 oz.) frozen pineapple juice concentrate, thawed
1 cup water
½ cup white wine or additional water
1 package (8 oz.) dried apricots, chopped
¼ tsp. ground cinnamon

Combine all ingredients in a saucepan. Cover, simmer ½ hour; stir occasionally. When most of the liquid is absorbed, remove from heat. Transfer to storage container, refrigerate. Serve with bread, toast or crackers.

Makes approximately 2½ cups, 30 calories per Tbs.

Fresh Cranberry Topping

2 cups raw cranberries
1 can (6 oz.) frozen apple juice or cider concentrate, undiluted and defrosted
1 envelope powdered pectin

Combine ingredients in blender or food processor using the steel blade. Process until cranberries are chopped. Store in a covered jar in the refrigerator. Use as a topping for frozen yogurt, vanilla ice milk, or spoon over crepes, cheese blintzes or sliced bananas.

Makes 2 cups, under 20 calories per Tbs.

Russian Raspberry Sauce

1 can (6 oz.) frozen orange juice concentrate
1 pt. ripe fresh raspberries *or* 10 oz. package, frozen unsweetened
Pinch of grated orange or lemon peel (optional)

Allow orange concentrate to defrost. Wash and hull berries (or defrost frozen berries). Slice very thinly lengthwise. Stir undiluted concentrate (and grated peel, if desired) into berries. Chill in the refrigerator. Use as a topping for thin slices of chiffon cake, or over frozen low-fat yogurt or ice milk.
Makes 6 servings, 90 calories each (sauce only).

No-Sugar-Added Berry Sauce

1 pt. fresh strawberries or raspberries *or* 10 oz. package frozen
unsweetened strawberries or raspberries
¼ cup undiluted, unsweetened red or purple grape juice

Wash and hull berries (or defrost, if frozen). Combine with grape juice in blender container (or food processor, using the steel blade). Cover and process with short on-off motions until berries are coarsely chopped, not pureed. Use as a topping for thin slices of chiffon cake, low-fat ice milk or frozen yogurt.
Makes 6 servings, 25 calories each with strawberries, 40 calories each with raspberries (sauce only).

Hot Blueberry Sauce

1 pt. blueberries, fresh or frozen unsweetened
¼ cup grape juice

Put berries in saucepan. (If berries are frozen, allow them to defrost in a saucepan, to retain juices.) Add grape juice and heat to boiling. Spoon hot sauce over thin slices of chiffon cake, sponge cake, low-fat ice milk or frozen yogurt.
Makes 6 servings, 50 calories each (sauce only).

Hot Pineapple Sauce

1 can (16 oz.) crushed pineapple, packed in juice or light syrup,
   undrained
1 tsp. vanilla extract
2 tsp. cornstarch
2 tsp. lemon juice (optional)
Dash of cinnamon or mixed apple pie spice

Combine ingredients in a saucepan; heat and stir until simmering.
Spoon over thin slices of chiffon cake, low-fat ice milk or frozen
yogurt. Store extra in refrigerator and reheat as needed.

Makes 6 servings, 55 calories each (sauce only).

15

Salad Drinks

When you have no time to eat right, you can always take to drink! The blender (and more recently the food processor) makes short work of turning raw fruits and vegetables into nutritious beverages that are as easy to take as they are to make (breakfast-skippers take note!). With the addition of healthful protein-rich ingredients like skim milk, yogurt, cottage cheese and eggs, it's easy to whip up a whole meal you can sip through a straw or pack into a Thermos bottle.

These recipes demonstrate the essential difference between mere drinks and juices on the one hand and drinkable salads on the other. Juice, after all, is the liquid of fruits or vegetables, separated from the valuable pulp and fiber. While juices may retain enough flavor and vitamins to make them satisfactory, they don't really do much to satisfy the appetite. They are, after all, primarily water!

These brawny blender beverages are made from the whole fruit or vegetable, with all its appetite-appeasing appeal intact.

Banana Shake for Two

1 very ripe banana
2 tsp. honey or sugar or equivalent sugar substitute
2 tsp. vanilla extract
Ice cubes and water to equal 2 cups
⅔ cup nonfat dry milk powder

Combine in covered blender; process on high speed until ice stops chinking. Serve immediately.

Makes 2 servings, 160 calories each with honey; 155 calories each with sugar; 140 calories each with sugar substitute.

Peach Yogurt Summer Nog

2 very ripe peaches, peeled and pitted
1 cup low-fat peach or vanilla yogurt
8 oz. seltzer

Chill all ingredients. Combine in blender container; process until smooth. Serve in punch cups (sprinkled with cinnamon or nutmeg, if desired).

Makes 6 servings, under 55 calories each.

Peachy Cream Orange Float

1 package (10 oz.) frozen peaches, unsweetened
1 cup plain low-fat yogurt
1 cup fresh skim milk
2 Tbs. brown sugar (optional)
1 eating orange, peeled and diced
Ground cinnamon

Partially defrost peaches. Combine with yogurt, milk, and sugar (if desired) in blender. Blend until smooth. Stir in orange. Pour into 4 glasses. Top with a shake of cinnamon.

Makes 4 servings, 140 calories each; with sugar 160 calories each.

Strawberry Pear Shake

3 juice-packed canned pear halves
⅓ cup juice from can of pears
4 large strawberries
⅔ cup plain low-fat yogurt
1 tsp. sugar or fructose or equivalent sugar substitute (optional)

Process in a blender or food processor with the metal blade, until almost smooth.
Makes 2 servings, 105 calories each.

Strawberry Pineapple Frappe

1 can (6 oz.) unsweetened pineapple juice (¾ cup)
4 or 5 large hulled strawberries, fresh or frozen
4 or 5 ice cubes

Blend until all ice is crushed. Serve in tall glass with fresh mint leaves, if desired.
Makes 1 serving, approximately 120 calories.

Watermelon Blush

2 cups diced, seeded, chilled watermelon
12 oz. cold water or club soda or ginger ale or lemon soda (regular or diet)
Ice cubes
Mint leaves or lemon slices

Puree watermelon smooth in blender or food processor. Combine with cold water or soda over ice cubes. Garnish with mint leaves or lemon slices.
Makes 3 servings, 30 calories per serving with water, club or diet soda; 65 calories per serving with regular ginger ale or lemon soda.

Balkan Fruited Iced Tea

Choose among: diced, peeled apples and pears; peeled, sliced
peaches; sliced strawberries; pitted cherries; melon cubes
Lemon juice
Honey
Strong cold tea

Prepare fruit. Add 1 tsp. each lemon juice and honey for each ½ cup
fruit. Store in refrigerator. To serve, pour cold tea over ½ cup fruit
mixture in a tall class. Serve with a long spoon.
Each serving, under 75 calories.

Strawberry Lemonade

1 package (10 oz.) frozen sliced, sweetened strawberries
1 cup lemon juice
½ cup honey or fructose or equivalent sugar substitute
6 cups cold water
Ice cubes

Defrost berries. Combine with lemon juice and sweetener in covered
blender container. Blend until strawberries are pureed. Combine with
cold water and ice cubes in a pitcher. (Add fresh berries, if desired.)

Makes 6 servings, 150 calories per serving with honey; 125 calories
per serving with fructose; 65 calories per serving with sugar substitute.

Yogurt Sherbet Fruit Float

3 Tbs. plain low-fat yogurt
1½ Tbs. defrosted undiluted unsweetened frozen fruit juice
concentrate (orange, tangerine, pineapple, etc.)
½ cup chilled seltzer or club soda or sparkling water
Ice cubes
¼ cup berries or diced fresh fruit (optional)

Stir yogurt and fruit juice concentrate until smooth. Combine with
seltzer or club soda and ice in a tall glass. Garnish with fresh fruit, if
desired.

Each serving, approximately 75 calories (¼ cup strawberries, 15
calories).

Gazpacho Cocktails

Half of a small cucumber
3 cups tomato or tomato-vegetable juice
5 or 6 stuffed green olives (optional)
Dash of Tabasco sauce *or* pinch of garlic powder (optional)
Celery (optional)

Have all ingredients ice-cold. Pare cucumber and cut into chunks. Combine in the blender with tomato juice. Add olives and seasonings, if used; blend until smooth. Pour over ice; add celery, if desired.

Makes 4 servings, 150 calories each (10 calories more with optional ingredients).

Bloody Maria—Add vodka or gin to taste. Each ounce of 80-proof liquor is 65 calories, 100-proof is 85 calories.

Sangría

1 bottle (⅘ qt.) Spanish Rioja or other dry red wine
1 can (6 oz.) undiluted frozen orange juice concentrate, defrosted
1 unpeeled lemon, thinly sliced
1 unpeeled orange, thinly sliced
1 golden delicious apple, unpeeled, diced
1 red delicious apple, unpeeled, diced
Ice cubes
16 oz. water or club soda

In large pitcher, mix wine, undiluted orange juice concentrate, fruit, ice cubes and water or soda; stir well.

Makes 10 servings, 125 calories each.

Sangría Blanco—Substitute Chablis or other dry white wine for the red wine.

Nonalcoholic Grape Sangría—Dilute 2 cups red grape juice with 2 cups cold water and substitute for the wine. Use white grape juice or unsweetened grapefruit juice for a nonalcoholic white sangría. Makes 10 servings, 95 calories per serving with grape juice; 85 calories per serving with grapefruit juice.

Blueberry Kir Spritzer

3 oz. dry white wine
3 oz. club soda
Ice cubes
1 Tbs. Crème de Cassis liqueur
2 Tbs. fresh or frozen unsweetened blueberries

Pour wine and club soda over ice cubes. Stir in Crème de Cassis and fresh or frozen berries.

Makes 1 serving, 130 calories.

16

The Home
Salad Bar

If you want to toss a party, but you're short on time, why not let your guests toss their own? Serve a salad bar! Salad bar entertaining is an adaptable idea that can be accommodated to almost any size or sort of gathering, any budget, any location. Your salad bar party can range from a portable picnic in the park to a fancy, festive buffet sparkling with crystal and candlelight. Your salad bar can be a first course, or the whole meal. It can be fast or fancy; an impromptu bounty of fresh ready-to-eat foods harvested in a single shopping trip, or the culmination of a month of planning. Salad bar eating is fun indoors or out, any season, poolside or hearthside.

The salad bar idea is borrowed from restaurants, where it has become the most popular notion since tipping. It's a help-yourself table where a variety of greenery is displayed, along with dressings and toppings. Patrons assemble their own salads while waiting for their entrees. Sure beats bread!

It's an idea with all-around support. Waiters love having one less item to write down. Management likes it because there is less waste. Nutritionists are ecstatic about the idea—making salad is a much better way to pass the time than ordering extra martinis. And, most of all, diners love it because everybody has his own idea of what the perfect salad should contain.

The salad bar at home has special appeal to weight-watching guests who prefer a do-it-yourself salad over one already tossed and drenched in somebody else's favorite, fattening salad dressing.

As the host or hostess, you'll find that a do-it-yourself salad table is less wasteful than providing one big bowl of already-dressed greenery. Leftover salad with dressing turns limp and must be discarded while unused salad can be bagged in plastic and returned to the refrigerator.

How to Arrange a Home Salad Bar

The centerpiece for your salad table is a big bowl of crisp lettuce. (In warm weather set the bowl in a larger bowl of crushed ice.) Surround the lettuce with smaller bowls of sliced, unpeeled cucumber; tomato wedges or cherry tomatoes; sliced red onions; and crisp radishes. For a more extensive salad bar, add bowls of red or green sweet bell pepper, sliced raw mushrooms, drained canned artichoke hearts, carrot curls and whatever greenery looks good on market day.

To add protein and appetite appeal, you might add wedges of hard-cooked egg, lean ham cubes, julienne strips of white meat turkey or chicken, shredded Swiss or cheddar cheese, or bacon bits. Smoked fish, cold shrimp, crabmeat, or flaked white tuna might be provided at a luncheon where salad is the main course.

Bowls of favorite homemade salad dressings should be offered, or substitute bottled dressings if you're in a hurry. For an informal meal, there's no reason to serve commercial dressings in separate bowls. Simply assemble a variety of bottled dressings and put them in a decorative basket. The labels are self-explanatory and will save you from explaining which dressing is which.

Remember to set out your salad bar ingredients in the order that they'll be used. Big bowls should be first in line (not the usual too-scanty salad bowls). Then come the lettuce, onions and other basics, followed by the optional ingredients. Finally, the dressings and toppings complete the salad bar.

For a lunchtime gathering, a salad bar can be the main course. Augment it with crusty loaves of French or pita bread, crisp crackers or bread sticks, plus iced tea, lemonade or tall drinks. If you're having a cookout, a salad bar can keep everybody from congregating around the grill. And a crisp do-it-yourself salad is a much more appealing accompaniment to barbecue fare than the usual heavy, starchy, mayonnaise-laden salads.

Salad Bar Suggestions

Leafy Greens: lettuces, such as romaine, Boston and iceberg; chicory; escarole; spinach leaves; watercress; endive; cabbage, both red and green.

Vegetables: cauliflower or broccoli florets; asparagus; avocado; green and wax beans; celery; fennel; hearts of palm; brussels sprouts; bean sprouts; cucumber; zucchini and yellow squash; artichoke hearts; beets; pea pods; water chestnuts; bamboo shoots; onion rings; scallions; mushrooms; tomatoes and cherry tomatoes; carrots—sliced, curled, shredded; red and green bell peppers cut into rings, squares or strips; pimiento; radish; olives.

Meats, Poultry and Fish: miniature meatballs, hot or cold; strips or cubes of lean ham, roast beef, chicken, turkey; pepperoni or salami (or turkey ham or turkey salami); shrimp, crab and lobster; oysters and clams; salmon; tuna; sardines; anchovies.

Potatoes, Pasta, Grain and Beans: tabouli; macaroni; rice mixtures (white, brown, saffron, wild); hot or cold potato salads; fruit and noodle mixtures (hot or cold); chickpeas; two- and three-bean combinations.

Cheeses: Swiss, Jarlsberg, Parmesan, Gouda, Gruyère, Edam, Gorgonzola, cheddar and Monterey Jack in strips or cubes; blue, Roquefort and feta, crumbled; farmer, cottage, ricotta in bowls (plain or mixed with fruits, vegetables, herbs or flavorings).

Fruits: oranges, pineapple, apples, blueberries, strawberries, raspberries, nectarines, peaches, pears, melon, grapes, figs, dates, mixed dried fruits, spiced crab apples.

Relishes: pickles (slices, spears, miniatures); pickled watermelon, cauliflower, or onions; tomato aspic cubes (or other gelatin combinations); deviled eggs; chutneys.

Dressings (regular and low-fat): French, Italian, Russian, Thousand Island, cheese styles, creamy cucumber, yogurt, oil and vinegar (with plain, wine, cider, or tarragon vinegars), mayonnaise (plain or flavored with spices, herbs or fruit juices).

Toppings: croutons; bacon or soy bits; minced chives, mint, or oregano; almonds, walnuts, pecans, pistachios, peanuts or macadamia nuts (chopped, sliced, whole, toasted or raw); pine nuts; sesame, caraway and poppy seeds; chopped egg; capers; chilies; olives; seasonings; dried herbs; hummus; tahini.

Index